TRAGIC PATTERNS IN JACOBEAN AND CAROLINE DRAMA

TRAGIC PATTERNS IN JACOBEAN AND CAROLINE DRAMA

by Larry S. Champion

THE UNIVERSITY OF TENNESSEE PRESS
KNOXVILLE

for M.H.C. *and* F.O.C.
the onlie begetters

Library of Congress Cataloging in Publication Data

Champion, Larry S
    Tragic patterns in Jacobean and Caroline
    drama.

    Includes bibliographical references and
    index.
        1. English drama—17th century—History
    and criticism. 2. English drama (Tragedy)—
    History and criticism. I. Title.
    PR678.T7C5   822'.051   77–8159
    ISBN 0-87049-217-9

Acknowledgments

Portions of the material in Chapter II have appeared previously in more extensive form in *Shakespeare's Tragic Perspective,* published in 1976 by the University of Georgia Press. Also, portions of this study in somewhat different form have appeared in *PMLA ("'Tis Pity She's a Whore* and the Jacobean Tragic Perspective," 90, 1975, 78–87), in *Studies in Philology* ("Tourneur's *The Revenger's Tragedy* and the Jacobean Tragic Perspective," 72, 1975, 299–321), in *Texas Studies in Literature and Language* (Webster's *The White Devil* and the Jacobean Tragic Perspective," 16, 1975, 447–462), and in *English Studies* ("Tragic Vision in Middleton's *Women Beware Women,"* 57, 1976, 410–424). Permission to reprint this material is gratefully acknowledged. I also wish to express my appreciation to North Carolina State University for supporting this publication through the Faculty Research and Professional Development Fund.

Contents

TRAGIC PATTERNS IN JACOBEAN AND CAROLINE DRAMA

I. Prologue

The seventeenth century has frequently been described as the beginning of the modern age. Certainly the civil conflict which gripped England in the mid century was the result of fundamental social, economic, and philosophical conflicts involving the way man lives and explains his life, a conflict which shook old beliefs and perceptions to their very foundations and in which the role of empirical data gained an ascendancy not relinquished to this day. Just how deeply the currents of change ran is illustrated in the sheer wordiness of the revolution. Between 1640 and 1661 well over twenty-two thousand printed sermons, speeches, pamphlets, and newspapers argued particular positions in the struggle. And this clash of ideas and of ideologies throughout the century had both its material and its spiritual dimensions. On the one hand, a historian like R. H. Tawney can explain the events as a shift in the political structure to accommodate the ascendancy of the new gentry who had risen to power in the sixteenth century over the old-fashioned landowners;[1] or H. R. Trevor-Roper can concentrate on a massive decline of the small landowners beset with inflation;[2] or Lawrence Stone can describe the increasingly effective organization on both the national and the county basis of the "local landed elite . . . to resist the political, fiscal and religious policies of the Crown, and the parallel shift to new mercantile interests in London, organized to challenge the economic monopoly and political control of the entrenched commercial oligarchy."[3] On the other hand, the philosophers speak of the replacement of a theological explanation by an empirical one: Latin Averroism, emphasizing man's naturalistic and scientific dependence on the world, vied openly with Humanism, which stressed his freedom and glory;[4] the Western mind turned from "the contemplation of the absolute and eternal to the knowledge of the particular and contingent";[5] the world became "hard, cold, colourless, silent and dead" as the

3

"Cartesian philosophy . . . became the predominant view of modern times."[6]

In any event the Interregnum merely brought to the surface ideological clashes set in motion a century and a half earlier—from points so diverse as the pedagogic idolizing of classical antiquity and veneration of its "ancient speculation and skepticism"[7] to the juxtaposing of capitalistic enterprise with medieval forms of trade and industry so as to provoke "perhaps the period of the greatest economic confusion in our history."[8] Giordono Bruno's and Thomas Digges' Copernican pronouncements and the increasing Puritan antagonisms toward the Crown, William Harvey's anatomical discoveries and the Midlands agricultural riots of 1607, the accumulating empirical data from both the microscope and the telescope and the virtual bankruptcy of over two-thirds of the English earls and barons in 1600, the government's inadequate control over the written word and the phenomenal growth of London from some sixty thousand in 1500 to some four hundred and fifty thousand in 1640—all such seemingly unrelated activities contributed to a new, and to many a profoundly disturbing, *Weltanschauung*. Theodore Spencer describes it as one of the occasional periods in history when fundamental concepts are examined and redefined with unusual vigor and urgency,[9] a comment itself penned at a moment for England of grave military danger and imminent sociological change and scientific development. The global conflict of the 1940s and the atomic age which it ushered in undoubtedly involved both a reshaping of life-styles and a redefining of fundamental values. In fact, however, that more recent era reflects no greater fragmentation of both personal and social values than did the struggle some three centuries earlier. If the Puritan triumphs in 1642 suggest a resurgence of rigid moral values, they more significantly represent the repudiation of a political institution which one hundred years earlier had successfully weathered a confrontation with Rome and Catholicism. Moreover, it is surely not entirely wrongheaded to consider this new political alliance with conservative and traditional morality a wishful momentary retreat for many to the comforting limits of the old moral concepts.

Divergent forces were obviously at work in the sixteenth century —with the "subversive and cynical mutterings of a Montaigne or Machiavelli, . . . [the] irreverent and ambiguous antics of a Rabelais or an Agrippa, . . . [the] irrational excesses of a Luther or a Calvin,"

to use Hiram Haydn's phrases.[10] Even so, the essential unity of the
three interrelated God-centered hierarchies of the cosmos, society,
and man is a consistent theme of Castiglione, Elyot, Palingenius,
Davies, La Primaudaye, Romei, Bodin, Du Bartas, Hooker, Raleigh,
Smith, and numerous others. It was near the end of the century,
with the Renaissance and the Reformation having worked as mutual
catalysts, that England began to develop what Patrick Crutwell has
described as "a new mentality, . . . critical, dramatic, satirical, complex, and uncertain."[11] In effect, the bond was forever broken between the material and the spiritual worlds; and, as previous criticism has well documented,[12] once the mental frame of reference
was adjusted, all values—whether religious or sociological—were subject to reexamination. The results were sobering, at times even
terrifying. Put in admittedly oversimplified terms, the Englishman,
enduring political agitation and uncertainty in the first decade and
outright chaos in the fifth—and unable through science and cognitive reason to support a teleological philosophy as comfortably as
had been possible through the unquestioned assumption of a
supernatural presence with unlimited control—faced an uncharted
future predicated on purely human terms. If, in actuality, man's
inhumanities to man were no less severe under the Church Universal
with God's ordinance undisputed, or under knighthood with its
avowed service to God and King, the philosophic differences were
profound. Now there was no universally accepted ideal, no restraint
upon man's appetite; the "pole is fall'n, . . . the odds is gone," and
the "universal wolf, / So doubly seconded with will and power"
might well "make perforce an universal prey / And last eat up itself."
In different terms, the possibility of a world populated with those
for whom man is his own measure and bodies but gardens "to the
which our wills are gardeners," is far more terrifying than a world
filled with those whose villainy is countered by a conscience which
admits the presence of God—even with Satan, whose wanton destruction is inevitably hedged by the assumption of God's providential
control.

My present concern is not to review at length the numerous and
complex factors which contributed to the seventeenth-century
English mentality, but to examine how one literary form—dramatic
tragedy—reflects the period of political and philosophical transition.
It is a natural choice both because the theater was one of the pre-
eminent forms of public entertainment in London during the early
decades of the century and because tragedy by its very nature

demands a logical accommodation for man's agony and suffering. The Jacobean and Caroline stage worlds mirror an age still informed by the fundamental moral precepts of the Western Catholic tradition—but an age also in which this faith is being seriously eroded or at least challenged by the tenets of empiricism. Obviously, the plays are not allegories; with rare exceptions they are not even suggestive of particular contemporary events, and there will certainly be no attempt here to relate them directly to the political and social context. At the same time, the manner in which a tragic hero exercises critical moral and ethical choices and eventually comes to terms with life even in confronting death represents, in literary terms at least, what the author apparently believes to be one valid approach to existence as he comprehends it. And, in turn, a consistent pattern from one play to the next comprises a significant record of the artists' emotional responses to the intellectual upheavals which were shaping their brave new world. The playwrights may indeed not represent the philosophic forefront of the age; they undoubtedly are writing in many instances for a middle-class and probably fairly conservative audience. They are nonetheless grappling with the issue of moral intelligibility in the accommodation of suffering, tragedy, and death. And they are doing so in the midst of contemporary intellectual crosscurrents which lend their stage worlds a degree of genuine credibility no mere fiction could hope to approximate.

The debt to recent critics will be obvious in the chapters which follow. Among the many cited in the notes, several are notable for the general breadth of their analysis. Una Ellis-Fermor (*Jacobean Tragedy*), for example, effectively reminded us forty years ago of the tensions and uncertainties which set the Elizabethan tragic spirit apart from the Jacobean; her positing of three phases of drama is provocative, though her description of the final tragic stage (after 1610) as one of relaxed tensions is hardly applicable to the stage world of Webster, Middleton, and Ford, however appropriate it may be for the sensationalism, the easy reconciliations, and the exploitations of intellectual and moral fashion which characterize the ubiquitous tragicomedies. Muriel C. Bradbrook (*Themes and Conventions of Elizabethan Tragedy*), a few years later, did much to sustain the interest. Both T. B. Tomlinson (*A Study of Elizabethan and Jacobean Tragedy*) and Robert Ornstein (*The Moral Vision of Jacobean Tragedy*) are concerned, in varying ways, with the ethical nature of the Stuart tragic worlds; Ornstein,

with F. P. Wilson (*Elizabethan and Jacobean*), calls attention to
their traditional moral position; and Tomlinson, at least in some
instances, sees a sordid attempt to cater to the depraved tastes of
the audience, a theme J. A. Bastiaenen (*The Moral Tone of Jacobean
and Caroline Drama*) argues with overly rigid consistency. Irving
Ribner (*Jacobean Tragedy: The Quest for Moral Order*) and George
C. Herndl (*The High Design: English Renaissance Tragedy and the
Natural Law*) focus more directly on the philosophic implications
of the changes taking place during the period and the various manners in which tragedy mirrors the decline of belief in the carefully
ordered Christian universe. Alfred Harbage (*Shakespeare and the
Rival Traditions*) may too narrowly define the distinctions between
plays written for the children's troupes and those written for adult
companies, but in addressing the interaction of the two he broaches
a topic of vital importance to an understanding of early seventeenth-
century drama. And more recently Arthur Kirsch has examined
what he considers the three most significant components of the
Jacobean theater—tragicomedy, satiric tragedy, and the private
stage.

The intent of this study is not to survey the period anew on any
such broad thematic, philosophic, or generic grounds, but rather,
building upon these previous investigations, to concentrate at some
length on a close reading of the relatively few Jacobean and Caroline
tragedies generally acknowledged as the most powerful apart from
Shakespeare's. Numerous other works will receive brief notice, and
an early chapter offers an overview of the development of Shakespeare's tragic perspective. But primary attention will be directed
to the various dramaturgical components and structural devices
through which the playwrights, in those major works, develop and
sustain the spectator's interest in the various protagonists and the
particular values they reflect, through which—in other words—they
create the vision of a fragmented and decadent society and, by carefully controlling the spectator's response, provide a compelling and
convincing aesthetic experience.

A cynically satiric spirit is evident in most of the titles examined
individually in this study, just as it informs the bulk of Jacobean
and Caroline tragedy as a whole. Indeed, the resurgence of verse
satire in the last decade of the sixteenth century is one of the significant early literary responses to the general social ferment. Consciously acclimated to the Elizabethan world, this new form—unlike
medieval satire—found its targets in social and economical abuses.

"Where the standard targets of medieval satire had been the clergy and professional men who were more concerned for their individual welfare than the good of the Christian commonwealth, the common butts of the new satire are the members of the rising middle class, the new-made knights, the yeoman's sons come to London to the Inns of Court, the merchant adventurer who buys a great estate and a coat-of-arms."[13] No doubt encouraged by the acerbic struggle in the late seventies and eighties between the Puritans and the Anglicans which took primary focus in the Martin Marprelate tracts and responding to profound religious and social convulsions, such authors as Joseph Hall, John Marston, Everard Guilpin, Thomas Middleton, William Rankins, John Donne, John Davies of Hereford, and George Wither[14] attack those very qualities of man now presumably freed from traditional moral constraints. Through the delineation of a scene over which presides a neo-Stoic satyric figure, a savage and insolent swaggerer who trenchantly proclaims himself the scourge of villainy and testifies to the use of Reason to shape one's life and to endure the evils of the world, the satirists mirror a growing disenchantment with the instability of the traditional moral and social values and their mounting apprehension concerning the inability of the New Learning to provide answers which are either spiritually satisfactory or physically operable.[15]

England's golden age of drama not accidentally coincides with these tumultuous years. Building upon these same tensions and influenced by the rage for satire, the stage provided another, and ultimately more important, reaction to the trauma of philosophic adjustment. Certainly the most obvious impact came in comedy, which Ben Jonson in *Every Man Out of His Humor*—perhaps motivated by the ban against the further printing of satire (Campbell, p. 56), perhaps by the satirist's search for protection in the dramatic persona (Peter, p. 205)—attempted to make a recognizable equivalent of formal verse satire. In the ensuing years—whether named Macilente (*Every Man Out of His Humor*), Chrisoganus (*Histriomastix*), Horace (*Poetaster*), Thersites (*Troilus and Cressida*), Lampatho Doria (*What You Will*), Jacques (*As You Like It*), Malevole (*The Malcontent*), Vincentio *(Measure for Measure)*, or Prince Phoenix (*The Phoenix*)—the satirist was one of the dominant figures on the stage, exposing both the folly and the vice in those around him. While the degree of rant and the particular form of criticism varies widely from one play to another, the pronounced

influence of the satiric figure is convincingly demonstrated by
Alfred Harbage, who classifies as satiric comedies forty-three of
the fifty-five extant plays produced in private theaters between
1599 and 1613.[16]

The impact upon tragedy was equally pervasive but more subtle.
Characters as diverse as Hamlet and Timon, or Vindice and Bosola,
stem in part from the satyr satirist. By its very nature, however,
satire requires a stasis in which, as Kernan describes it, "the two
opposing forces, the satirist on the one hand and the fools on the
other, are locked in their respective attitudes without any possibility of either dialectical movement or the simple triumph of good
over evil" (p. 31). Mature Elizabethan tragedy, on the other hand,
is constructed upon a situation in which to some degree the central
figures grow in comprehension of self and surrounding. In such a
form the satiric in one manner or another is subsumed in the tragic,
perhaps as one phase of the protagonist's experience (characteriz-
ing, for example, his initial view of society), perhaps as the condition to which a character is reduced through agony and frustration,
perhaps as the posture of an adversary whose values constitute a
foil to those represented by the principal.

Whatever the literary mode, this remarkable resurgence of satire
was the direct offspring of Renaissance man's pessimistic concern
about his own nature, the scope and function of self-serving
machinations, and the limits of evil in the universal scheme of
things. With its "more exact, more searching, more detailed in-
quiry into moral and political questions," as F. P. Wilson has observed,[17] the seventeenth century slowly experienced "the transfer of authority from the humanistic to the scientific epistemolo-
gy."[18] Certainly, this transition contributed directly to what critics
in various ways have described as the darkening scene of Jacobean
and Caroline tragedy. For such a "mentality of crisis . . . obsessed
with the contradictory nature of things,"[19] the stage provided "a
dialectic of ironies and ambivalences, avoiding . . . the simplifica-
tions of direct statement and reductive resolution."[20]

Generalities concerning something so multifaceted as Renaissance
English drama are inherently dangerous, and categories refuse to
fit securely on an art form which reflects the dynamic spiritual
quality of the age. Nevertheless, critics for years have noted a
marked distinction in emphasis between the tragedy of Marlowe
and the early Shakespeare at one end of the chronological spectrum
and the work of the principal playwrights of the later years.

Marlowe's central figures gain heroic stature by defying the mental
and physical limitations man has previously accepted as inviolable;
they do not so much deny God's existence and governance as exude
the excitement—and the inevitable frustration—of man's assumption of unlimited power. Such essentially is also the case with
Hamlet and Othello; neither refutes God, but each is involved in a
psychomachia in which ultimately he must suffer the consequences
of appropriating to himself the prerogatives of God. These tragedies,
in other words, do not challenge the traditional values concerning
the metaphysical dimensions of life. Such works as *King Lear* and
Macbeth pose a more problematical view of the universe, but in
each the central conflict builds primarily on the protagonist's conception of his own role in relationship to that of the controller of
the universe. Each in his death confirms his assumptions of a
teleological universe operating under divine law, although the spectators must also reckon in both plays with a force of destruction
almost primeval in nature. In any case each of these tragedies from
Tamburlaine through *Macbeth* in varying degrees focuses on the
experience of a central figure whose guilt, suffering, and tragic
insight are registered essentially on the private level of the individual. The precise nature of the tragic experience will vary, but the
essential framework is consistent. The action has come to focus on
a single figure of noble stature, a concept of tragic character which
Glynne W. Wickham describes as "one of the genuinely original
and creative contributions of Elizabethan actors and playmakers to
the theatre of their time,"[21] and the experiences and development
of this protagonist during a limited part of his life provide a fundamental unity. Facing some critical decision or provoked to some
critical act, he is not without a live and sensitive conscience and
not without at least a latent conviction that he is "the cause of his
own undoing"[22] and that he is responsible for the consequences of
his actions both for himself and for others.

The protagonist is placed, to be sure, within an Elizabethan world
of opposing values in which the rigidity of old orders was already
badly shaken, and the pulls of religious ties on the one hand and
social ties on the other were roughly equal.[23] He faces an awareness
of the contraries of human existence, which A. P. Rossiter terms
"ambivalence"[24] and Norman Rabkin "tragic complementarity."[25]
The resulting paradox lends dignity to the hero's inevitable error
and subsequent misery; it projects him, in the eye of the beholder
at least, beyond naked, unmediated suffering, and beyond the

despair which results from suffering which has no context larger than the individual experience of pain. In the full pattern this central figure will experience some form of an anagnorisis, either wisdom spawned by suffering followed by reconciliation and spiritual peace or tragic insight resulting from the "power to endure and the power to apprehend,"[26] even if he himself is incapable of regeneration, followed by a restitution of harmony in the order of man and the order of nature.

Whatever the case, the dominant focus is on the intensely personal experience of the protagonist. A potentially great and noble man, blinded by some manifestation of pride, commits a disastrous act of egocentricity for which he must suffer the full public and private consequences even as through agony he achieves the insight and self-knowledge possible only after self-love is placed in proper perspective. Through various structural devices the playwright guides the spectators' reaction, forcing them to share the struggle within the soul at the same time they observe the larger design of the action. This double vision demands that the spectators be bound emotionally to the protagonist at the same time they are detached from him, that they credibly and sympathetically experience the dilemma of the character although, through their more expansive perception of the physical and metaphysical forces which control the stage world, they also sit in judgment on his decisions and anticipate the consequences.[27]

In Shakespeare's final plays and in the work of Jonson, Tourneur, Webster, Middleton, and Ford, this double vision persists as a central feature—but the perspective shifts in a vitally significant manner. Notably, for instance, there is no fully articulated transformation in the protagonist. With no such moment, the spectator is perforce left without the comfort of a satisfactory aesthetic accommodation for the existence of pain, suffering, and evil. Tragedy, in general terms, comes to be envisioned more clearly as the consequence of a combination of destructive human forces from both within the individual and from without; the individual's disaster is seen as but a single manifestation of the social cancer which has produced the dilemma. Evil as an external force operating against the individual is broadly manifested, to be sure, in tragedies such as *Lear, Macbeth, Hamlet, Othello, Edward II*, indeed even simplistically in the morality plays. The essential difference, however, is the focus. In these earlier works the spectators' interest is predominantly on the individual man and his private accommodation of error in a teleological universe, and admittedly *Lear* and *Macbeth*—subject in this respect to widely divergent interpretations—are perhaps best considered as transitional pieces. In the later tragedies, while sporadic moments of internalization might well suggest a psychic struggle within such characters as Antony, Coriolanus, Vittoria, Vindice, and Orgilus, the central figure is seen in large part through the other characters, each of whom is tainted by lust or consumed with self-interest. In other words, though the flaw and the potential of the principal figure command sufficient interest to afford tragic impact to his downfall, the spectators are also forced to consider more directly the significance of the evil that exists in the characters around the central figure.

This delicate but crucial shift in perspective occurs in various manners. Shakespeare, for example, in his final tragedies utilizes the very structural devices by which he previously has depicted the private, inner struggle with passion and thus has provoked close emotional rapport between the spectators and the protagonist to block such a relationship. The soliloquies no longer reveal a moment of crucial decision; instead, spoken by the principal, they simply establish a particular state of mind; or, spoken by a minor character, they emphasize the forces of evil which operate on the protagonist from without by signaling the complexity of the situation he confronts. Instead of one or two choric characters who rivet attention on the central figure, Shakespeare now utilizes multiple figures to direct the spectators' attention through soliloquies to the public dimensions of evil. Similarly, Jonson juxtaposes the arrogant hubris of his central figures with the emerging policy of the equally villainous characters who surround them; the spectators, alone in a position to observe the evil at every hand, are forced to provide— and to test the limitations of—their own personal scale of values as a gauge by which to respond to decisions and actions on stage which precipitate the tragedy and destruction. Webster, likewise, does not minimize the lust and avarice which precipitate Vittoria's downfall. But his sharpest focus is upon those around her who play an active role in her developing tragedy—the brother whose every value is dictated by survival and social gain, the Machiavellian Francisco intent upon blood vengeance at any cost, the Cardinal who readily uses religion as a mask behind which he serves his own vindictive interests, and the adulterous lover willing to commit double murder to gratify his lust. Middleton's Beatrice-Joanna, for another example, commands the spectators' major interest, to be sure. But their view transcends her individual experience and focuses upon the general tragedy of human abuse in which she is villain as well as victim. While her tragic situation is resolved on moral grounds, the fact that significant figures—who are responsible in part for the tragedy and with whom the spectators have shared private perceptions—are required neither to answer morally to their decisions and actions nor directly pay the consequences impresses upon the spectators a deep sense of the corruption of human society and of the ethical ambiguities intrinsic to it. Similarly, Ford depicts the incestuous relationship of Annabella and Giovanni as abominably sinful and destructive; yet their affection, if unrighteous, is also intensely sincere, and the playwright places equal emphasis upon the treachery and hypocrisy of the society whose morality the lovers have rejected. Giovanni's love is set in the context of rival wooers, each in his own way more despicable—Grimaldi, who in cowardly fashion attacks Soranzo in the darkness, murders an innocent victim, and then runs to the Cardinal for holy protection; Bergetto, who is too stupid to develop into much more than a buffoon; Soranzo, who on the one hand refuses to acknowledge his own previous affair with Hippolita and on the other hypocritically and mercilessly beats his pregnant wife for a liaison she refuses to deny.

In a word, the major Jacobean and Caroline dramatists seem to be striving, through the experience of the individual, to give dramatic focus to the tragedy of an entire society. Their tragic worlds are more pervasively ambivalent than those of their Elizabethan counterparts, reflecting more poignantly the increasing tensions of a world no longer capable of accepting the old values without question and yet unable to provide satisfactory alternatives. Admittedly, in the earlier tragedies the protagonist faces choices or alternate paths of action which at the moment defy clear moral judgment. But in meeting his death the protagonist to a large extent resolves such ambiguity by acting in accordance with certain positive social and metaphysical values which emerge (Brutus, Hamlet, Othello, Bussy, Lear) or in defiance of them (Faustus, Hieronimo, Macbeth). In the later plays, on the other hand, the ambiguity is never resolved; by positing the viability of divergent codes of value, the stage world precludes the possibility of the spectators' unquestioned and unexamined assumption of traditionally accepted values. With the protagonist flawed by a passion which destroys his ability to guide his own destiny and the surrounding characters manipulating him to serve their own material and emotional ends, the spectators—

even when the stage is strewn with corpses—are not provided the easy assurance that virtue has prevailed on this or the other side of the grave; nor are they convinced that society has been effectively purged of the potential for the recurrence of such tragedy.

It has been argued that these dramatists were simply reacting to the jaded tastes of a theatrical clientele which demanded a greater degree of violence and was amused by an exposure of the salacious and the vicious in social mores.[28] Certainly in a period of philosophic transition, when traditional values are being openly challenged, there are always those who will cater to the sensationalistic possibilities of the moment. And, not surprisingly, many of the plays in one way or another do merely titillate through their freshly daring positions in defiance of traditional morality or social decorum— John Stephen's *Cynthia's Revenge, or Maenander's Ecstasy,* for example, or Anthony Brewer's *The Lovesick King, or The Perjured Nun,* John Suckling's *Aglaura,* William Sampson's *The Vow Breaker, or The Fair Maid of Clifton,* or George Glapthorne's *The Parracide, or Revenge for Honour.* The more profound plays, however, reflect a social theme alive to contemporary issues,[29] a theme not effectively to be accommodated by the dominant focus of earlier Elizabethan tragedy.[30] Without exception the playwrights represented in this study are probing and experimenting in structure and in theme. If it stretches credibility to assert that they—like Jonson— would through their art counsel the very center of the kingdom, assuredly they do achieve a tragic vision both of universal significance and of particular relevance to their own times.

The Jacobean and Caroline dramatists, more specifically, through emphasis on "people driven on by unruly and irrepressible energies, by sexual instinct, by scramble for advance, and by the temptations of high places," explore a view of life more somber and pessimistic than their Elizabethan counterparts.[31] Gone is the dominant emphasis on the Titan hero aspiring to boundless knowledge or power and capable of great achievement—albeit an accomplishment tainted by hubris. Gone too is the preoccupation with the internal struggle or with the single vicious antagonist and the flawed hero as the only significant aberrations from a world in which conventional moral values constitute the accepted norm. This shift in focus neither minimizes the tragedy of the individual and the value of the insights which he gains prior to his death nor mitigates the individual's responsibility for his actions and their tragic consequences. The central figure lends coherence to the events of the plot, and his

experience reflects one way in which a character comes to terms
with life's mysteries; indeed, the tragic insight to which the
protagonist of these plays is led almost invariably supports the
concept of traditional morality. But the illumination is presented
in such a manner as to leave lingering and unresolved doubts among
the spectators. Predominant focus is not only upon the individual
character, his flaw, and his tragic experience, but also upon the
characters who surround the protagonist and who manipulate him
for selfish purposes. Consequently, the playwright is able through
his stage world to offer an observation about society and the age
more far-ranging and frankly more pessimistic than would be the
case through the more restricted focus. The later Shakespearan
tragedies (indeed from *Lear* forward) and the major Jacobean and
Caroline productions consistently tend through carefully controlled dramatic structures to mirror a corrosive and malignant environment, and thus their work collectively stands as an artistic
reflection of the troubled spirit of an age in fundamental transition.
In a word, this perspective—exploring the "nature of reality [rather]
than the nature of heroism"[32]—is broader, demanding judgment
both on the flawed protagonist and on the corrupt society, the
surrounding characters who through deceit and passion for self-
gratification share the responsibility for provoking such a flaw.

Various structural modifications contribute to this focus. Shakespeare, for example, by developing a second figure to whom is transferred at least a part of the emotional impact of the tragic illumination arising from the protagonist's experience, is able to avoid the
total emotional commitment to the protagonist which would block
the spectators' realization that the judgment against evil must fall
equally upon the individual and upon those around him; he also
can stress a similar fact about the wisdom, heroism, compassion, or
sacrifice which the protagonist achieves—that such a quality, in
touching and influencing the life of another, also has its public
dimension. Both Webster and Tourneur double the antagonists in
order to increase the intensity of the malignance and to broaden
the base of its operation against the protagonist. Tourneur, moreover, in *The Atheist's Tragedy* and Jonson in both *Sejanus* and
Catiline move the principal villain to center stage, and the spectators share the private perceptions as their schemes unfold. Middleton, through a consistent tone of satiric detachment, a carefully
modulated subplot, and numerous soliloquies in characters surrounding the central figure, reflects an age of dubiety and

unscrupulous individualism, a mercenary world in which morality has its price and violence is the rule rather than the exception. In *'Tis Pity She's a Whore* Ford doubles the protagonists, and their conflicting insights gleaned through suffering sharply underscore the metaphysical ambiguities of the stage world; moreover, while far from blameless themselves, they reflect also in their struggle the tragic waste of lives destroyed by the value structure of a pervasively decadent society. The protagonist is likewise doubled in *The Broken Heart,* and the conventional lines between protagonists and antagonists are totally blurred. Here the societal aspect of tragedy gains further emphasis through the delineation of Penthea and Calantha, virtuous and blameless characters who are destroyed in spirit and in body by the actions of others who use them for self-advantage.

Generally, then, the Elizabethan focus is on the individual's aspiration in the context of assumed moral absolutes, however ambiguous the nature of his choices might be; for the Jacobean dramatist, on the other hand, what Arthur C. Kirsch has called the "metaphysical reverberations"[33] are frequently missing as the individual struggles in the face of moral relativism and pervasive decadence. Like *Hamlet, Othello, Lear,* and *Macbeth* these plays involve a collapse of the protagonist's personal world, but it is a world which integrally involves the actions of others and their relationship to the central figure. While obviously any tragedy delineates the protagonist *in* his context, the perspective is determined by the focus and the emphasis, in turn involving the specific structural devices by which the playwright controls the spectators' interest and directs their concern to particular characters and issues.

A study of this nature necessarily must establish somewhat arbitrary limitations on the material it covers; and, if for no other reason, one would hasten to qualify any sweeping assertions concerning Jacobean and Caroline drama. At least nine hundred sixteen plays and entertainments were completed between 1603 and 1642, well over seven hundred of them after 1610.[34] While comedy as in the Elizabethan period was the predominant form, there were one hundred fifty-eight tragedies, only nineteen of them composed by playwrights included in this present analysis. Moreover, there is no attempt here to account for the marked increase in popularity of the tragicomedy, of which over one hundred were produced or for the one hundred thirty-five masks and royal entertainments staged during the thirty-nine-year period. Neither is there coverage of such significant playwrights as John Marston, Thomas Heywood, George

Chapman, Philip Massinger, and James Shirley, who account for at least eighteen tragedies.

At the same time, if this analysis has its genuine limitations, it is not based on a random sample which distorts the full evidence. For one thing, only eighty-four English tragedies are extant from the forty-year period, fifteen of which are not in print. Moreover, the tragic work of the significant playwrights not covered in some detail is not anomalous in tone and structure to the plays to be discussed at some length. Chapman's five pieces, written between 1604 and 1611, all deal with the tragic conflict between the rights of the individual and the claims of the State. If in spirit his protagonists like Bussy, Cleremont, Byron, and Chabot reflect the unbounded aspiration of Marlowe's titans, they are crushed by the external forces of inexorable law and royal absolutism. Certainly in *Antonio's Revenge* and *The Wonder of Women, or Sophonisba,* Marston combines a mosaic of the various deeds of violence and intrigue from the tragedy of blood with an instinctive conception of the power of a dark atmosphere and social corruption which appears again in later pieces like *Macbeth* and *The Duchess of Malfi.* Paris and Antiochus, Massinger's tragic heroes in *The Roman Actor* and *Believe As You List,* likewise represent the individual of integrity in conflict with adverse societal forces, and both Charolais in *The Fatal Dowry* and Sforza in *The Duke of Milan* are attended by close confidantes, Francisco and Romant, who are largely responsible for provoking the principal to disastrous conduct—the one as a means of avenging a sister's honor and the other as a means of redressing private wrongs upon the surrounding characters who have wronged him. Thomas Heywood's *A Woman Killed with Kindness,* which (according to Henslowe's account was completed in March, 1603) may be the last great tragedy of Elizabeth's reign, seems to point toward the broader focus of later years. Instead of concentrating intensely on a single figure, Heywood uses comments by the wronged husband Frankford, his adulterous wife Anne, the seducer Wendoll, the servant Nicholas, and various others to create a mélange of perspectives which stresses the social experience of tragedy. Shirley, certainly the most prodigious Caroline playwright, pushes the focus even more completely beyond the individual. In a manner not unlike that of Middleton and Ford, he creates diverse reactions to a tragic dilemma in the Duke of Florence, Sciarrha, and Amidea (*The Traitor,* 1631) and in the Duchess, Hernando, and the Cardinal (*The Cardinal,* 1641), leaving the spectators to sort the pervasive moral ambiguities.

One final admission: since the dramatists obviously did not write with one particular focus in mind until 1603 and then suddenly modify it when James came to the throne, the labels "Elizabethan" and "Jacobean-Caroline" can never prudently be forced to suggest mutually exclusive points of view. *Selimus,* for example, which in the early 1590s capitalizes on the sensationalism of the barbaric Turks, anticipates the thoroughly decadent society and the moral ambiguities of later years; so for that matter do the horrific aspects of *The Jew of Malta* and the extensive depravities of *Edward II.* Conversely, the formidable dominance of personality and the tragic intensity of a character like Vittoria Corombona around 1612 or Beatrice-Joanna in 1622 are strongly reminiscent of earlier titanic figures. The germinal seeds of any specific period are present in the age which precedes it. Without pressing categories too far, however, the general design and the principal emphases are reasonably firm, and the terms are generally convenient for describing two intellectual as well as chronological phases of the English Renaissance and the tragic works which inevitably tend to reflect the spirit of the age. Shakespeare's work bridges the substantial transition in temper, and his plays provide a touchstone for analyzing those which follow. While all subsequent authors leave their individual stamp, to be sure, their vision of a fragmented society and the *mise en scène* for tragedy are remarkably consistent, and the emphasis upon the societal aspects of tragedy grows progressively sharper. The structural experimentation by each of these playwrights is the clearest indication of the continuing vitality of the form well beyond the universally acknowledged golden era.

II. Shakespeare
—FROM ELIZABETHAN TO JACOBEAN

As the single major playwright active over a period of two decades
at the turn of the seventeenth century, Shakespeare provides a body
of material crucial to an understanding of the changing emphases
of tragedy in the early years of the seventeenth century. Tragedy
inevitably mirrors the *Weltanschauung* of an age since it seeks both
physical and metaphysical accommodation for ethical questions
measured in the context of suffering and individual culpability,
and nowhere can one gauge more clearly than in Shakespeare's
stage worlds the fundamental changes between 1590 and 1610 in
man's view of himself and his role in the universe and in his society.
The differences in perspective are determined, not only by the
personality of the central figure himself, but more significantly by
the manner in which his experience is depicted—that is, whether
primary emphasis focuses on the private nature of the character's
decisions and their consequences or whether his actions are given
a broader scope, whether his decisions are perceived primarily as a
consequence of his individual impulses or whether they are seen
to result in large part from the manipulations and desires of those
surrounding him, whether the consequences of the sequence of
events and the tragic illuminations which may accrue are of a major
significance only to the protagonist or whether they ramify into a
larger comment affecting other principals or society at large—and
by the teleological frame in which the actor is placed.

It is neither possible nor necessary to retrace the full scope of my
earlier study of Shakespeare's tragedies,[1] but, in establishing a context for the subsequent discussion of individual Jacobean and Caroline stage worlds, a brief glance at the central distinction between
his tragedies written before and just after the turn of the century
and his final works composed following James' ascent to the throne
will be helpful. The earlier plays are characterized primarily by the
intensely personal quality of the tragic experience and the firm
metaphysical boundaries within which it is set. Whatever the

attitude toward a particular value may be at any given moment in
a play, the existence of supernatural control is assumed, as is a
proper code of human conduct guided by right reason. The protagonist, the antagonist, and perhaps a small group of additional
characters are viewed as temporary aberrations in what the spectators assume to be a God-controlled world in which Christian
morality will ultimately prevail. Certainly such a setting in no way
minimizes or limits the tragic experience for the individual, but it
does restrict it to precisely that—the tragedy of the individual.
There is no dominant focus upon the society beyond the individual, and there is no fundamental questioning of the teleological
frame.

This concern for focusing the spectators' vision upon a central
figure whose tragedy is the result of individual error in a world of
moral absolutes is evident even in Shakespeare's earliest work.
Richard III, for example, is not profound tragedy by the later
standards. Richard as a character is wooden; his capacities for evil
fascinate the spectator, his macabre delight perhaps even blunting
their moral responses to the abominations against nature. There is
no growth in his character, in other words, and his villainy is
melodramatically countered by his simplistically virtuous adversary
Richmond. Nevertheless, two patterns of action—the curses uttered
against the tyrant King and the remorse experienced by those whose
fall from prosperity precedes that of Richard—tightly control the
assumed metaphysical dimensions of the stage world. Most important is the execration of Queen Margaret in Act I. Not only does
she prophesy the King's anguished fall; she also provides a virtual
outline of the action of the drama. Twice beseeching God to inter-
vene in order that she may accomplish her revenge (iii, 110, 136 ff.),[2]
she predicts King Edward's death "by surfeit," the death of her own
"Prince Edward," the misery of Queen Elizabeth when she shall
outlive her present glory, and the premature deaths of Rivers and
Hastings. Her curse of Richard specifically invokes heaven's "indignation" to be "hurl[ed] down" on this "slave of nature and the son
of hell" when his "sins be ripe."[3] Further, her plea that "the worm
of conscience still begnaw [his] soul" underscores Shakespeare's
intention to depict a spiritual struggle within Richard. The ghosts—
of Prince Edward (son of Henry VI), Henry VI, Clarence, Rivers,
Grey, Vaughan, Hastings, Prince Edward (son of Edward IV), Anne,
and Buckingham—also curse Richard's bloody ascent to the throne.[4]
Indeed, the combined total of thirty-five lines spoken by these

spirits who appear in Richard's dream the night before his fatal confrontation with Richmond trigger the spiritual anguish of his final soliloquy. Each apparition, after recounting the usurper's sins, chants his grisly refrain, "Despair, and die!" The spirit of Buckingham, last to appear, charges Richard to "die in terror of thy guiltiness! / . . . Fainting, despair; despairing, yield thy breath!" (V, iii, 171, 173).

Shakespeare does not question the nature or the validity of the ghosts. These spirits, after all, represent the final stages of Margaret's curse, and Shakespeare is at some pains to establish the credibility of the supernatural machinery of the play. When Richard asserts, for instance, that Margaret's misery is the result of his father's curses upon her, Margaret responds:

> Did York's dread curse prevail so much with heaven
> . . . .
> Can curses pierce the clouds and enter heaven?
> Why then, give way, dull clouds, to my quick curses!
> (I, iii, 190, 194–95)

A few lines later she proclaims herself a "prophetess" (300), observing that her maledictions will "ascend the sky / And there awake God's gentle-sleeping peace" (186–87). In the final act, for another instance, Richmond—whose efforts are endorsed by the spirits—is directly associated with God and the enforcement of His will for England publicly and for Richard personally; if Richard is God's scourge, surely Richmond is His minister.

Clearly, Shakespeare constructs a theologically affirmative stage world in which the omniscience and omnipotence of the divinity is assumed, even by those who experience only misfortune and misery. Equally clearly, he attempts to construct a human circle in which the conscience is alive and sensitive to the values centered on that God. More precisely, Shakespeare preplots Richard's final reflective moments on various occasions throughout the play as, in the face of death, character after character—Clarence, Grey, Rivers, Vaughan, Hastings, Buckingham—turns his thoughts to the state of the soul and the sinful nature of his earthly life.[5] So, too, Richard's ending is passionate. His frenzied cry for a horse on the battlefield and his refusal of rescue from Catesby with the decree that he has "set [his] life upon a cast, / And I will stand the hazard of the die" (V, iv, 9–10) are surely intended to be the actions not of courage but of desperation.[6] Through the emphasis on the macrocosmic divine control and the microcosmic spiritual reflection preceding death, the drama, in a word, projects a positive world in which the tragedy of the individual, whatever his awe-inspiring qualities, is seen as the consequence of his violation of moral law and in which the vision of society is that of a healthy body subordinate to God's law and through it capable of purging itself of a diseased member.

In *Richard II* the authority of God is again flatly assumed. The hand of divinity operates directly through His anointed, and this relationship is alluded to time and again by Richard and his supporters and tacitly acknowledged through King Henry's "guilt of conscience" in the final scene. Bolingbroke, admittedly, defies the political power of the King. But he is no Richard III who delights in evil for its own sake; nor does he, like Iago or Edmund, ever challenge the power of heaven. To the contrary, he refers to his "divine soul" (I, i, 38) and to "God's grace" (iii, 37), and he later ascends the throne "in God's name" (IV, i, 113). This value structure is further enforced through the elaborate emphasis on knighthood, an order founded in service "to God" and "King"—as both Mowbray and Hereford frequently reiterate. Moreover, four references to the forthcoming War of the Roses (III, iii, 87–88; IV, i, 133–38; IV, i, 322–23; V, i, 57–59) fortify the religious dimensions of the play by recalling God's ordinance beyond Bolingbroke's successful usurpation. That is, though the violation of religious sanction wreaks no disaster within the scope of the play, the spectators are assured that God's inexorable justice will ultimately prevail. The prophecies also enable Shakespeare to set the play within the fifteenth-century political-historical context with which his spectators were familiar and, as recent criticism has suggested, to allow those in the audience to draw certain analogies between Richard's reign and that of Elizabeth.[7] Thus these anticipatory devices function within the play to heighten the tension and to suggest the power of heaven inextricably bound to the kingship; they also function beyond the play to broaden the scope of the issues and thereby provoke a richer emotional and intellectual response.

The world of *Julius Caesar*, though obviously not Christian, is nonetheless a world in which the existence of the gods is unquestioned.[8] The play opens, for example, at the feast of Lupercal, a day on which the tribunes direct the citizens to "Pray to the gods to intermit the plague" (I, i, 54). Caesar also takes note of the religious day and its "holy chase" (I, ii, 8). From this point, references to the Roman deities are scattered freely throughout the action. It

is also a world in which the intervention of the gods is assumed,
even though the nature of the intervention is subject to diverse
interpretation. The events of the night preceding the murder provide
a ready example: Casca, labeled Shakespeare's "mouthpiece" by
V. K. Whitaker,[9] believes, for instance, that the "tempest dropping
fire" (I, iii, 10) and the strange sights such as the lion in the Capitol
(20) and "men, all in fire, walk[ing] up and down the streets" (25)
are "portentous things" (31) to a world which has "Incense[d the
gods] to send destruction" (13); Cassius, to the contrary, would
read the "strange impatience of the heavens" (61) as "fear and
warning / Unto some monstrous state" (70–71) if Caesar remains unchecked; or, at another moment, he relates the tempest to the work
the conspirators "have in hand, / Most bloody, fiery, and most
terrible" (129–30); Calpurnia sees the tumult as a forewarning to
Caesar (II, ii, 31), Caesar as the gods' test of his courage (41). The
spectators, however, who see beyond the limited vision of the
individual, are aware of the impending disaster for Rome, for Casca,
and for Brutus; and they inevitably tend to associate the turbulence
with some teleological power, however inscrutable, which not
unconcernedly observes the human condition.

Ultimately, of greater significance than the metaphysical setting
is the experimentation by which Shakespeare attempts to develop
the spectators' consuming interest in the protagonist. One obvious
key to the power of *Hamlet* and *Othello* is the rapport between the
audience and the principal—the delicately sustained balance of
simultaneous emotional involvement and objective judgment; and,
again in the early tragedies Shakespeare is demonstrably probing to
achieve such a relationship. To this end in *Richard II* and *Romeo
and Juliet* he primarily utilizes external devices—choric figures and
foil characters—while in *Richard III* and, more effectively, in *Julius
Caesar* he employs the soliloquy and the aside to rivet attention
upon the private agitations of the central figure.

The stage world of *Richard II,* for example, is filled with a procession of characters who constantly maintain an intense focus
upon the King, emphasizing at one moment Richard's heinous mis-
management of his office coupled with his moral lassitude and at
another the sanctity of the kingship which forbids a subject to
oppose the divinely ordained monarch, and at still another moment
Richard's personal distress. The result is a powerful ambivalence in
the figure of Richard. God's vicar on earth capable through sensitivity of evoking the aura of mystery which surrounds medieval

royalty as envisioned by an Elizabethan audience, he at the same
time is thoroughly decadent in his self-centeredness;[10] intent upon
catering to his personal pleasures, he lacks the vital concern for the
security of his kingdom as well as the masculinity and decisiveness
which characterize an effective leader.

To compound the ambivalence, Bolingbroke's development as a
foil character is far more powerful than that of Richmond in
Richard III. Whereas Richmond for all intents and purposes is not
introduced until the fifth act, Bolingbroke figures in the play from
the opening scene, and his eventual struggle with the King is inevitable by the end of Act I. At the same time, Bolingbroke is not,
like Richmond, a simplistic figure of virtue acting as the hand of
God rendering justice to a tyrant and bringing peace to a strife-torn
land. Not only is he a political usurper against God's anointed; his
own motives are ambiguous from the beginning. The spectators,
never able flatly to condemn him for moving in defense of his
inheritance and in defiance of the parasites who surround Richard
and yet never able to make an emotional commitment to a character whom they perceive but dimly as one who, whatever the justification, defies the value structure established in the stage world,
are thus thrown all the more powerfully back upon Richard albeit
both in sympathy and in disdain. In a word, Richard—though a
dissipated figure and though juxtaposed with an ambitious cousin
who seems to possess all the monarchical traits which the ruler
lacks—is set within the religio-political context of divine right and
surrounded with numerous choric characters who in a variety of
ways call attention to his dilemma.[11]

The single genuinely significant moment of internalization occurs
in the final act, in which Shakespeare brings the protagonist as close
to an anagnorisis as Brutus and far closer than Titus, Richard III, or
Romeo. Here the spectators' rapport with Richard is most nearly
complete as in his lone soliloquy—his single performance without
an on-stage audience—he muses on the many roles which a person
is forced to play in life. So also, overhearing discordant music, he
compares his own life to broken time and unkept proportion (V, v,
44), admitting that he had no ear to recognize the "true time
broke. / I wasted time, and now doth time waste me" (48–49). Although from this point he again laments excessively the sighs, tears,
and groans that mark his present time, and although he dies with
the conviction that his soul will mount and that his seat is on high
(111), the moment is not without power; coupled with his anoma-

lous moment of physical valor as he slays two assassins before receiving his fatal wound, the scene elevates Richard as close to tragic stature as any figure in Shakespeare's early plays.[12]

Again, in *Romeo and Juliet* Shakespeare does not attempt to depict directly a continuing internal struggle coincident with the physical tragedy. He does, however, seem determined to control our attitude toward the central characters. Such an observation about this tragedy as well as others is not intended to suggest that Shakespeare worked rigidly from a priori positions and that his plots and characters did not frequently evolve in many respects during the process of composition. It does suggest, however, that Shakespeare and his major Elizabethan and Jacobean contemporaries were conscious artists, that they had a fundamental design and direction in mind as they created their stage worlds, and that in broad terms at least they consciously or unconsciously utilized various structural devices effectively to sustain the spectators' interest in and to orchestrate their responses to the principals and the central concerns of the action. In *Romeo and Juliet*, for example, Shakespeare extensively employs the soliloquy—indeed Romeo and Juliet soliloquize more than Hamlet, with nineteen soliloquies and one aside (a total of 237 lines) as compared with Hamlet's eight soliloquies and one aside (a total of 223 lines)—to establish a close rapport and a sense of intimacy between the audience and the protagonists. To be sure, these soliloquies involve no self-analysis (that is, no expression of conscious struggle and conflict of values which would provide the philosophic dimensions vital to the decision-making process), but they do at critical moments signal the integrity of the youthful romantic vows.[13] The most striking example is in Act II. Certainly in the early scenes it is difficult to take Romeo seriously as (like Lysander with the flower in *A Midsummer Night's Dream* or like Proteus in *The Two Gentlemen of Verona*) he is wrenched from one object of adoration to another. Yet Shakespeare would presumably see one as fatuous dotage and the other as devoted affection and would see Juliet's love at first sight as unfaltering. To be sure, there is humor in these affairs of the heart, especially in Romeo's traumatic transition. But Shakespeare concentrates ten soliloquies in Act II, six by Romeo and four by Juliet—overwhelming the spectators with ardent statements of devotion in order to convince them of the sincerity of the young lovers. Still another instance is Romeo's soliloquy in which he announces his intention to reveal all to Friar

Lawrence and to request immediate marriage. Again he does not, even for a moment, ponder the immediate or future consequences of such a request and weigh one value against another. But the soliloquy does force the spectators to accept his intentions as honorable, and their disapproval on either moral or pragmatic grounds is further disarmed.

The play is also structured in the final acts to provoke maximum sympathy for the lovers as their tragedy culminates. Regardless of the extent of their guilt to the point of Tybalt's death, both Romeo and Juliet—in the action which follows—confront reversals in companionship, creating dilemmas in the face of which they are woefully inept. Juliet, for instance, sees her emotional and physical support methodically stripped away. Her first shock comes from her father, who peremptorily insists that she agree to a marriage despite her emotional state. Next, the nurse betrays her by capitulating to the father's demand that Juliet wed the County Paris. Romeo is betrayed; Paris is available; the father is insistent: to the nurse the only solution, spoken "from [her] soul," is for Juliet to be "happy in this second match" (III, v, 229, 224). Finally, the Friar's desertion in the tomb leaves Juliet totally without support, and the spectators cannot deny that the steadfast devotion to Romeo which prompts her to join him in death excels any fidelity which she has found outside the tomb.[14] Romeo's predicament is even more pathetic. He leaves Juliet and Verona assured that Friar Lawrence will

> find a time
> To blaze [his] marriage, reconcile [his] friends,
> Beg pardon of the Prince, and call [him] back.
> (III, iii, 150–52)

The Friar promises further to "find out [Romeo's] man" and send him news "from time to time" (169, 170). Never again, though, does Romeo have conversation with Juliet, the Friar, or any of his kin; and he is utterly oblivious of the events which transpire after his banishment. The only news he receives is that Juliet is dead, and, with no message from the Friar, he can only presume he has been deserted. His suicide in the tomb—provoked by mistaken assumptions of Juliet's death and providing no redeeming qualities of insight or self-analysis—is ultimately the most painful moment for the spectator.

Shakespeare, then, methodically constructs and maintains a

sympathetic portrayal of Romeo and Juliet. The spectator is by no means oblivious of the excesses of passionate love, and on brief occasions both principals anticipate the worst possible consequences; but, with no internal struggle and with other figures manipulated to reflect the admirable characteristics of the young lovers, the structure of the play literally does not permit the audience to develop a critical posture. The play may not glorify young love, but it certainly does not condemn it, as Roy Battenhouse would have it.[15] The simple truth is that it forcefully projects a sympathy for Romeo and Juliet as victims of a wide variety of coincidences and pressures.[16] While Shakespeare makes use of the feud as a major obstacle preventing the normal development of young and impetuous love, it is certainly not the only barrier, and Shakespeare never permits social criticism to become the dominant thrust of the play. The spectators' interest is primarily the pathos of youth's attempting to accommodate itself to the ambiguous and conflicting demands of the adult world, not—as in the playwright's final pieces—on the decadence and corruption of the society itself.

More extensively in *Richard III* and *Julius Caesar,* Shakespeare seeks to make the devices of internalization an effective analytic instrument. In the former, for instance, Richard's twelve soliloquies create the eye—albeit jaundiced—through which the spectator observes the action. Such a device, as well as providing a mechanism (through Richard's meticulous plotting) of anticipating the forthcoming action, permits the audience to view directly the unholy combination of zealousness and shrewdness which comprise his character in equal parts. More importantly, it makes possible at least the dim beginnings of philosophic depths in the central figure —through his sporadic expression of fear and, above all, through the spiritual despair voiced in his final soliloquy. Starting from his dream, he desperately berates "coward Conscience" for afflicting him; his flesh trembles; he recognizes himself as a "murderer" and a "villain" and, Faustus-like, would fly from himself. His "conscience hath a thousand several tongues" as his "several sins . . . Throng to the bar, crying all, 'Guilty! guilty!' / I shall despair" (V, iii, 194, 199–201). In a remark reminiscent of his earlier desire for his mother's blessing and his subsequent affiliation with Buckingham, he laments, "There is no creature loves me; / And if I die, no soul shall pity me" (201–202). So powerful are the effects of these moments that he for the first and only time openly admits his fear to another (213, 215), informing Ratcliff:

> By the apostle Paul, shadows to-night
> Have struck more terror to the soul of Richard
> Than can the substance of ten thousand soldiers
> Armed in proof and led by shallow Richmond.
>   (217–20)

It is above all in the delineation of Brutus, though, as numerous critics have remarked, that Shakespeare reveals momentary evidence of the power which characterizes his major plays.[17] Although by comparison with subsequent work the tragedy is flawed by a blurring of focus and fails to project a meaningful anagnorisis in Brutus,[18] the fact remains that the agony of Brutus' decision is set forth with remarkably profound emotional impact. The strength of the characterization is found in Act II in the lengthy first scene in which the audience perceives in Brutus the transformation of political idealism into the ideology of violent revolution. Actually, he commits himself in his first soliloquy; through the psychic struggle which then ensues, his spirit too will eventually assent.[19] In this initial statement (II, i, 10–34), prompted and goaded by Cassius in the earlier scenes, he observes that Caesar must die (10); he must be attacked for the general good (12); to give him a crown is to give him a "sting" (16); an absolute ruler forgets the meaning of remorse (18–19); an ambitious man "Looks in the clouds, scorning the base degrees / By which he did ascend" (26–27); a serpent is best killed "in the shell" (34). Certainly at this point, however, he is capable of separating fact from fancy, and his whole being seems to well up in rebellion against the sophistry of his rationalization. He admits, for example, that he "know[s] no personal cause to spurn" Caesar (11), that the crown "*might* [italics mine] change his nature" (13), that he "*may* do danger" with the sting (17). He admits also that he has never "known when [Caesar's] affections swayed / More than his reason" (20–21). Again, though, "Caesar *may*, . . . augmented, . . . run to . . . extremities" (27, 30, 31). Clearly, Brutus' case against Caesar is pitifully weak and problematical— and no one, at this particular moment, knows it better than he.

The second soliloquy (44–58), shifting the grounds of his reflection to himself, projects the egocentricity which will blind him to these distinctions between what Caesar is and what he may be. Gullible victim to the "messages" which Cassius has planted in his home, Brutus all too willingly "piece[s] . . . out" (51) the implications of the plea for him to "Awake, . . . Speak, strike, redress" (46–47). With a touch of smugness he recalls the feats of his ancestors in driving Tarquin from the streets. And the touch is but prelude to full seizure as, envisioning himself as Rome's present saviour, he pledges himself to the city and vows that it shall receive its "full petition at the hand of Brutus" (58). In the space of an incredibly few moments, then, pride has converted concern into an opportunity for heroics, and it is no longer convenient to consider Caesar's guilt a mere possibility.

The misery and torment of Brutus' inner hell reaches its height in the third soliloquy (61–69) two lines later. Describing such agitation as "a phantasma or a hideous dream" (65), he likens the struggle in "the state of a man" (67) between "The Genius and the mortal instruments" (66)—the spiritual and the physical—to "an insurrection" (68–69). Similarly, in the fourth soliloquy (77–85) he is plagued by the guilt which attaches to the covert and stealthy movements of the conspirators. The plot will "show [its] dang'rous brow [only] by night, / When evils are most free" (78–79). Either by day it must "find a cavern dark enough / To mask [its] monstrous visage" (80–81), or it must cloak true intent "in smiles and affability" (82). If for the moment he can manufacture the courage of desperation in the assurance that hypocrisy, skillfully practiced, is incapable of perception, certainly he has lost it in the fifth soliloquy (229–33) as—like Henry IV obsessed with a commitment inherently tainted—he laments that he is deprived of "the honey-heavy dew of slumber" (230) which comes so naturally to a mind uncharged with "figures," "fantasies," and "busy care" (231–32). In his aside before Caesar is struck down, this hypocrisy is the focus of Brutus' particular agony; to Caesar's remark that they "(like friends) will straightway go together" (II, ii, 127), he can only mutter in remorse that his heart "erns to think upon" the deception which festers behind the cloak of friendship (129).

In no other play does Shakespeare cluster soliloquies so thickly within a single scene, a point even more remarkable in light of the fact that this work presumably follows two tragedies in which the devices of internalization are of minimal significance. Granted, there is a general falling off in the last half of the play. Brutus' additional soliloquies are insignificant, and at no time can he bring himself to admit that he has been used by another who has hidden dishonest intent behind his courage and integrity. Consequently, despite the powerful development of the early acts, Brutus in the final analysis is only slightly closer to true self-knowledge at the conclusion of the play than are Shakespeare's early protagonists. Even so, the focus in the final acts is not on the social scene, but on Brutus, whose deeply disturbed nature belies the superficially stoic posture of innocence.[20] Coupled with Antony's explicitly developing villainy (which deflects the spectators' judgment upon Brutus) and with Cassius' unrestrained admiration for and Lucius' innocent devotion to him, Brutus continues to be a compelling figure. He muses philosophically about the uncertain end of "this day's business" (V, i, 123) and of the desirability of "leap[ing]" in the pit himself rather "Than tarry till they push [him]" (v, 24, 25) because "Night hangs upon [his] eyes; [his] bones would rest" (41). He even relates the catastrophic events to the spirit of Caesar which "walks abroad and turns our swords / In our own proper entrails" (V, iii, 95-96) and which appears to convince him that his "hour is come" (v, 20).[21] And in his most affecting moment, as he runs on his sword, he exclaims that he "killed not [Caesar] with half so good a will" (51).

Clearly Shakespeare's plays are exploring various avenues to tragedy, and in *Hamlet, Othello, Lear,* and *Macbeth* the internal and external structural devices coalesce to produce his most powerful achievements in personal tragedy. Each protagonist a titan in his own particular manner who passionately defies those who oppose his will and each destroyed by an intensity of personality which provokes both admiration and condemnation, these central figures are the logical descendants of Marlowe's overreachers and Shakespeare's early protagonists. Indeed, they are the last of the genuinely Elizabethan tragic heroes. Again what characterizes these tragedies is the focus on the intensely private experience of the central figure whose activities and the forces they set in motion represent temporary and awesomely destructive aberrations from a world in which natural harmony is an attainable goal (at least in the mind of the tragic figure—and the perspective renders this the single most important fact) and in which metaphysical authority is assumed.

Hamlet quite obviously invites comparison with Tourneur's Vindice, and the comparison offers a signal illustration of the difference in focus between the Elizabethan and the Jacobean perspective. Both are sardonic individuals impelled to revenge by the death of a loved one and as such both form the center of dramatic

interest for the plot; both with genuine disgust look upon a decadent court in which the ruler himself is the prime example of the
pervasive corruption; both are possessed of a barbed, satiric wit
which titillates the audience even as it castigates the general moral
license; both grow increasingly more vicious as they develop in
their role of purger. The crucial difference, however, is the metaphysical frame in which Hamlet operates; he eventually must come
to terms with the irrevocable and absolute moral values which he
assumes to obtain in his universe. This in turn leads him through a
personal crisis in which the spectators' abiding concern is the individual's accommodation to his corrupt environment. Conversely,
Vindice never recognizes a higher moral value than his own vendetta; and, though he fails to realize it, his passion slowly transforms
him from a self-appointed moral avenger into a vicious monster
little better than the depraved creatures whom he opposes.[22] In
this case there is no personal crisis demanding the spectators' attention; instead, they are forced to observe and to judge the extensive
social corruption, and the tragedy becomes as much an indictment
of aggregate man and his political institutions as of the individual
who forms its narrative center.

Again the single most significant feature in determining the private focus in *Hamlet* is the soliloquy, here used in a strikingly bold
manner to accentuate the complexity of the protagonist's character. To be sure, the assertion is commonplace that the essential
power of *Hamlet* results directly from the spectators' descent into
the Dane's "war within himself." But the crucial ingredient is not
the number of soliloquies; it is the structural arrangement by which
they reflect diverse, even polarized, aspects of his total personality.[23]
In effect, they function in this play as a device for complication,
not for clarity. Here the soliloquy does not establish a vision of a
consistent personality; since the decision of one moment is forgotten or ignored in the next, the soliloquy does not project a pattern
of narrative anticipation; it is not used for any conscious articulation of commitment to passion; nor—following the precipitous actions which leave a trail of human carnage from Gertrude's bedchamber to the great hall of the castle—is it used to describe any
moment of insight: indeed there is no soliloquy whatever after IV,
iv—Hamlet's final words prior to his sea-adventure.

The protagonist's eight soliloquies, to be more specific, are
clustered within fourteen of the twenty scenes of the play as
marked in modern editions, from I, ii, to IV, iv. During this section

of the play Hamlet does not achieve vengeance—for himself or for
God; he pierces neither Gertrude's soul nor Claudius' body. He
does, however, face the moments which impel him to an irrevocable stand against his uncle-King and to an impulsive attack in Gertrude's bedchamber—moments which forever dispel his glimpses of
stoic dislocation from the intrigues swirling around him. When the
pirates release him on Danish soil, he is no longer the contemplative
man; however much one might argue the point, there is not one
shred of evidence in the play that Hamlet, having been previously
bent on private and personal revenge, is concerned with finding the
proper "public" moment for the king's execution.[24] He is now
simply a man determined to act. And, quite frankly, he never wor-
ries further over the moral implications of such action—at least
insofar as the spectators are permitted to see within him. Granted,
he is now convinced that a providential God is in His heaven once
again and that a part of His providential scheme is for murder to
reap its proper rewards. Under the umbrella of this conviction, he
is able to accommodate everything from the proxy execution of
Rosencrantz and Guildenstern to the double slaughter of Claudius
with the sword and the cup. On the other hand, to insist that
Hamlet following his sea-change is a man totally purged of passion
is to disregard his essential nature in the last four scenes. He is anything but dispassionate as he leaps impulsively into Ophelia's grave
and grapples with Laertes in a dispute over whose love for the
maiden was greater, as he is piqued to a more than passing interest
in the possibility of besting Laertes at fencing ("Since he went into
France I have been in continual practice" [V, ii, 199–200]), and as
in high fury he forces the king (the "incestuous, murd'rous, damned
Dane" [314], to "Drink off" the last dregs of the "potion."

At the risk of oversimplification, the difference between the
Hamlet of the first four acts and the Hamlet of the final act is that,
in Act V, he is a man prepared to face the fortunes of life with both
consistency and conviction; his actions move almost predictably
toward the final confrontation between uncle and nephew in which,
already fatally wounded, he will find the provocation to accomplish
a vengeance whose moral justification he now flatly takes for
granted. It is true that he has achieved this conviction far too late
to save himself either from moral stain or physical harm; his rash
impetuosity which resulted in Polonius' death has long since
marked him for destruction. But the Hamlet of the end of the final
act of the play is a man of undivided mind and philosophy; his

actions and his thoughts—as expressed in dialogue with Horatio and others—are of a piece.

The earlier Hamlet sorely lacks this coherence of personality; his psychic complexity results from the various aspects of his spirit, each struggling for predominance and control.[25] At one moment he is profoundly concerned with the moral implications of murder despite the apparent justification; at another he is disturbed at the possibility that the ghost (and hence the justification) be false; at another he possesses a fire-eyed determination to strike down the tyrant King whatever the ramifications spiritual or political; at another he ponders turning the knife against himself rather than facing these cruelly enigmatic issues; at another his words reflect an awesome frenzy not far short of madness. Critics on occasion have seized upon one single aspect as the real Hamlet; similarly, in order to achieve a coherence of personality, an actor may emphasize the angry young man, or the melancholy Dane, or the moralist, or the incipient madman.

The sheer enigma of the character, however, is that he is all of these faces; the Hamlet of the first four acts cannot be reduced to a single complexion without distortion and oversimplification. And the key structural feature is the soliloquy. By convention the spectator must accept the character's word in soliloquy as straightforward and sincere; at such moments pretensions and façades crumble, and the character stands before us—and before himself—for what he is. In the soliloquies of Shakespeare's other tragic protagonists, the character realizes to some degree the nature of his predicament. He senses the mounting tensions and attempts to describe either the decisions or the course of developing events which impel him to disaster. Hamlet's soliloquies, to the contrary, provide no such guidance for the spectators. They are emotional reactions to the thoughts or events of the moment, and consequently they lack the significant continuity which would reflect a genuine comprehension of himself or of his relationship to the events which surround him.

In effect, the gap between what the spectator knows and what the protagonist knows is wide indeed. Not only are the spectators aware of the external forces which gather against the Dane, culminating with the venom-tipped rapier and the poisoned wine; they also see him more fully than he sees himself. That is, they are forced into the position of comparing and evaluating the many faces of the protagonist—something of which he himself is incapable, despite his intensively introspective nature. If to see is not totally

to comprehend, these spectators nonetheless are compelled to become a vital part of the dramatic process as the pattern of Hamlet's
actions in the first four acts assumes form and meaning essentially
in the mind of the beholder. In a very real sense, then, the critics
speak of *Hamlet* as the most universal of plays; the initial stages of
the tragic experience are determined by the manner in which the
spectators put together the pieces of the puzzle to provide the
answers or assumptions which the play itself refuses to yield; the
"experience of the audience on the stage (which includes all the
dramatis personae) is shared by that in the theatre."[26] The spectators, for example, must ultimately decide for themselves the question of Hamlet's sanity at any given point in the eleven of fifteen
scenes in which he appears through IV, iv; they must determine the
nature of the ghost,[27] the extent of Gertrude's guilt, and the son's
precise attitude toward both her and that guilt; they must draw
their own conclusions concerning the nature of Hamlet's relationship with Ophelia; in the early scenes at least they must determine
whether Hamlet's hesitation to move against the King is occasioned
by moral fortitude, physiological or psychological incapacity, personal vindictiveness, sincere doubt, or arrant cowardice—whether,
for example, Hamlet's moral impasse is the accidental by-product
of Shakespeare's placing the pagan concept of revenge within the
frame of Christian morality, or whether he deliberately juxtaposes
the two systems to produce just such an enigma. There, obviously,
is no single face which the pieces of these first four acts must or
can be made to depict, and the actors or critics who force the
protagonist into a rigid mold make a mockery of his essential complexity. In a word, the impact of the drama emerges from the
continuing mystery of Hamlet prior to his sea-change, a mystery
created fundamentally through the soliloquies.

Equally important, the metaphysical ambiguities of the play are
essentially resolved in the final act. Following his sea-adventure,
Hamlet no longer is frenetically inconsistent in his approach to the
destruction of Claudius. No longer does he question the moral
justification of the act; now he flatly considers it to be "perfect
conscience / To quit him with this arm" (V, ii, 67–68). No longer
is he a man whose obsession with the corruption and depravity of
the world and its inhabitants is exceeded only by his desire to
escape from it. Now he asserts that "There's a divinity that shapes
our ends, / Rough-hew them how we will" (ii, 10–11). "Heaven"
was "ordinant" (48) in his escape from death in England through

the manipulations that send Rosencrantz and Guildenstern to their destruction (deaths which "are not near [his] conscience" [58]). Hamlet is now "constant to [his] purposes" (190), prepared for every alternative. Nothing, he now proclaims, happens by accident: "There is special providence in the fall of a sparrow. If it be now, 'tis not to come; if it be not to come, it will be now; if it be not now, yet it will come. The readiness is all" (209–11). He acknowledges a divine purpose within him: "Yet have I in me something dangerous, / Which let thy wisdom fear" (i, 249–50). Hamlet is now a man who, albeit too late, is able to articulate his love for Ophelia, able to exchange forgiveness freely with Laertes. Instead of his earlier callous attitude toward death and the human corpse, now the prince is incensed that the gravedigger "has . . . no feeling of his business. . . . Did these bones cost no more the breeding but to play at loggets with 'em?" (i, 62, 85–86); his remarks concerning Yorick (201–15) reveal a sympathy and affection foreign to the earlier Hamlet. Here, too, is a man concerned that his "story" be told fully and accurately, lest a "wounded name . . . shall live behind [him]" (ii, 333–34). And, in giving his voice to the election of Fortinbras, he now is capable of looking beyond his death to the stability of the country. The final words of both Horatio and Fortinbras underscore the nature of Hamlet's tragic growth.

Spectators may not be universally happy with a God who condones blood revenge and utilizes human agents to expedite His divine wrath, but the thrust of the play—which "emphasizes the mystery of existence by illuminating the nature of human responsibility"[28]—is clear. The protagonist finds a peace of soul and mind only after he accommodates himself to a will and purpose greater than his own. This peace of soul which the play proclaims is of this world, not of the next, to be sure; nonetheless, it comes only with the purgation of an ego which at the outset prompts him to judge all else in terms of his own frustration and despair and which later hardens into the cynical assumption that decisions of death and life (the slaying of Polonius, the sparing of Claudius) rest only with his own distorted logic.

Othello, perhaps Shakespeare's most intensely personal tragedy, forces the viewers inside the mind of a man, noble and talented but incipiently wrathful and jealous, where, even as they observe the total sweep of the action, they must confront the full emotional impact of his destruction. If the dramatist is to succeed, the interest must arise, as in Hamlet and—less successfully—in Brutus, from the ever intensifying pressures mounting in Othello's spirit rather than from the external events of the plot itself. To this end he creates in Iago an antagonist whose soliloquies and asides in the early acts provide a rich perspective of dramatic irony and whose comments guide the spectators' attention to both Othello's present nobility and his potential weakness. These same structural devices of internalization are transferred to Othello in the last half of the play; and, in successive scenes which reiterate the situation of the protagonist's decision and intensify his spiritual agony, the spectators' interest is increased progressively to the climactic moments of the murder and the subsequent heartsick despair of tragic waste coupled with the self-knowledge which results from his suffering. One may continue to speak of the cosmological implications—the storm which provides a macrocosmic "foretaste . . . of what is to happen in Othello's soul,"[29] the symbolic movement "from *the city* to barbarism, . . . from order to riot, from justice to wild revenge and murder, from truth to falsehood,"[30] the universal nature of the struggle between the higher and lower faculties of the human spirit. But, for all practical purposes, the dramatic focus is sharply limited: the time is condensed, too sensationally for many; and the action is single, permitting no diversion of interest. Othello's agony—involving the actual murder and the recognition of his error —is more isolated than that of any other Shakespearean tragic hero.

  Viewed only from the outside in the first half of the play, Othello is a man who acts with understandable assurance and confidence. By III, iii, however, his willingness to listen to Iago's insinuations,[31] first about Cassio, then about Desdemona, takes a dreadful toll, and the remainder of the tragedy the spectators experience, not through the eyes of one who with burning joy intrigues to trap another, but through the eyes and soul of the victim who must bring himself to admit both the crime of passion against the fair Desdemona and also the stupidity and naïveté which render him susceptible to jealousy. Questioning the prudence of marriage, Othello considers his age and his color, concluding with a touch of typical pomposity that marriage is "the plague of great ones; / Prerogatived are they less than the base" (273-74). At this point the general is visibly disturbed, as Iago notes on three occasions within the scope of ten lines (214-24). By the end of the scene Othello has himself seized the initiative, agonizing that his "occupation's gone" (357).

> If there be cords, or knives,
> Poison, or fire, or suffocating streams,
> I'll not endure it.
>
> (388–90)

It is the supreme irony of the play for Othello to kneel ritualistically and "in the due reverence of a sacred vow" to "engage [his]
words" to "yond marble heaven" (460ff.). Iago's most precious
moment must surely be the Moor's response to his request to let
Desdemona live:

> Damn her, lewd minx! O, damn her! damn her!
> . . . I will withdraw
> To furnish me with some swift means of death
> For the fair devil. Now art thou my lieutenant.
>
> (476–79)

The structure of the last half of the play is remarkably firm as,
following III, iii, the spectators' attention is drawn toward Othello's
private struggles with progressively increasing intensity. More specifically, in four successive waves Shakespeare repeats and intensifies Othello's commitment to passion, thus building the tension to
a maximum peak just before the murder in Act V. Othello's fateful
decisions are made, to be sure, at the end of III, iii, without the
benefit of one shred of evidence; and nothing essentially changes
between this scene and V, ii. What the spectators do see, however,
is the progressive deterioration of Othello's mentality as he grows
more determined to commit the action to which a moment of hot
passion has already forced him to agree.[32] The first such wave (III,
iv, 32–98) occurs immediately after his decision, as he confronts
Desdemona before the castle, addressing her as "chuck" and demanding the handkerchief which he believes she has given to Cassio
and which he asserts has "magic in the web" (69). As his anger
waxes hotter, he for the first time becomes overtly disrespectful
to his shocked and bewildered wife, stubbornly demanding the
"napkin" in threatening grunts that become almost bestial: "Ha!
Wherefore? . . . Is't lost? Is't gone? Speak, is't out o' th' way? . . .
Say you? . . . How? . . . Fetch't, let me see't. . . . Fetch me the
handkerchief! My mind misgives. . . . The handkerchief. . . . The
handkerchief! . . . 'Zounds!'" (78ff.).

In the second wave, which follows immediately (IV, i, 1–209),
Iago is at further work upon the Moor's diseased mind. Far bolder
now, he graphically describes Desdemona's liaison with Cassio,

their kissing in private, their being naked in bed together, the hand-kerchief she has given him as a love token, Cassio's blabbing of lying "With her, on her; what you will" (34). Othello's white-hot passion renders him literally incoherent ("Pish! Noses, ears, and lips? Is't possible?—Confess?—Handkerchief?—O devil!" [42–43]) moments before, in physical collapse, he reveals to the spectators and to the immensely pleased Iago the extent of the inner corro-sion.

The third wave (IV, i, 210–56) provokes Othello to strike his wife in public. Lodovico arrives with orders for Othello to return to Venice and for Cassio to replace him in command (an order which, assuming sufficient time has elapsed, sharply points up how ineffective the Moor's command and his communication with his home base have become). Again, when the orders remind him of Cassio, his speech becomes fragmented ("Fire and brimstone! . . . Are you wise? . . . Indeed? . . . I am glad to see you mad. . . . Devil! . . . O devil, devil!" [227ff.]); and, when he overhears Desdemona indicate pleasure that Cassio is to assume command, he strikes her impulsively in what amounts to a painful preplotting of the perversely contemplated deed he will shortly thereafter enact in the privacy of his bedchamber. In the "brothel scene" (IV, ii, 1–94), the fourth wave, both Othello's misguided sense of honor and his language are at their most extravagant. Openly confronting Desdemona with charges of infidelity, he brands her "chuck" (24), "strumpet" (81), "weed" (67), and "cunning whore of Venice" (89), guilty of deeds at which "Heaven stops the nose" (77), the "moon winks" (77), and the "bawdy wind . . . Is hushed" (78–79); her honesty equates with "summer flies . . . in the shambles, / That quicken even with blowing" (66–67). Claiming that she has trans-formed his heart into a "cistern for foul toads / To knot and gender in" (61–62), he is furious that she has made him "A fixed figure for the time of scorn / To point his slow unmoving finger at!" (54–55).

Othello, in his soliloquy in Act V, the spectators see as a man whose mind has been virtually paralyzed by the monstrous obses-sion with his own sense of justice. Torn between revulsion for his wife's degradation and affection for the woman he earlier loved beyond measure, he nonetheless moves with awesome resolution to the fulfillment of his role as both judge and executioner. His final conversation with his wife is replete with Christian terms: "Repent," "prayed," "Unreconciled," "heaven," "grace," "spirit," "soul," "amen," "confess," "sin," and "oath" (10–54 *passim*).

Shakespeare

THE
UNIVERSITY OF WINNIPEG
PORTAGE & BALMORAL
WINNIPEG, MAN.   R3B 2E9.
CANADA.

39

Beneath this façade of piety, however, is the bloody passion which causes his eyes to roll (38), which prompts him to "gnaw . . . [his] nether lip" (43), and which bursts forth in the cruelty of his "strumpet! . . . strumpet!" (77, 79) in defiance of her request for time "but . . . [to] say one prayer!" (83).

His tragic insight begins within seconds, as the shock of Emilia's call rings from him, "My wife! My wife! What wife? I have no wife. / O, insupportable! O heavy hour!" (V, ii, 98–99). And while in life she could not persuade him of her innocence, her dying words to Emilia (which, in returning love for hatred, make no mention of his brutal act) apparently do. Confronted on every side with evidence of the stupidity and cruelty of his deed, his momentary reactions range from the painful "O! O! O!" (199) to his "why should honor outlive honesty?" (246). A conscious self-debasement (not unlike Lear's, "I am a very foolish fond old man") is involved in his admission that it is only a "vain boast" that one "can control his fate" (265–66), an assumption which had been at the very center of his earlier proclamations concerning "the cause" and heavenly justice.[33]

In *Othello* Shakespeare sets forth his least complicated structure to concentrate the spectators' attention on the inner hell of a man blinded by pride and circumstance. The villain as an external pointer who establishes multiple layers of dramatic irony and the successive waves of action which reflect Othello's mounting passion combine to achieve an intense focus on the isolated figure who agonizes over a deed committed in the privacy of his bedchamber. In *King Lear,* most likely Shakespeare's next tragedy chronologically, the movement is reversed—outward and all encompassing rather than inward and restricting. The disastrous errors of passion, the immediate and eventual consequences, and the painful joy of self-knowledge are enacted in the public arena and the effects and ramifications are registered on several macrocosmic levels.

Viewed in the context of the total canon, *Lear* and *Macbeth* are transitional tragedies in which Shakespeare begins to move from the Elizabethan to the Jacobean perspective. Like the earlier plays they are above all else personal tragedies, drawing their emotional power from the private dimensions of experience in which the spectators share with the protagonist, in the one instance the heart-rending path back to right reason following a sudden destructive act of temper, in the other the agonizing process of succumbing to the temptation of ambition and the methodic corrosion which thereafter

renders life meaningless and abhorrent. Like earlier figures the
protagonists literally dominate their stage worlds, and it is primarily the exercise of Herculean will and prodigious ego which impels
the disastrous act. At the same time, as a consequence of specific
structural innovations, both the causes and the ramifications of
tragedy seem to be extended. For one thing the agents of evil are
multiplied, and the spectators—confronted with their oppressive
presence—sense a more extensive corruption in the frame of the
human community. For another, the metaphysical dimensions of
the stage world no longer support the unchallenged assumptions of
teleological design which serve to assure the spectator that, however monstrous the temporary deviation, positive values will be
reestablished and will prevail. If this is not yet a societal perspective, it is a reshaping of the concept of the very ontology of tragedy
and a direct reflection of the modulating social and philosophic
concepts which form the basis of such a dramatic vision.

The difference, it bears repeating, is primarily in the structure—
the devices by which the audience is made an emotional part of the
experience. Most obvious is Shakespeare's use in *Lear* of the double
plot, among his tragedies a feature unique to this work. Lear and
Gloucester face similar dilemmas, are guilty of similar misjudg-
ments, and must pay similar consequences.[34] Their full cycle is
delineated, not (as with Hamlet, Othello, and Macbeth) through
the usual devices of internalization, but through the Fool (for Lear)
and Edgar in disguise as Tom o' Bedlam (for Gloucester)—characters
whose most significant dramatic function is to provide the principals
an effective means by which to express their innermost thoughts.
Finally, through soliloquies and asides the playwright establishes
three major tragic pointers to guide the audience's response to this
experience—Edmund as spokesman for the self-interest which ever
stands ready to profit from the prideful naïveté of others and Kent
and Edgar (apart from his disguise) as spokesmen for the dis-
interested self-knowledge vital to man's successful completion of
his journey through this tainted society, knowledge which enables
one both to have a clear vision of reality by removing self from the
center of his universe and also to realize human love in its profoundest sense. These characters, unlike the Fool and Poor Tom,
perform roles important to the narrative itself, but they also sporadically function as spokesmen for the polarized values which
both destroy and regenerate Lear and Gloucester.

In a broad sense, Lear's mad scenes (III, ii, iv, vi) are the emo-

tional equivalent of Gloucester's blinding; the mental anguish of
the one and the physical anguish of the other compel the sufferer
to recognize the truth and to confess the stupidity of his earlier
judgment.[35] At this point they are, however, far indeed from a
reassertion of right reason; both swing wildly from the position of
disregarding the significance of human responsibility in a teleological universe controlled by benevolent deities to the position of
disclaiming the possibility of such responsibility in a nihilistic one.
Gloucester is now "made [to] think a man a worm" (IV, i, 33); "As
flies to wanton boys, are we to th' gods; / They kill us for their
sport" (36–37). In despair he renounces the world as no longer
bearable and collapses in what he assumes to be a fall to death and
to release from a meaningless life. So also, Lear—beyond the
delirium of his madness—proclaims the world a place fit only for
copulation (IV, vi, 113) and justice merely a system by which one
man exploits another (148–52); man is but a "natural fool of
fortune" on "this great stage of fools" (188, 180).

Both Gloucester and Lear emerge from this despair in Act IV.
Gloucester in scene vi, amazed to be alive, swears that never again
will he permit his "worser spirit" to tempt him to doubt the purpose of life (214). Lear in scene vii awakens in Cordelia's arms, admitting that the tears of contrition "Do scald like molten lead"
(48) and acknowledging that he is "a very foolish fond old man"
(60), "old and foolish" (84). Even in prison he and Cordelia—
reunited in love—will profess to read the riddle of existence, to
"take upon [themselves] the mystery of things / As if [they] were
God's spies" (V, iii, 16–17). Finally, both men face a brutal test of
their convictions in Act V, and both suffer a momentary regres-
sion—Gloucester when he hears that Cordelia's forces have been
defeated and Lear when he carries the dead daughter on stage. The
despair is but momentary, however; caught between the beauty of
selfless love which they have discovered and the cruel forces of
nature which demand full payment for earlier destructive forces
set in motion by pride's misjudgment, each dies of a broken heart.
Gloucester's "flawed heart . . . 'Twixt two extremes of passion,
joy and grief, / Burst [s] smilingly" (iii, 196, 197–99), and Lear
breathes his last while gazing on Cordelia: "Do you see this? Look
on her! Look her lips, / Look there, look there" (iii, 311–12).
While one can never be absolutely certain whether Lear does or
does not assume his daughter to be alive as he holds her in his arms,
the fundamental significance of the drama does not rest on this

particular point.[36] Belief that she is alive can certainly increase his
joy, just as belief that she is dead can add power to his profound
despair. But the impact of his final moments results from the
combination of both emotions held in heart-rending tension. He is
ecstatic over the newfound love which through her he has experienced while at the same time he is tormented by her tragedy
for which ultimately he is responsible.

    With the parallel experiences of Lear and Gloucester, the two
internal pointers who prompt the principals to soliloquy in dialogue,
the three external pointers who establish the range of values within
which the critical choices occur, as well as the minor pointers and
the various foil relationships, Shakespeare has devised in *King Lear*
a "complex polyphonic development of . . . themes."[37] Structure is,
of course, largely determined by the playwright's thematic intentions and the kind of character he depicts. Certainly, in this play
a primary concern is to reveal the spiritual struggle within both
Lear and Gloucester and to compel the audience to emotional
identification with and involvement in both the agony and the joy
of their growth in tragic insight. But the soliloquy would hardly be
a natural medium of expression for men hardened by pride to crass
insensitivity and unaccustomed to introspection. Far more effective and credible is a second character, viewed by the audience as
objective, who can through conversation force the central figures
to react emotionally and reflectively. Moreover, Lear's mental
deviations on the one hand and the nihilistic despair coincident
with Gloucester's savage blinding on the other assume a more awesome significance against the grotesque background of the Fool's
riddles and the lunatic's whirling words. Both clothe profound
truth in outlandish language: the seeming absence of logic in the
Fool's phrases forces Lear to seek the meaning within himself; and
poor Tom's companionship and guidance, despite his own misery
and destitution, constrain Gloucester to search his own heart for
the charity which prompts such compassion without judgment.

    This structure, in addition, quite literally demands that the spec-
tators develop an intimate familiarity with a larger number of
characters than in any other Shakespearean tragedy. Such a circumstance, on the one hand, supports Shakespeare's obvious intentions to make the ramifications of this tragedy massive, funneling
out from the level of the individual, to the family, to the kingdom,
and to the order of nature itself. On the other hand, the theme of
play is also best served by such a structure. Lear and Gloucester

must learn the fundamental reality of existence—that humanity encompasses both the animal and the spirit. The insight which they must achieve does not involve an isolated decision concerning the ethics of ambition, or of vengeance, or of wasted opportunity; instead it is directly concerned with their spiritual relationships with others—and is meaningless outside that context. Although Cordelia, Edgar, and Kent are essentially static and stylized, Shakespeare through the soliloquy and the aside is able to underscore unambiguously their selflessness and thus to achieve the maximum emotional impact from the reconciliation of Lear and Cordelia, and Gloucester and Edgar, at the end of Act IV.

King Lear, in brief, is not about a supernatural heaven and hell, but about the human condition. As one critic has noted, "Almost every possible point of view on the gods and cosmic justice is expressed, from a malevolent, wanton polytheism to an astrological determinism, from an amoral, personified Nature-goddess, to 'high-judging Jove.'"[38] With every character invoking his own concept of a deity,[39] the play does not proclaim that there is—or is not—a god, and it most assuredly does not deny the horror and reality of death. What it does proclaim is that man is a responsible agent and that in the short span of this life he can most nearly experience the godlike ecstasy and comfort of heart through a love of mutual humility and concern, through a human relationship purged of self-interest. Through the complex pointers which converge on Lear and Gloucester, Shakespeare creates an effective structural base for a tragedy both microcosmic and macrocosmic; he achieves for the spectators a perspective of double vision—forcing them to share fully the protagonist's spiritual struggle while at the same time providing a sufficiently omniscient view to compel them to sit in judgment on his decisions and anticipate the consequences.

In *Macbeth,* Shakespeare pursues further the concept of tragedy set within a universe whose principal inhabitants lack clear assurance of teleological control. The effects of the tragedy, as in *Lear,* are registered on the level of the individual, of the family, of the state, and of physical nature.[40] Like Edmund, Kent, and Edgar—Banquo and Lady Macbeth function as external pointers who establish the frame of values within which Macbeth must make his decisions; through the devices of internalization, the spectator is compelled to share their inner struggles as well as Macbeth's, thus widening the scope of the tragedy beyond the intense focus on a single individual.

As with Lear, however, the major focus is once more upon the single tragic figure; to the spectators the surrounding features remain secondary to Macbeth's increasingly awesome descent into villainy. There is no full tragic cycle, no Lear-like regeneration or recognition at the moment of destruction. But there is pathetic regret; and Shakespeare carefully modulates the death of Macbeth's conscience and the parallel growth of his despair through four increasingly intense waves to the point of his death. At the same time, the playwright in the final act attempts to retain the sense of tragic illumination by transferring the anagnorisis, in part, away from the tyrant through significant emphasis upon the humanizing effects of suffering (in Lady Macbeth) and the restitution of national order (in Malcolm, Duncan's proclaimed heir to the throne).

As a backdrop for Macbeth's individual tragedy the playwright establishes a consistent conflict for supremacy between the forces of darkness and the forces of light. And he refuses to tilt the balance; in the cosmos of this stage world, a "humanly relevant quality only exists in relation to a particular human outlook and standpoint."[41] Certainly, this is not unequivocally God's world in which Macbeth's sinful aberration occurs in total isolation. The Weird Sisters do exist, after all;[42] they are seen by Banquo as well as Glamis, and their malicious obfuscations sorely try him as well, while to Lady Macbeth they are disastrous. If Malcolm as God's vicar is eventually established on the Scottish throne, Macbeth lies dead, in part a victim of the witches. Innocents also like Lady Macduff, her son, young Siward, and nameless victims of the final battle are sacrificed to the perverse ambition fed by the withered hags.

By the same token, the simplistic assertion that the play is fatalistic mocks the philosophic complexity of the tragedy.[43] The mysterious creatures of the heath clearly do not hold ultimate authority to compel the mortals of this stage world to destruction. For one thing, Banquo is able to withstand the temptations inherent in their prediction that his descendants shall rule the kingdom. Admittedly, the drama focuses only sporadically and briefly on his inner turmoil; moreover, since the prophecy refers only to those of future generations, the temptation for him presumably is far less immediate. He does, however, respond both to ambition and to conscience; and he is depicted as one free to choose his own path. Unlike his companion, Banquo does nothing at the price of principle or soul, and any argument which affirms his villainy simply must read into the text what the playwright does not provide. On several further occasions the witches themselves admit their limited powers. In discussing their various activities in I, iii, for example, the first witch is enraged against a sailor whose wife has insulted her. With the aid of her fellow spirits, she will "drain him dry" (18); unable to sleep, he, like "a man forbid" (21), "Shall . . . dwindle, peak, and pine" (23). Significantly, however, she holds no power of life and death; "his bark cannot be lost" (24). Thus, a mere eleven lines prior to Macbeth's entrance the witches would seem to indicate that, though they can hound and taunt through the manipulation of surrounding circumstances, they cannot in the final analysis either force decisions or destroy for failure to comply with their desires. When Macbeth seeks them out to demand further insight into his destiny, they—with their charms "firm and good" (IV, i, 38)—can answer only that they are creating "A deed without a name" (49). The illusory apparitions they will display have no reality and no name; only he, duped by such appearance and subject to "an interplay of relations or circumstances as important as the motives themselves,"[44] can subsequently make the decisions and commit the deeds which will give truth to their vision. For that matter, their divinatory powers in the first act are suspect. The spectators hear of Cawdor's treason and Macbeth's appointment to the title in scene ii; the witches of the heath, who prophetically announce the position to Macbeth in the following scene, obviously are in the vicinity of Duncan's camp and might well also have had quite logical access to the information.

With the powers of witchcraft far more limited than the protagonist realizes, *Macbeth* is a tragedy of free will. But this free will involves the constraints of the human condition, the "infra-personal levels of [Macbeth's] own being."[45] The Christian God of Macbeth's universe takes the initiative neither to save nor to destroy; He exists as an idea, aloof, removed, even indifferent. At the other extreme are man's regressive and animalistic instincts. The mortal with his limited, finite view and his constant doubts must struggle to restrain himself within boundaries of justice and morality tacitly assumed to exist, whether for religious or societal convenience. The witches represent nothing more or less than the particular circumstances surrounding him which entice him to regard himself as the measure of all things. For Macbeth, to submit to these lesser gods is to unleash an ambition which, undisciplined, grows to Marlovian dimensions

in its myopic obsession. In essence, to the spectators, if not to
those who inhabit this stage world, Shakespeare makes clear through
the structure of the play that the witches are a dramatic depiction
of totally egocentric values and that they are carefully balanced by
the assumptions of higher Christian values. Set into this philosophic
caldron is the individual man whose tragedy, through the devices of
internalization, the playwright forces the spectators simultaneously
to share and to judge.

    Aside from the nature of the philosophic context, the most signif-
icant feature of the play for our present purposes is the conclusion.
While the waves of Macbeth's increasing passion do indeed maintain
the spectators' dramatic interest to the moment of his defeat by
Macduff,[46] the conclusion does not cast the focus on the protagonist
in the manner one has come to expect in Shakespeare. To provoke
the tyrant to a renewed moral awareness would be not only melodramatic but antithetical to the pattern of his intensification; moreover, such a dramatic turn would concentrate and reduce the implications of the tragedy, whereas, as we have noted, several features
throughout the play have pointedly widened the perspective. Shakespeare, in short, was constrained to move outside the protagonist
for the effective achievement of some form of an anagnorisis. In this
play, and even more so in his subsequent works, the causes of tragedy
and the pattern of interrelationships between their public and private
dimensions are far too complex to be served by a moment of recognition, however profound, with implications for the protagonist
alone.

    The essence of the anagnorisis in Shakespearean tragedy is, of
course, a sense of regeneration in the face of destruction, of crucial
insight and self-knowledge coupled with tragic suffering and waste.
In the middle plays the impact of this moment has been registered
in the individual, his understanding honed by adversity largely of his
own making. With the movement toward a broader vision of tragedy
in *Lear,* Shakespeare doubles the anagnorisis, presenting offstage in
Gloucester and onstage in Lear the painful wisdom gained from
their wheels of fire. Still, however, the essential focus is on the old
king. In *Macbeth,* Shakespeare spreads this experience over several
characters. Certainly Macbeth himself, with the blend of bravado
and despair in this erstwhile leader of men, attests to tragic destruction of human potential. This distressing waste is compounded by
the madness and apparent suicide of Lady Macbeth, whose development in the final act suggests also the nascent quality of tragedy.

There is no moral awakening, to be sure (again something which would be quite out of character). But her perturbations do mirror a mounting horror and an inability to live rationally with her atrocities of the past and her husband's of the present. Obviously, her destruction is assured. But the sparks of humanity stirred by her suffering in the waning moments signal again the cognitive effects of tragedy for her and thus for the spectators. Like Lear, she would appear to be sanest at the point the world would brand her mad.

In effect, the dominant emphasis of the final act is highly abstract. There is pathos, but no essential restoration in the man Macbeth, who in order to assure his authority would have had "Nature's germains tumble all together / Even till destruction sicken" (IV, i, 59–60). Instead, the anagnorisis focuses beyond the personal action on the emergence through disaster of a kingdom in which cure is possible only by a drastic purge and health can be maintained only if the individual—like a single member of the human anatomy—acts in compliance with the needs of the total body politic.[47] Macbeth himself is powerful and terrifying testimony to the self-destructive qualities of uncontrolled ambition. In no small way this terror results from Shakespeare's growing insistence that the free will which leads one to a commitment to such ambition is gravely subject to the physical and social conditions which create his opportunities and to the manipulations of others who stand to share his glory or to profit from it.

Shakespeare's final tragedies, *Timon of Athens, Coriolanus,* and *Antony and Cleopatra,* have always been considered something of an anticlimax. To be sure, each of the plays—especially *Antony*— has had its admirers who argue all the more passionately and, not infrequently, persuasively in order to compensate for this assumption. Moreover, these works have been much in evidence of late; both the Royal Shakespeare Company and the American Shakespeare Theatre have included *Antony and Cleopatra* in recent seasons, with *Coriolanus* as well featured in England. But the fact remains, whatever position the scholar may take from the armchair of his study, that as stage plays these works over the years have been less in demand than most of Shakespeare's earlier tragedies.

The greatest irony is that, while the final works may not be as effective as stage pieces, they are in some respect philosophically the profoundest. Their primary concern is not with a dramatic vision of man's *psychomachia,* but with the manner in which human interactions inevitably contribute to tragedy; not with heinous moral crimes which involve the private dimensions of the soul, but with the social dilemma in which guilt and provocation can be attributed to no single individual. These final heroes are still fair game for those bent on a search for a tragic flaw, but Shakespeare stresses more sharply than before the significance of the evil that exists in those characters around the central figure. Specifically, he depicts three views of noble manhood—the generosity of Timon, the physical heroism of Coriolanus, the leadership and magnanimity of Antony—corrupted and ultimately destroyed by their own passion in combination with the greed, lust, and thirst for power of those who manipulate them to their own material or emotional ends.

The chronology of the last tragedies is at best an educated guess. Of the three, however, *Timon of Athens* is the least successful in the opinion of most critics and would most clearly appear to reflect the difficulties resulting from Shakespeare's shifting tragic perspective. Admittedly, the character of Timon is relatively rigid in its movement from prodigality to misanthropy. Since the spectators do not share the crucial moments of decision in which he weighs various value judgments and articulates his choice of misanthropy, Shakespeare is demonstrably minimizing the tragic experience.[48] Timon's character is not flat, however, and the playwright gives it dramatic interest through development from prodigality, to naïvely idealistic rationalization, to self-pity, to a hatred which grows by degrees from his desire for immediate vengeance in kind, to his denunciation of false friends, his repudiation of his homeland and his few faithful companions, and finally his awesome execrations upon the entire race and his attempts to utilize his newfound wealth to provoke its destruction by war, rapine, and disease.

This characterization culminating in total misanthropy some would explain as a result of Shakespeare's source, others as an abortive attempt at or preliminary sketch for the kind of tragedy of his previous years. The play also has been an object for much special pleading: possibly it is unfinished, "roughed out" and then "abandoned," possibly to be taken up by another playwright.[49] Or perhaps it represents a particularly dark period of Shakespeare's life, a period when he was "spiritually and intellectually rudderless."[50] Or, possibly, it represents a consciously different kind of play—a tragical satire in the spirit of Jonson's *Sejanus* or his "so-called comedy" *Volpone,* a moral exemplum or morality or dramatic fable, an Elizabethan pageant or "show" prepared for private stage performance and depending not on plot but on a series of contrasting scenes written on a central theme.[51] None of these views is patently impossible; Shakespeare, as one can demonstrate time and again, was a practical playwright sensitive to the demands of popular tastes and opportunities. And, with no contemporary reference to a performance and no publication of the piece prior to 1623—when it was apparently inserted hastily into the First Folio, one simply cannot disprove those who claim the play to be fragmentary.

A significant part of the answer is surely to be found in Shakespeare's general artistic development. Consciously or unconsciously he is moving to a broader tragic focus, a perspective in which the protagonist's flaw and his experience consequent to error are central to the design of the play but in which, also, the emphasis is sharply upon the public dimensions of evil as a major contributing factor to the individual's tragedy and as a responsive participant in the illumination or human transformation it provokes. Such a focus results from minimizing Timon's sympathetic qualities and shifting—or at least attempting to shift—the anagnorisis to a second character, Alcibiades, whose response to Timon's plight provides the insights which redeem humanity from Timon's general curse. Admittedly, to a degree at least, this experiment with the protagonist miscarries as dislocation from Timon becomes dangerously extensive; and the spectators, forced to choose between the misanthropic principal and the hypocrites who surround him, are left strangely alienated and confused.

The structure of the play strongly suggests that Shakespeare is consciously striving for this broader tragic perspective. In the early acts Shakespeare surrounds the central character with various commentators on the state of his wealth, effectively establishing Timon's improvident nature on the one hand and the avaricious duplicity of his friends and associates on the other. In this role of lavish dispenser, Timon is clearly susceptible to flattery, taking an obvious pride in his ability to meet another's needs and doing so without regard for the merit of his gifts or the state of his own affairs. And it is to these shortcomings, rather than to any virtues of largess, that the spectators' attention is directed through the remarks of the surrounding characters.

Certainly the most extensive commentary on the evils both within and around Timon is provided by the caustic objurgations of

Apemantus, who observes the situation without involvement and of whom it is said that he loves "few things . . . better / Than to abhor himself" (I, i, 59–60). In isolation his misanthropic diatribes would be dismissed as the utterances of a diseased mind. But flanked by the remarks of those additional characters who focus our attention on just such moral erosion, Apemantus' chilling attacks seem not only credible but strangely appropriate. In the latter part of the play the focus on the heinous culpability of the central figure is again only a part of the perspective. As the extent of Timon's derangement becomes apparent, Shakespeare through additional minor figures also intensifies the repugnance of those whose avarice and hypocrisy have helped to mold the misanthropy. Lucullus, for example, in an aside delights in the arrival of Flaminius because he anticipates a gift from Timon, yet, when he hears that his friend wishes to receive rather than give, he offers the servant a reward to say "thou saw'st me not" (III, i, 42). Flaminius, in a soliloquy moments later, berates this "disease of a friend" with "such a faint and milky heart" (50, 51). In another scene strangers discuss the "monstrousness of man" in which "policy sits above conscience" (III, ii, 71, 86) as they observe Lucius, Timon's friend, weaving an elaborate web of lies to avoid loaning him money.

Shakespeare, then, sharply depicts the opprobrium both of Timon and of those around him. But it is virtually impossible to maintain that he is writing satiric tragedy, since he quite obviously does not intend for the spectators' sympathy and sense of values to be totally disengaged. More specifically, in the experience of Alcibiades and his development as a character foil to Timon, the playwright apparently attempts to provide a variation in the anagnorisis and the restitution of right reason in the individual and in the society at large which are characteristic of his earlier trage-dies.[52] The Athenian soldier figures in only four scenes, speaking a total of one hundred fifty-seven lines. His last three appearances, however, provide an experience which is woven into the last por-tion of the play as a parallel to that of Timon. Juxtaposed to the scene in which Timon, enraged at the greed and hypocrisy of his friend, plans his mock feast in revenge is Alcibiades' appearance before the Senate to plead for the life of a battlefield companion accused of murder. Irritated by his persistent argument, the sena-tors peremptorily banish him; and, like Timon, he reacts with the blind wrath and fury of injured pride:

> I hate not to be banished;
> It is a cause worthy my spleen and fury,
> That I may strike at Athens.
>
> (III, v, 111-13)

Alcibiades' banishment, like Timon's self-renunciation, results in
total estrangement from his homeland. As in IV, iii, the misanthrope
curses society and provides gold for those who will destroy it, the
soldier readies his army for a devastating attack upon Athens. Here,
however, the similarity ends. Timon repudiates the overtures of
repentance from the senators, refuses to aid the besieged city, and
dies in bitter isolation tossing the final curse against the human
race from his grave. Alcibiades, on the other hand, entertains the
emissaries from the city, agrees to withhold his attack in return for
autocratic powers, and—though still tainted by a degree of self-
interest—is resorbed into the society from which, like Timon's, his
departure had been so violent.

The relationship between Timon and Alcibiades is tenuous, to be
sure. The soldier's decision to spare the city is not based upon a
close personal association with Timon—either in some desperate
hope that the misanthrope is still capable of resorption into a
normal society—or in horrified reaction to the nature of Timon's
grotesque death. The thematic parallel is powerful, however, and
Shakespeare apparently depends upon this similarity to relieve the
increasingly aberrational actions of Timon through the emergence
of a second figure whose resulting illumination or capacity for compassion provides the rationale for tragedy.

In the final analysis, the significance of *Timon of Athens* rests not
only on whether the work in itself is or is not effective drama, but
also on the manner in which the tragedy reflects the genuinely ex-
ploratory nature of Shakespeare's art. Indeed, the complex structure of the piece provides a signpost for charting the perspective of
Shakespeare's final tragedies as the focus broadens from the anguish
of the individual's internal struggle and his conflict with the metaphysical dimensions of his universe to a larger vision of the multiple
human forces intrinsically responsible for his destruction and their
relationship to the fundamental insights achieved concomitantly
with the desolation and death. Certainly, in this respect *Timon*
provides the groundwork for more powerful and more successful
efforts in both *Coriolanus* and *Antony and Cleopatra.*

In Coriolanus, more so than in Timon, sporadic moments of
internalization provide the spectators glimpses of a psychic struggle,

but again the protagonist is seen in large part through the tainted eyes of the other characters, each of whom perceives the attributes of the principal figure through the filter of his own self-interest. And again Shakespeare has chosen a narrative in which the central figure is not directly guilty either of abdication resulting in destruction of family and kingdom, or of murder—whether in the name of state, God, or self.[53] With the character thus innocent of an act involving a heinous moral aberration which aesthetically requires a profound cathartic experience based on virtues of good and evil upheld by the play, the dramatist without violating the ethical frame of reference is able to block an intensely personal commitment to the protagonist and to force the spectators to evaluate his actions from several points of view and in constant relation to the motivations and value judgments of those around him.

Certainly in comparison with Shakespeare's earlier tragic figures, Coriolanus is intellectually shallow. To a large degree the spectators' attention is riveted externally upon the martial valor and the insufferable arrogance which seem to make up his personality in equal parts. Admittedly, no one is his rival on the field of battle. At sixteen he bravely confronted Tarquin, and in battles since that time, brow-bound with the oak, he consistently has proved the best man in the struggle. The pride of the man is equally furious.[54] The plebeians he considers beneath him in birth and pitifully subordinate in martial skill and courage. These common citizens are to him but dissentient rogues, scabs, curs, hares, geese, a sick man's appetite, fragments, and rats; the news of impending war he welcomes as a means to vent Rome's musty superfluity.

Such constant emphasis on extreme valor and pride tends to reflect only the outer shell of the man. Moreover, Shakespeare carefully avoids soliloquies, asides, or personal dialogue at those crucial moments when an inner struggle would presumably be most intense. As Coriolanus considers the position of consul and how he must achieve it, for example, the spectators get no real insight either into any lust for power or into any foreboding discomfort that a position of power unsought and undesired is being thrust upon him. Even more critical, the audience is not permitted to see his private emotional reactions to banishment which lead to his decision to join Aufidius in order to seek personal vengeance against an ungrateful homeland. Similarly, no soliloquy in Act V reiterates the significance of his decision to acquiesce to his mother's pleas and spare his homeland.

Unquestionably, then, the characterization of Coriolanus is far less complex than that of the protagonists of the middle plays. On the other hand—and this is a fact all too easily overlooked by the critic[55] who hastens, sometimes peremptorily, to judge the character by the measure of introspection in the earlier protagonists—he is by no means totally stylized or static. The spectators on several occasions do perceive, beneath this outer shell, the internal struggles where at least a degree of essential dramatic growth occurs.[56] Most obviously, in reaching the crucial decision to spare Rome at the behest of mother, wife, and child, Marcius is aware of the disastrous consequences which he must personally face. Coriolanus seems to realize that no honorable reconciliation is now possible— that he has become involved in a situation from which there is no escape: to destroy Rome will vitiate whatever is human in him as he destroys family and friend to achieve the fruition of his bitter revenge; to exercise mercy will alienate Aufidius and the Volscians in whose hands he has quite literally placed his life. He senses that his decision, in effect, will involve his sacrificing himself in order to save others; foolishly—by the standard of both the world and the ego—he will toss away a victory which is assured (V, iii, 183– 89).

All things considered, the tragic experience of Coriolanus—the movement from obdurate self-will to a moment of mercy and self- lessness involving an act which costs his life as a result of the forces of evil earlier set in motion by his passion along with the painful achievement of at least a degree of self-knowledge enabling him more truly to perceive the forces which motivate those around him —is in basic design not unlike those of the earlier protagonists. Yet, Shakespeare has quite clearly structured the play so as to bar the spectators from sharing fully the intense struggles of the soul which would provoke them to total emotional identification.[57] In effect, with Coriolanus having not one line of aside and only limited soliloquies, not for the most part critically located, Shakespeare draws the spectators back from the central character even while, more successfully than in Timon, sketching him in sufficient detail to force them to view the tragedy in part through his eyes.

Central to this broader perspective, the essential complexity in Coriolanus' character results from the external structural devices —the multiple choric figures and the double foils—which control the spectators' response. Before his first appearance on stage and his diatribe against the commoners, a group of citizens pointedly

blur the spectators' attitude toward them.[58] One of the citizens
maintains that they should consider Coriolanus' services to the city
and the full effects of any charge brought against him; the others—
bats and clubs in hand—aver that he is chief enemy to the people,
a very dog to the commonalty; they would prove that they have
not only strong breaths but strong arms too by killing him and
demanding corn at their own price.

By the same token, the spectators see the dehumanizing effects
of battlefield training before they are caught up emotionally in
Coriolanus' valorous exploits in scenes iv–xiii and his idolatrous
aggrandizement by his military colleagues Lartius and Cominius in
I, ix, and II, ii. Volumnia describes to the sensitive Virgilia (who
recoils in alarm) her past rejoicing in her son's martial excursions.
She has always been pleased to let him seek danger and to hear his
drum as he returns with bloody brow. So, too, she hears with
obvious delight that her young grandson in one of Coriolanus'
moods cruelly ripped to pieces a gilded butterfly. Such details
obviously temper the spectators' admiration for the military hero
who fights without regard to fear like a well-tuned precision
machine. Moreover, there are several subtle suggestions of
fanaticism in Coriolanus' behavior. When he enters the gates of
Corioli and shouts for others to follow, the soldiers flatly refuse
to be a part of such foolhardiness, and later even Lartius observes
that Coriolanus outdares his senseless sword.

There is, then, in the opening act no simple and single response
to what superficially appears to be either the protagonist's vice or
his virtue. Similarly, while two soldiers contrast further his haughty
contempt for the common citizens with his blunt honesty and noble
service (II, ii, 1–34), and while Coriolanus pridefully offers himself
as candidate for consul only to be banished when in a fit of wrath
he alienates the people, the factors which motivate first the tribunes
and then his mother and the patricians to manipulate him for their
own selfish interests become painfully clear. Sicinius and Brutus
(whom Menenius describes as unmeriting, proud, violent, testy, and
ambitious) emerge as direct adversaries, fearing not so much that
the people will lose liberty as that they themselves will lose power
and authority over them. Convinced that their office "may, / During
his power, go sleep" (II, i, 211–12), they determine to set the people
against him and to prod his arrogance with barbed remarks. To this
end the designing pair persuade the people to revoke their acceptance of Coriolanus as consul; then they literally bar Coriolanus'

path, confronting him with news of the revocation of his appointment and with fresh charges of his insolence. When Coriolanus in a
vitriolic rage calls for the senators to abolish the power of the
tribuneship, Brutus and Sicinius have accomplished their aims.
They accuse him of manifest treason; he is a traitor, a "foe to th'
public weal [who] . . . deserves death" (III, i, 175, 207).

In effect, the self-concerns of Brutus and Sicinius on the one
hand, of Volumnia on another, and of the patricians on yet another precipitate a situation for which Coriolanus—despite all his
faults—is not directly responsible. Thus Shakespeare in the middle
portion of the play carefully holds in balance the spectators'
response to the protagonist through the comments, actions, and
intentions of the surrounding characters. In the climactic moments
he draws a richly sympathetic focus on Coriolanus' act of selflessness through the further development of Volumnia and Aufidius as
character foils. Certainly, as an emissary for peace in the final act,
Volumnia is concerned for the welfare of the city. But her abiding
obsession with shaping Coriolanus into a politician who can sacrifice principle to policy surfaces again in her assertion that her son
must reconcile the Romans and the Volscians so that both sides
will acknowledge his heroism and magnanimity. Meanwhile,
Aufidius, in his lone aside (V, iii, 200–202), clearly reveals that the
Roman's magnanimous act will be his certain destruction. Planting
his supporters in the crowd and accusing Marcius of treason, he sets
the stage for assassination, then with a ready explanation gains
control of the assembly and emerges with total authority.

Considering the complexity of the total design, one would do
well to pause before condemning the play simply because—in terms
of the protagonist's experience and the total dramatic effect—it fails
to do what its tragic predecessors do. The tragedy, to be sure, is
possible as a consequence of a fundamental flaw in the protagonist;
but the dominant thrust of the play is that the tragedy actually
occurs as a result of the diverse forces and pressures brought to
bear by those around him who manipulate him and others to
selfish advantage. In the fact that those succeed who are willing to
practice policy at the expense of integrity and without regard for
the consequences to others the tragedy reflects the darkest side of
humanity.

On the other hand, as with Alcibiades in *Timon of Athens,*
apparently Shakespeare does again intend in Aufidius' final moments to reflect a transfer of the anagnorisis to a character whose

critical dilemma closely approximates that of the central figure and whose destiny is inseparably related. At the moment Coriolanus is struck down by the frenzied mob, the Volscian leader avers that his own rage is gone and that he is struck with sorrow. Responding, perhaps, to Coriolanus' finest moment, Aufidius will become a mourner through whom Marcius "shall have a noble memory" (V, vi, 152). Granted, there is not the full emotional catharsis which results from close identification; there is not even absolute conviction that Aufidius' words are motivated by virtue rather than by pragmatism and practicality. What is clear, though, is that potentially Coriolanus' most positive influence upon his fellow man is achieved through a single act of human compassion. His tragedy, like Macbeth's, is that his own selfishness must destroy him before he can discover that potential. The essential difference, on the other hand, is the focus; where *Macbeth* distinctly emphasizes the personal despair of a life withered and destroyed by vaulting ambition, *Coriolanus* stresses equally the central figure's transformation and the response of others to this moment of human perception.

In *Antony and Cleopatra,* whether actually his last tragedy or not, Shakespeare achieves his most powerful delineation of the secular values between which man struggles to make the choices for a successful life. Gone is a clear distinction between virtue and vice, between material and spiritual choice.[59] The drama operates within the world of man, within the conflict created out of the struggle for power and influence between a Roman emperor and an Egyptian queen.[60] And the values of these two worlds are equally tainted.

Cleopatra's world, for instance, is decadent and enervating. Nowhere do the spectators have even the slightest sense of the queen's concern for her kingdom and for the welfare of her subjects; nowhere are they convinced that her affairs with heads of the Roman state, past or present, are motivated by any sort of determination to protect her nation at any price. To the contrary, she utilizes her unlimited power and her limited beauty for the gratification of her own vanity.

The Egyptian world is also morally vitiated.[61] For one thing, it reeks of sensuality. The bawdy wit of Iras and Charmian in the opening scene (over where best to have an additional inch of fortune in a husband and over how delightful it would be to see Alexas cuckolded) is prologue to Cleopatra's own banter with Mardian after Antony has departed for Rome.

If there is no moral fiber in Cleopatra and her court attendants, so also no such quality is to be found in Octavius and his associates. Robert Ornstein aptly remarks that "the decay of Roman idealism is so advanced that it is difficult to say whether a Roman thought is of duty or disloyalty."[62] In any event, Shakespeare methodically undermines the spectators' confidence in the Roman leaders through reflection of Lepidus' dissipation and Octavius' duplicity. Ironically, for example, despite all the references to the orgies of the East, the only such scene in the play involves the western leaders on Pompey's barge. Disconcerting also is the Roman marriage by which Octavius intends to ensure perpetual amity with Antony. Arranged wedlock—born not in love but in material convenience—was, of course, conventional practice both in Shakespeare's day and in Caesar's. Even so, the context of heated words followed by histrionic displays of affection results in a union which looks cynical indeed to the friends of the triumvirs, who have no illusions about the game they watch. Moreover, on his individual initiative he removes Lepidus from a position of command, denying him "rivality" and seizing him after "having made use of him in the wars 'gainst Pompey" (III, v, 6–10). His claim that he is merely responding to Antony, who has returned to Egypt to dole out kingdoms to Cleopatra's brood, is clearly *post factum;* Antony's actions subsequent to this power play merely provide Octavius a convenient excuse and a ready response to Octavia's queries.

Between these two worlds Antony is a pawn manipulated to best advantage; each attempts to use him for selfish ends: Cleopatra bemoans in III, iii, that, were Antony gone, she knows not through whom she would command; similarly, Enobarbus appropriately observes to Octavius that, if he borrows Antony's love for the instant, he may return it again when Pompey is no longer a threat; and Menas admits that policy was more important in the marriage of Octavia and Antony than the love of the parties. In short, unlike the situation in the middle tragedies in which the protagonist has a particular path of action ultimately recognized as desirable, Antony has no "correct" choice through which to calm and control the turbulent forces of his spirit. Indeed, no such moral structure is assumed. As in Webster's view, a character must transcend the moral ambiguities which surround him. With all values tainted, the protagonist—if he is to achieve tragic proportions—must through his suffering come to envision a potential integrity and selflessness beyond that which can be found in the society of his stage world.

Antony at the outset is no better and no worse than those around him. Certainly there is nothing magnanimous about him; he is an opportunist capable of affection only for himself and ready to compromise truth to protect his reputation and suffer his vanity. In a word, his wheel of fire is built from equal parts of his own blind egocentricity and of the callous avarice of his associates who stand to profit from his alliance or from his destruction. As his tragic experience unfolds, he by degrees is conditioned to hold himself accountable for his actions; at the same time, by achieving a full measure of responsibility and thereby regaining something of the magnanimity which his associates constantly recall in the man antecedent to the play, Antony is able to overcome the defensive and accusative nature which has led him to gauge others only by the standard of self-gain or self-gratification.

The development of this integrity in Antony's character can be traced in the eighteen scenes from the moment of his first military disaster to his death at the conclusion of Act IV. Although he is by no means ready to accept the blame for the naval defeat in III, xi, his apprehension for the safety of his attendants is significantly new. Admitting that he has lost command, and that his very hairs do mutiny—with the white reproving the brown for rashness, and the brown reproving the white for fear and doting—he implores his subordinates to divide among themselves the treasures of his ship. A similar touch appears in IV, v, when Antony makes a point of stopping to converse with a common soldier who earlier had warned him not to fight by sea. His comment, "Would thou and those thy scars had once prevailed / To make me fight at land" (2-3), though brief, acknowledges both the old soldier's bravery and his wisdom. For another example, before renewing his struggle against Caesar, Antony calls together his household servants in an unusual display of sentiment. After clasping each of them by the hand and praising their honesty and their devotion to service, he addresses them as his honest and hearty friends and invites them to burn this night with torches. A similar display of affection occasioned by a sense of foreboding disaster occurs two scenes later as Eros and Cleopatra arm the aging titan for battle. In a touching moment Eros, almost overcome with emotion, fumbles badly in attempting to buckle the armor and Cleopatra can do little better.

Antony's final confrontation with Cleopatra is even more remarkable. On three previous occasions he has subjected her to vicious and cruel tongue-lashings. Following her desertion in battle, he maintains that she knew he would follow and thus give the victory to Caesar; when he overhears her in conversation with Thyreus, he berates her as a "kite" (III, xiii, 89), a "half blasted . . . boggler" (105, 110) "found . . . as a morsel cold upon / Dead Caesar's trencher" (116–17); when the Egyptian navy capitulates to Rome, he threatens to kill her, branding her a "foul Egyptian [who] hath betrayed me" (IV, xii, 10), a "triple-turned whore [who] . . . / Hast sold me to this novice" (13–14). Now, however, as he faces what in a sense is her cruelest trick—the report of her suicide which prompts him to fall upon his sword in remorse—his passion is spent. This serenity is the strongest possible affirmation of Antony's growth in self-knowledge.[63] As with Enobarbus, he knows full well that *he* has forced the crisis; whatever the queen's true nature this final ploy is her response to his threats. Moreover, Antony's affection has grown far beyond mere sensual desire. When he receives news that she is still alive, his last request is for reunion with her. Facing her with not a semblance of reproach on his lips, his dying efforts are to give her counsel. He instructs her to seek her honor and her safety of Caesar, to trust none about Caesar but Proculeius. Finally, he implores her not to lament or sorrow, but rather to remember him in his former fortunes when he lived the greatest and noblest prince of the world.

The major impact of the play occurs in the final act with the transferral of the anagnorisis which focuses the spectators' attention upon the societal responses to—as earlier upon the causes of—the individual tragedy. Admittedly, a tainted society prevails beyond the tragedy it has occasioned. Octavius, standing over the dead Cleopatra, pompously asserts that the death of this famous pair of lovers will redound to his glory. Obviously, this is the same world leader who, rankling under the weight of a triumvirate, in turn cast off Lepidus and defied Antony's authority.[64] Nor, presumably, has society improved—whether it be the turncoat Egyptian naval force or the fickle Roman populace. If human nature is still tainted, however, individual lives have not remained untouched by Antony's experience. Through Cleopatra and her attendants—far more effectively than in Alcibiades in *Timon of Athens* or Aufidius in *Coriolanus*—Shakespeare forces the spectators to realize this fact. Indeed, Antony, like the Duchess of Malfi, is dead at the end of Act IV, and the final thrust of the drama—for Cleopatra as for Bosola—is on the catalytic effect of his death upon even the most tainted of those who have helped to produce it.

Perhaps the most significant structural feature of the last scenes of the play is the extensive dialogue between Cleopatra and her attendants which achieves the conventional effects of soliloquy. Charmian and Iras, who live and die with Cleopatra, exist only in dramatic combination with her; like the Fool in *Lear,* they function as internal pointers or objects of dialogue through whom the spectators are able to see beneath the deceptive layers of the Egyptian queen. We have no reason to doubt the sincerity of her comment to them that, since with Antony dead all is but nought, it is no sin to rush into the secret house of death. With that huge spirit now cold her only friend is resolution and the briefest end. They will do it after the high Roman fashion and make death proud to take them. In similar dialogue later she asserts that her desolation does begin to make a better life. Steadfast in the face of Caesar's lengthy personal protestations that he will use her with pomp and majesty, she informs her attendants, "He words me, girls, he words me, that I should not / Be noble to myself" (V, ii, 191–92). At this moment—*prior* to Dolabella's warning of Caesar's plans to apprehend her within three days—she sends Charmian with a message for the asps secretly to be brought. Further, she instructs her attendants to dress her in full royal array—crown and all. When she receives news of the arrival of a rural fellow who brings the asps, she speaks again of the noble deed which will bring her liberty; and there is not the slightest hint of hesitation: "My resolution's placed. . . . I am marble-constant" (238, 240). Moments later, applying an asp to her arm, she has immortal longings and hears Antony call to praise her noble act.

The spirit of Antony, in brief, pervades Act V, and Cleopatra best reflects a primary characteristic of Shakespeare's final vision that tragedy is a social as well as an individual phenomenon. Since the flawed central figure is manipulated by the selfish interests of those around him, they inevitably must share the guilt of his destruction. But they are also capable of responding to the tragic insights which he achieves. The final significance of life, Shakespeare again seems to be saying, lies in the manner in which one is touched by and in turn touches the lives of those around him. To be sure, *Antony and Cleopatra* lacks the intense inner focus, the powerful emotional involvement, of Shakespeare's middle tragedies. As in *Timon* and *Coriolanus* the spectators, blocked from total commitment to the protagonist, are forced to view the emerging tragedy in the full context of the pervasive evil which produces it. Of these final plays, however, *Antony and Cleopatra* is clearly the most powerful. Through the structural devices which force the spectators to consider the causes and the effects of Antony's destruction from a wide variety of angles and which project his tragic insights beyond his limited individual experience, Shakespeare has largely overcome the problems of the two preceding plays in achieving a perspective which involves the social dynamics of tragedy even while it effectively centers on the tragedy of the individual.

Shakespeare's final tragedies, then, in spirit are akin to those of Jonson, Tourneur, and Webster. Critics may describe the dominant thrust of Jonson's tragedy as political, of Tourneur's as satiric, and of Webster's as grotesque, but these are all variations upon a single theme—the plight of the human being in a physically corrupt and a metaphysically uncertain world. Tragedy is engendered in the flaw of the individual, but it is nourished and fed by the social context, by those whose relationship with the protagonist is determined by self-serving ends. It is no longer envisioned as a Faustus in the privacy of his own soul deciding to pursue knowledge at whatever expense or a Hamlet struggling within himself to define the moral constraints of his commitment to revenge. It is instead both a personal and a social phenomenon in which the causes and the consequences of tragedy are depicted in terms of human interaction. Set in a world of conflicting human demands, this tragedy requires that human dignity be achieved without the guidance of assumed moral absolutes; while the classes and the particular issues may differ radically, the tone and temper are the ancestors of modern social drama.

III. Jonson

—SEJANUS, CATILINE

Although Ben Jonson wrote several tragedies before the turn of the century, only two pieces survive—both written well after the enthusiasm and optimism of the Elizabethan era had begun to wane, and both with Roman settings which only thinly veil their contemporaneity. Both *Sejanus* (1603) and *Catiline* (1611) portray a consummately decadent society in which ultimate values are frankly relative and belief in the efficacy of the gods depends upon the convenience of the moment. The primary concern is neither the topical vanities of dress and manner nor the innocuous incongruities and duperies arising from man's greed, as in Jonson's comedies, but the dreadful consequences of ambition—on both the personal and the public level—when man has abandoned all social and religious values. Indeed, the most significant characteristic of these stage worlds is the pervasively grim view of human nature unable to purge itself of those who through the abuse of power destroy themselves as well as those around them. In the final analysis, just as the spectators in Jonson's major comedies must provide the scale of values against which both gull and guller must be judged, so in these works tragic illumination is possible only for those whose association has been vicarious.

The stage world of *Sejanus,* more specifically, assumes no metaphysical values which lend causal credence to man's tragic plight; nor does a psychic struggle become its own justification by focusing on the interior movement of spirit and the insights gained through suffering or on the heroic commitment to private values.[1] Sejanus, like Richard III, is committed at the outset to political self-aggrandizement. More completely than his English counterpart he has quite extirpated any semblances of moral conscience, and he too must methodically eliminate the not inconsiderable number who stand between him and absolute power. In both, self-confidence, fed by success, grows to monstrous proportions which culminate in flagrant public defiance of the gods.

The context of this defiance, however, signals the fundamental difference in the philosophic dimensions of the two stage worlds. As we observed in the preceding chapter, Richard's horrific actions are set firmly within the moral context of the Tudor myth; Richard is the scourge of God granted a few years of frenzied activity, but both his character and the historical context assure his fall in a world graced by God's blessings upon the emerging Tudor house. No fewer than sixteen characters through curses invoke God's heavy justice on Richard, eleven in the form of apparitions. Of these, the dominant figure is Queen Margaret; her execrations not only proclaim heaven's predomination and the King's anguished fall, but also provide a virtual outline of the action of the drama through prophecies of the precedent destruction of King Edward, Prince Edward, Rivers, and Hastings, whose agony and remorse lend emphasis to the fall of Richard himself. Moreover, Richard's adversary is a providential agent; character and motive beyond reproach, Richmond fights "in God's name . . . whose captain [he] account[s himself]."

Sejanus' diabolic machinations are unchecked by such external moral assumption. To be sure, references to the gods are frequent; omens and a statue of Fortune unreceptive to sacrifice figure on stage just prior to his fall. Jonson methodically, though, undermines the apparent efficacy of the gods with the result that the spectators can have little faith that the gods are more than names invoked and manipulated for personal gain.[2] Virtuous and vicious alike, for one thing, stake equal claim to the deities' favors. Arruntius and Silius, for example, alert to Sejanus' devious machinations, call upon Jove to protect them and the empire (I, 435; II, 470),[3] while at the other extreme the physician Eudemus—ready tool for Sejanus' plots—thanks Jove and Apollo that they "marke me out so" (I, 263). Both the senators unaware of the extent of Caesar's corruption (III, 141–44) and those like Regulus and Haterius privy to his dark practices invoke "all our gods . . . Phebus, Mars, Diana, Palace, Juno, Mercurie [to] guard him" (V, 693–96). Depending upon the individual perspective, Sejanus' extensive power reflects either the wisdom and justice (IV, 481) or the stupidity and blindness (IV, 259–76, 482) of the gods.

Such paradoxes cut to the very heart of the tragedy. The valiant Silius may well defend the justice of the gods, proclaiming in the opening moments that Rome's "ryots, pride, and civill hate / Have so provok'd the justice of the gods" to scourge them with Sejanus

(I, 57–58); he might even frantically reaffirm this justice of the
"equall gods" as the net of tyranny closes around him (III, 250).
Yet confident faith is no protection from the human deceit which
strikes him down. Indeed, the few individuals of courage and moral
integrity are methodically destroyed by the machinators whose
authority they threaten. Germanicus, for example, the gallant
general—husband of Agrippina and nephew of Tiberius, is poisoned
antecedent to the action of the play because his popularity poses
a threat to Sejanus' authority. A similar fate befalls Drusus,
Tiberius' son, whose vices are minor in comparison with those of
Sejanus to whom he stands opposed. Sosia, like her husband Silius,
is marked for the stalwart "furie in her brest" (II, 301); Cremutius
Cordus must be struck down because in his annals he by implication "doth taxe the present state" as "a profest champion, / For
the old libertie" (308, 311). The elimination of Agrippina's niece
"deare Claudia Pulchra" and the "innocent Furnius" (IV, 21, 22),
noted in a passing reference, reveals the wide-ranging net cast for
those who oppose the power structure: "No innocence is safe, /
When power contests. Nor can they trespasse more, / Whose only
being was all crime, before" (40–42). Sabinus is charged with
treason and "drawne from the *Gemonies*" (283) for speaking of
the corruption of the court; Nero is "banish'd into *Pontia*" (330),
Agrippina "confin'd to *Pandataria*" (335), and Drusus Junior is held
a "prisoner in the palace" (333). These forces of opposition, in
whom demonstrably in some instances and inferentially in others
the spectators must find the virtue and integrity which resist
Sejanus' vicious decadence, offer no genuine contest; all fall before
the "stale catamite" whose politic tyranny aims at the throne of
Caesar itself.

At first glance the spectators can take some degree of moral comfort in the fact of Sejanus' eventual fall—and the various portents
which lead them to anticipate it. Arruntius, for example, invokes
supernatural intervention against the blasphemer; and, as omen
piles upon omen, it would appear that the gods are indeed directing events toward the tyrant's destruction. Sejanus' statue belches
smoke, the head is mysteriously removed and a monstrous serpent
emerges from the trunk, his servants fall victim to a fatal accident,
the augury produces "no prosperous bird . . . but croking ravens"
(V, 63), and a new head with a rope around the neck is mysteriously
placed on his statue. When Fortune averts her face from Sejanus
rather than accept his sacrifice and he peremptorily dashes the

goddess' statue to the ground, his destruction seems assured—and indeed it occurs within five hundred lines. Yet, the ultimate results belie a society controlled by supernatural intelligence. Macro, who replaces Sejanus as Tiberius' "ready engine" (III, 747), is equally defiant of the gods. For the sake of rising in the emperor's employment, he would undertake to "make / The gods all guiltie" (732–33); man's true gods are reason, license, observance, occasion, and profit—"what else is, vaine" (743). Even Arruntius, whose faith in the gods has been unshaken throughout the play, berates a deity who through "the strange punishment" would attempt to "redeeme . . . crimes" and "make amends" for "ill placed favours" (V, 891–93).

There is, then, in Jonson's stage world no apparent sense of a teleological cosmic design which predicates the value and dignity of human life and consequently against which the suffering and pain resulting from error and the destruction and waste of human potential assume an overtly demonstrable tragic significance. At best Jonson has created a world in which some of the vicious are punished and none of the virtuous rewarded. At worst, he has depicted a human jungle in which corruption in high places— limited only by the capacities of man's sordid imagination—"destroys or corrupts all that it comes in contact with."[4] Inherent in the philosophic context are fundamental contradictions which block the spectators' assumption that the gods exist, let alone that they function in men's daily lives. The stage world of *Richard III* leaves no doubt on either count.

A second useful distinction can be drawn between the structure of Shakespeare's play and of Jonson's first surviving tragedy written some ten years later. Both works make obvious use of the choric or pointer characters. In *Richard III* the scrivener exists primarily to reveal the alarming increase in Richard's brazen callousness in moving against his enemies (III, vi); similarly the three citizens of II, iii, point explicitly to the dangers of a kingdom ruled by a child and the ripe opportunities for the "Duke of Gloucester," who is "full of danger." So, too, Queen Margaret's asides and her meeting with Richard's mother and Edward's widow (IV, iv) emotionally underscore the mounting opposition to Richard's vicious rule. Such scenes, however, are scattered sporadically throughout the drama, and they serve primarily to emphasize the Machiavellian adroitness and the barbaric human insensitivity of the central figure. In contrast, choric figures speak fully 60 percent of the lines in *Sejanus* (1,958 of 3,256).[5] These moments, frequently involving a scene within a scene, not only provide an extensive running commentary on Sejanus' rise and fall; more importantly they stress the social corruption that has permitted such a scoundrel to gain power and of which he is only a small part. In the opening lines, for instance, Silius and Sabinus consider themselves out of step with the world since they are not "good inginers" with the "thriving use" of "shift of faces," "cleft tongues," and "softe, and glutinous bodies" to render them "favour'd of the times" (I, 3–8); they "burne with no black secrets" (15) to gain blackmail; nor can they "lye, / Flatter, and sweare, foresweare, deprave, informe, / Smile, and betray" (27–29). When Satrius and Natta enter at a distance, they are immediately branded "Sejanus clients" who "change every moode, / Habit, and garbe, as often as he varies" (23, 34–35). They

> Looke well, or ill with him: ready to praise
> His lordship, if he spit, or but pisse faire,
> Have an indifferent stoole, or breake winde well,
> Nothing can scape their catch.
>
> (38–41)

Arruntius, in particular, denounces the general corruption of the state.

> The men are not the same: 'tis we are base,
> Poore, and degenerate from th' exalted streine
> Of our great fathers.
>
> (87–89)

Without the "soul / Of God-like Cato" or the constancy of Brutus, "All's but blaze, / Flashes, and smoke, . . . / There's nothing *Romane* in us; nothing good, / Gallant, or great" (89–90, 100–103).

   Through establishing such an elaborate commentary before Sejanus appears and then depicting his first two entrances as a scene within a scene, Jonson starkly affirms the societal dimensions of tragedy.[6] Indeed, for the entire five hundred eighty-one lines of Act I, Silius, Sabinus, Cordus, and Arruntius remain on stage proclaiming the depravity of society. They are passive, to be sure; though they perceive that Tiberius ("dead to vertue" but alive to "every act of vice") through exalting Sejanus "above the best of generalls" (416, 418, 545) provokes "the close approach of bloud and tyranny" (420), they sit idly by, able only to talk and to

dream of the halcyon days of the Republic when men could be
stirred to meet the challenge of the times. One of the grimmest
confirmations of the pitiful vulnerability of these few positive
voices lies in the fact that only one—Arruntius—survives the play,
and Sejanus well realizes that he "only talkes" (II, 299) and thus
can be used as a decoy; his "franke tongue / Being lent the reines,"
no one will suspect that the emperor intends malice against others:
"We must keep him to stalke with" (III, 498-99, 501).

Despite the impotence of these figures, though, they do serve as
a continuous reminder that this tragedy is the result both of Sejanus'
individual tyranny and of society's general corruption. They recognize clearly that the tyrant would be powerless without his spies
who have sold their integrity for lucre or political favor—the
"beagles," for example, who "haunt the house / Of Agrippina"
(II, 410-11) and thereby obtain libelous evidence on Sejanus'
enemies. Accused unjustly, Silius proclaims that the tyrant's law

> is but a forme,
> A net of Vulcanes filing, a meere ingine,
> To take that life by a pretext of justice,
> Which you pursue in malice.
> (III, 244-47)

The world is populated with "wolfe-turn'd men" (251), the "officious *Senate*" (320) comprised of the emperor's willing slaves. The
entire trial scene (III, 1-487) in which Silius and Cordus are arraigned is, like Act I, staged as a scene within a scene, and Arruntius
provides barbed observations about the proceedings. He praises
Silius for his courage and his example; Cordus, likewise, speaks
"freely, and nobly" (461), and those who guard Cordus are "two
of Sejanus bloud-hounds" (376). Tiberius is an "excellent wolfe"
(347) who ingenuously conceals the tremendous discrepancies
"betweene the brest, and the lips" (97). The senate, whose "faces
runne like shittles, . . . are weaving / Some curious cobweb to
catch flyes" (23-24); swayed by palpably false evidence, they are
"brainlesse" and the "*Roman* race most wretched" (472, 486).

Choric denunciations of the social corruption increase markedly
in the last two acts. When Sabinus, like Silius earlier, is tricked into
treasonous comments and arrested, he lashes out at the "most
officious instruments of state" (IV, 226) who have helped to snare
him, especially incensed that even the elderly and white-haired
have sold their integrity and become "reverend monsters" (222)

and "men of all uses" (227). Arruntius would "sooner trust Greeke-
Sinon, then a man / Our state employes" (360–61); he deplores the
wretched citizens who would have the emperor clearly tell them
who is in political favor that they "might follow, without feare, or
doubt" (425) and who, lacking such information, "beleeve, what
they would have" (492). His observations in the final moments
scathingly trace the actions of "my monster, / The multitude" (V,
879–80). As Sejanus in favor arrives at the tribunal, the crowd
"like servile huishers . . . proclaim his idol lordship" (450–51);
"officious friends / Flock to salute" him, anxious to receive "a
lord-like nod" (446–47, 448). The sensory images—heavy with
sexual implications—are strikingly repulsive:

> Gods! how the spunges open, and take in!
> And shut againe! looke, looke! is not he blest
> That gets a seate in eye-reach of him? more,
> That comes in eare, or tongue-reach? o but most,
> Can claw his subtle elbow, or with a buzze
> Fly-blow his eares.
>
> (506–11)

Such "tame slaverie, and fierce flatterie" (542) cease, however, as
the political wind (and along with it the fawning friends) shift.
The lord now a fugitive given fetters for wreaths, "strokes, for
stoops: / Blind shame, for honours; and black taunts, for titles"
(728–29), the mob "now, inhumanely ravish him to prison" (725).
    While the cancer of cruelty and selfishness, then, touches every
corner of society, the dominant dramatic focus is obviously on the
"magnificent monster"[7] Sejanus, whose rise and fall provides narrative coherence for the tragedy. Through eight soliloquies and one
aside, a total of one hundred seventy-six lines (over 68 percent of
the total lines spoken in soliloquy), Jonson develops a private level
of perception, thereby rendering Sejanus the more appalling because the spectators are forced to view the destruction of the innocent through his dreadful anticipation. Moreover, the spectators
can only sit in awe before one so unreservedly committed to self-
interest. Stained from his childhood days when he "prostituted
his abused body" (I, 214), he from the opening scene is a man
untroubled by genuine affection for others and unrestrained by
moral scruples of any kind. Shrewdly, he realizes not only that
Pallas' share in success is far greater than Venus' (373–74), but
also that, among his fellow men, "Ambition makes more trusty
slaves, then need" (366); so also he knows how to use fear as an

offensive weapon—how to "present the shapes / Of dangers, greater then they are (like late, / Or early shadowes)" (384-86)—and he recognizes the signal distinction between hot and cold passion:

> He that, with such wrong mov'd, can beare it through
> With patience, and an even mind, knowes how
> To turn it backe. Wrath, cover'd carryes fate:
> Revenge is lost, if I professe my hate.
>
> (I, 576-79)

Along with this Machiavellian policy he possesses a cruelly fascinating wit and an unholy delight in his machinations which ensnare those around him. On more than one occasion he refers to the swelling joys of his success, and he is almost masochistically ecstatic in describing his revenge against Drusus:

> If this be not revenge, when I have done
> And made it perfect, let *Egyptian* slaves,
> *Parthians,* and bare-foot *Hebrewes* brand my face,
> And print my body full of injuries.
>
> (II, 139-42)

More significant, Sejanus is also the sole dynamic figure in the play. Such development does not occur in terms of moral complexity, to be sure; in that sense Jonson's characters are static or "exemplary," providing a value construct from which "audiences may take their own moral bearings."[8] Certainly, too, there is no abortive attempt to force the audience to a sympathetic perspective such as we find in the momentary terror experienced by Shakespeare's Richard as he confronts spirits of his previous victims the night before his fatal encounter with Richmond. Comparison with Iago is more apposite. Although we cannot determine which of the two figures is the antecedent creation, together they establish a new standard in the dramatic delineation of Satanic evil. Both in the course of the action grow progressively more subtle and sophisticated in their ability to practice upon virtually everyone else in the stage world. Indeed, for fully half of the action Sejanus is essentially uncontested as he manipulates others—Eudemus, Livia, Lygdus, Tiberius, Augusta, Prisca, Varro, Afer, Latiaris, Rufus, and Opsius—to his own best advantage.

Sejanus' development as a Machiavellian schemer, more precisely, moves through four distinct stages culminating in his flagrant hubris at the point of his fall. In the initial stage (I, 1-581), though already a man of wealth, power, and influence because of his favored relationship with Tiberius, he acts with caution. Admittedly, he already knows the value of allies bound to him for position and material benefits; by selling Eudemus a tribuneship the opportunist is able to question the physician about his patient Livia, to test his moral integrity, and eventually to persuade him—for the promise of gain—to champion his cause as wooer by serving as panderer in establishing an adulterous liaison. Sejanus privately realizes that Livia, corrupted, will provide him the "way . . . to worke out" (370) his designs against Drusus. He realizes also the obvious advantage of lavish compliment, praising the physician's "art, and learning" (272) and general virtue and addressing him as "my Aesculapius" and "my friend" (355, 360). Sejanus at this point is essentially operating from a position of weakness, and he well knows that he has not the luxury of response in word or deed when Drusus strikes him publicly, then draws his sword and taunts him:

> Avoid mine eye, dull camell, or my sword
> Shall make thy brav'rie fitter for a grave,
> Then for a triumph. I'le advance a statue,
> O' your owne bulke; but 't shall be on the crosse:
> Where I will naile your pride, at breadth, and length,
> And cracke those sinnewes, which are yet but stretch'd
> With your swolne fortunes rage.
>
> (568–74)

Sejanus can vent his wrath only on the audience as he swears in soliloquy to pursue his practice against Tiberius' upstart son.

In the second stage (II, 1–500) he gains an invaluable ally in Livia, on whom again he lavishes praise as a "royall ladie," "bright, as the Moone, among lesser lights," whose "wisedome, judgement, strength, / Quicknesse, and will" serve to rarefy his own spirit (24 *et passim*). And he grows increasingly bold. Not only does he eliminate Drusus with Livia's aid; he is also able to convince Tiberius of the righteousness of moving against his enemies:

> All for a crowne.
> The prince, who shames a tyrannes name to beare,
> Shall never dare doe any thing, but feare;
> All the command of scepters quite doth perish,
> If it beginne religious thoughts to cherish.
>
> (177–81)

Silius, Sosia, and Cordus are marked for accusation by the senate, and Sejanus persuades Tiberius to trust him completely in devising

the false accusations. Moreover, increasing confidence prompts
him to manipulate the emperor's mother, Augusta, to feed her
son's suspicions concerning the family of Agrippina. His vision has
obviously expanded with his confidence; he assures Livia, for
example, that they shall "share the sov'raigntie of all the world,"
between them dividing the name of Caesar (37, 40); if that be but
a ploy to gain her stronger support, there is no duplicity in his
observations in soliloquy that the two of them will bear the prize
of world power (157) or that he "will rise, / By making [Tiberius]
the publicke sacrifice" (403–404). Markedly advanced also is the
pride and arrogance of the man. His schemes he describes as "my
art" (399), and he vows with singular pleasure to commit a "race
of wicked acts" so that the world may know his anger (151). And
for the first time he defies the power of the gods, swearing to
persevere in his course of action "though heav'n drop sulphure,
and hell belch out fire":

> Tell proud Jove,
> Betweene his power, and thine [my soul's], there is no oddes.
> 'Twas onely feare, first, in the world made gods.
>
> (160–62)

Sejanus, it is true, at this point is still forced to operate privately
and on an individual level, but both his self-assurance and his ambition have grown in frightening proportions as—in the absence of
belief in external and absolute values—he is molded by opportunity
and relentless self-concern as a child of the times.

In the third phase (III, 1–749; IV, 1–523) Sejanus, no longer
operating privately, systematically manipulates a group of high-
placed subordinates in order to destroy those who oppose him.
Delivering detailed notes, he informs the consul Varro and his associates of the charges which must publicly be drawn against Silius,
then slyly maintains absolute silence during the proceedings; as
Silius becomes increasingly furious and volatile, he observes with
seeming objective equanimity that the remarks to the consul are
most "insolent! And impious!" (III, 238–40). Likewise, in later
action Sejanus is not even on stage as others work in his behalf for
the praise and reward they expect from him. The Senator Latiaris,
along with Rufus and Opsius, lays the trap which brings Sabinus
down (IV, 93–114), and within two hundred lines the spectators
hear of Nero's banishment and Agrippina's confinement. Sejanus,
obviously, now moves with a boldness and cunning born of success,

and in a daring stroke he requests the emperor's approval of his
marriage to Livia, a union which would "strengthen [his] weake
house, / Against the-now-unequall opposition / Agrippina (III,
524-26). Rebuffed, he expresses his private disdain for Tiberius
and rejects the need for further support from him. By lulling the
"voluptuous Caesar" to concern only for gratification of personal
lust, he will effectively seize control of the imperial power:

> By this, shall I remoove him both from thought,
> And knowledge of his owne most deare affaires;
> Draw all dispatches through my private hands;
> Know his designements, and pursue mine owne;
> Make mine owne strengths, by giving suites and places;
> Conferring dignities and offices.
>
> (III, 613-18)

In the final act Sejanus is victimized by his own confidence, which
—bolstered by pride—has caused him to lose touch with reality and
has destroyed that wily perceptiveness that had made him a master
of men. It is true that events both planned and unplanned conspire
to strengthen his sense of security—his saving Tiberius' life when a
part of a farm house collapsed ("With which adventure, / He hath
so fixt himselfe in Caesar's trust, / As thunder cannot moove him"
[IV, 57-59]); the subsequent fall of his political enemy Sabinus;
and the punitive actions against Nero, Drusus Junior, and Agrippina
which seem conveniently to remove yet additional obstacles. Later
he gullibly and unquestioningly swallows Macro's intimations that
Caesar stands ready to confer upon him the "tribuniciall dignitie,
and power" (V, 363) and that Caligula lies in disgrace at Capreae.
Now, in a word, he is blind to the dangers around him and, thus,
ironically is susceptible to the same trap set earlier for his own
political enemies. His hubris is blatant as in soliloquy he terms himself "great, and high": "My roofe receives me not; 'tis aire I tread:
/ And, at each step, I feele my advanced head / Knocke out a starre
in heav'n" (57-59). And in his brashest moment he asserts himself
"no lesse than Jove" (205); Jove is his equal, Caesar his second, all
Rome his slave, and the Fates envious of his power.

Sejanus' character, then, develops consistently in the tragedy
from halting and covert operations to public assertions of unlimited
power. Despite the absence of any kind of moral progression, Jonson is demonstrably attempting to create a dynamic character
whose development will both interest and horrify the spectators.

Of greatest significance, though, in a consideration of the developing perspective of Jacobean tragedy, is the manner in which the
collapse of this figure is accommodated to the philosophic context
of the stage world. In other villain-dramas of the period a counterforce develops which through the eventual destruction of the
protagonist reflects some sense of the ultimate victory of right
reason and the authority of God. Whether it be death's conquest
of Tamburlaine, Richmond's overthrow of Richard III, the
governor's trick which hoists Barabas with his own petard (given
the hypocrisy of the Christian governor and the avarice of the holy
friars, the values which prevail are admittedly seriously vitiated,
but unlike that of *Sejanus* the focus in this play centers upon the
single personality whose destruction seems to purge the stage
world of a cancerous evil), or Charlemont's successful resistance to
Damville, for example, a superior and positive force prevails, in
terms of the value structure established in the fictional world; and,
consequently, the causal construct of the events supports the
assumption of a society ultimately controlled by metaphysical
teleological design.

    In *Sejanus,* to the contrary, the developing counterforce is
equally as tainted and corrupt as the individual it opposes. It is
Tiberius who first voices suspicion of Sejanus' intentions and who
is responsible for setting in motion the forces which eventually
destroy him. And it is Tiberius, of course, who retains the primary
position of power following Sejanus' fall. This emperor, though,
throughout the play is accused of tyranny by a wide range of
characters. Through his sycophant Sejanus, he but ratifies his own
bloody political designs to tread down "rites / Of faith, love, piety"
(II, 175–76). He is "an Emp'rour, only in his lusts," a monster
"forfeited to vice / So far, as no rack'd vertue can redeeme him"
(V, 376, 373–74); at his "slaughter-house at *Capraea*" he "studie[s]
murder, as an arte" and practices his "strange, and new-commented
lusts" upon his "boyes, and beauteous girls" (388 *et passim*). He
may well perceive in Sejanus' pride a more dreadful enemy "then
all fell Agrippina's hates" (III, 636) and determine, through Macro,
to "raise one ill / Against another, and both faithfully kill" (657–
58), but certainly it represents no individual perception gained
from moral insight and no social purgation, either of which might
lend ethical justification to the waste and destruction of such
tragic events and thus provide the spectators in Tiberius an object
of effective sympathy.

Nor does Macro in the spectators' eyes ever rise above Tiberius' assessment as a poison by which he must expel and destroy another. A Sejanus in miniature, he proclaims himself "without ambition: / Save to doe Caesar service" (667–68), yet privately admits that the way to rise is to obey and please" (735); Sejanus' "fall / May be [his] rise" (748). Indeed, his amoral self-centeredness places him in the forefront among the dramatic depictions of the Renaissance New Man:

> He that will thrive in state, he must neglect
> The trodden paths, that truth and right respect;
> And prove new, wilder wayes: for vertue, there,
> Is not that narrow thing, shee is else-where.
>   (736–39)

Never once does he flinch in this resolve. Hearing of Sejanus' new-found favor following the accident at the farm house, he determines to strike before the danger redounds upon him. To that end he convinces Caligula to join Caesar at Capraea and to avow humility to his uncle preferable to living in "hourely fear . . . [of] bold Sejanus' authority" by appointing consuls opposed to him. Arranging the accusations, prompting those who are to deliver them, directing the military forces which might conceivably be needed, and then disarming Sejanus by visiting him and reporting Tiberius' intentions of honoring him, Macro virtually single-handedly stages the senatorial proceeding which breaks Sejanus' power. With smug satisfaction he then proclaims that Sejanus lies "as flat, / As was [his] pride advanc'd" (V, 745–46). And he is not satisfied with simple victory; he is intent upon provoking the "torture [of] / So meriting a traytor" (680–81). Tearing off Sejanus' robe and insultingly plucking his beard, he incites the frenzied mob to "use th' ingratefull viper, [and to] tread his braines / Into the earth" (678–79). Well might Arruntius prophesy—in the midst of shouts of praise to Macro as Rome's savior—that "this new fellow . . . will become / A greater prodigie in *Rome,* then he / That now is falne" (751–53).

What then is left to provide a fundamental base for the audience's sympathy? Certainly not Caligula, who, though he has escaped Sejanus' clutches and enjoys the favor of Caesar, already belies the corruption of his maturity; Macro's favor with Caligula is the result, as Pomponius reports, of willingness to prostitute his wife to the young prince's appetite, to "looke up, and spie / Flies in the roofe,

when there are fleas i' bed" (IV, 517–18). And certainly not the
body politic, which in the form of the mob emerges as yet another
villain in the final act. Allowing themselves to be used "to stamp
out their own liberty" (Hamilton, p. 275), they become "partners
in crime with their oppressors" (Ornstein, p. 198). More specifically, their willingness to endure and even to adulate a tyrant above
the law, yet to destroy him without recourse to the law, forces us
to view them as the mindless tool of those who lead them:

> The rout, they follow with confused voyce,
> Crying, they'are glad, say they could ne'er abide him;
> . . . .
> And not a beast of all the herd demands,
> What was his crime? or, who were his accusers?
> Under what proofe, or testimonie he fell?
>
> (V, 786–87, 793–95)

An "eager multitude" who "never yet / Knew why to love, or hate,
but onely pleas'd / T' expresse their rage of power" (759–61), they
are seen in their most execrable light when their feverous passion is
allayed only by decapitating Sejanus and literally tearing his trunk
into small pieces,[9] deflowering his daughter, and strangling both
daughter and son despite the "unripe yeares" which proclaim their
"childish silly innocence" (V, 843–44). The "black, and bitter execrations" (866) of Apicata, Sejanus' estranged wife, delivered while
tearing her hair and beating her breasts and womb become at once
the most pitiful moment of the play and the severest condemnation
of the monstrous rabble. In light of such moral relativism the final
irony results from placing a pious and straightforward moral concerning the wisdom and justice of the gods and of the grave consequences of insolent man's denying their powers (898–903) in the
mouth of Terentius, a slight and inconsequential character whose
five previous appearances on stage as Sejanus' sponge have confirmed only the bias of his perspective and thus his peculiar inap-
propriateness for such a choric role.

For fully half of the play the spectators have shared Sejanus'
level of perception. But as Tiberius and Macro counter and eventually overcome his power and as each in turn engages in soliloquies
which reveal his machinations against the other, the perception
fragments, and the spectator alone is in a position fully to visualize
the depravity of a society in which each principal, motivated by
vicious self-interest, struggles desperately against the others.[10] Like

Shakespeare in *Timon of Athens, Coriolanus,* and *Antony and Cleopatra,* Jonson utilizes a group of minor characters who through extensive choric commentary direct the spectators' attention equally to the flawed central figure and to the corruption of those around him who by manipulating him to their own advantage play an active role in his developing tragedy.[11] Like Webster he doubles the principals committed to villainy in order to increase the intensity of the social malignance and broaden the base of its operation. And like Ford, he provides no acceptable resolution to the metaphysical ambiguities of the stage world and to the tragic waste of lives destroyed by the value structure of a pervasively decadent society. In *Sejanus* "the evil survives" (Burton, p. 411) and the "tragic events only reaffirm Sejanus' own relativism, which is now turned back upon him" (Dessen, p. 72); with the audience perhaps aware that Arruntius in a few years would commit suicide, the tragic effect "is intensified by the historical context" (Thayer, p. 120). By the same token, by forcing the spectators vicariously to face the worst potentialities of human nature, the tragedy—as Barish aptly observes—"acts to inhibit their further actualization in reality" (p. 24). Jonson's tragic vision stands or falls—not on what happens on stage—but on what happens in the galleries.

Jonson, to repeat, requires the spectators to utilize their personal values as a measure of judgment upon every character in the play. Cyril Tourneur in *The Revenger's Tragedy* (1606–1607) establishes a similar structure by presenting in Vindice a revenger whose methods grow progressively more vicious even as does the immorality of his victims. In his second tragedy Jonson develops the converse pattern; Catiline is monstrously malignant from the outset, but the spectators in subsequent scenes become increasingly aware of the duplicity and decadence of those who oppose him.[12] The deeply ambivalent situation which results in both instances— and which demands the audience's direct participation—is to become the hallmark of the most powerful Jacobean tragedy.

Catiline himself furnishes the narrative frame for an action involving the sickness of a society, its propertied class and the "new man" who must accommodate his virtues to the times, its politically disaffected and those who feed on such discontent, its harlots and the clients who visit them from high station.[13] While he speaks only 21 percent (742) of the lines in the play—compared with over 30 percent (1,048) for Cicero—he is the only character who establishes a private level of perception with the audience, delivering

three soliloquies and eight asides. Moreover, half of his lines occur
in Act I, in which he is the dominant figure and in which he serves
as a catalyst for those who normally might very well seek the
convenience of peace and its protection of vested interests.

Unlike Sejanus, Catiline does not develop in the course of the
action either in intensity of purpose or artistry of design. His commitment to self, his willingness to use the most vicious methods to
accomplish his purposes, his total lack of moral sensitivity—along
with the feverous pride reflected in his disdain for others and his
class consciousness—all are vividly established in his first appearance on the stage; in fact Jonson has consciously darkened Catiline's
character, transforming any touch of reforming zeal into false and
self-seeking ambition.[14] In his opening soliloquy Catiline rankles at
Rome's "no-voice, when [he] stood *Candidate*" for consul (I, 89),
declaring himself "a man, bred great, as *Rome* her selfe" and vowing to topple the "proud citie"—to live again the "labour of her
wombe, and be a burden / Weightier then all the prodigies, and
monsters, / That shee hath teem'd with" (83, 78, 95–97). Moments
later to Aurelia he describes the murder of his wife and son in
order to clear the way to "call her Queene / Of all the world" (109–
10).[15] Moreover, he takes macabre delight in his ability to use others
for his own hidden purposes. Lentulus, descended from the Cornelii,
foolishly believes he will be "a king in *Rome*" (138); the fiery
Cethegus, properly goaded, can be set to any deed, however
dastardly. Some, like Curius, "haue been degraded, in the *Senate*"
(150) and smart for revenge; others, like Lecca, Vargunteius, Bestia,
and Autronius, are fired by "meere ambition" (153); still others,
like "th'idle Captaynes / Of Sylla's troops" and "diuers *Roman*
Knights" (158) are so oppressed by want that they would "Runne
any desperate fortune, for a change" (161); others would gladly
destroy that law before which their own crimes stand condemned;
and some, "slight ayrelings" (167), can be won with dogs and
horses, a whore, or a young boy. With perfect aplomb Catiline can
proclaim his projected rebellion the "great, and goodliest action"
(338) by which to "redeeme our selues to libertie" (344) and to
"break the yron yoke" (345), yet in the same breath extol the
riches and brave spoil which the rebels themselves will seize:

> For our reward, then,
> First, all our debts are paid; dangers of law,
> Actions, decrees, judgements against vs quitted;

> The rich men, as in Sylla's times, proscrib'd,
> And publication made of all their goods'
> . . . .
> You share the world, her magistracies, priest-hoods,
> Wealth, and felicitie amongst you, friends.
>   (453–57, 463–64)

Underscoring the hideously grotesque qualities of this political
monster is his forcing each conspirator to partake of a sacrament
of human blood drawn from a murdered slave and his turning
furiously upon a young page whose very squeamishness reveals a
normality which must be repudiated.

With remarkable impact, then, Catiline is established as the
dominant figure of the play, and a spectator might well anticipate
that—whether in the mold of Tamburlaine, or Richard III, or
Macbeth—the action will focus on his personal encounter with
tragedy. Yet, to the contrary, Catiline after Act I grows increasingly victimized by the action he has precipitated; he suffers no
qualms either moral or physical, to be sure, but the spectators'
attention is shifted increasingly to others, likewise tainted in varying degrees, whose political fortunes dictate their opposition to
him. For one thing Catiline's power progressively declines following the opening scene. In Act III, again rejected in his bid for the
consulship, he registers his disdain in a series of asides, then in a
sudden, uncontrollable fit of spleen spits his venom openly upon
Cato and the prevailing power structure, an action which Cato
counters with obvious disdain. Catiline may again confidently rally
the forces of rebellion—plotting the assassination of Cicero, nam-
ing the day for general attack, and vowing to "Strew sacrifices" in
"heaps" and to "Make the earth an altar. / And *Rome* the fire"
(624–25). And in his second major soliloquy he may boastfully
refer to his assorted companions as stales with which he stalks who,
like the "brethren sprung of dragons teeth" (736), shall destroy
each other and leave him alone to bear the glory. There is now,
though, a critical difference. Since the audience at this point
realizes that Cicero has informants at the heart of the rebellion and
hence knows the leader's every word almost as soon as it is uttered,
Catiline no longer looms an awesomely monstrous figure; instead,
from this new perspective his public threats and private self-
assurance contain at least a touch of the thrasonical. So, too, in
Act IV when his fellow senators refuse to sit by him in the temple
of Jupiter Stator and subject him to a remarkably forthright tongue-

lashing, he reacts like a sulking bully whose bluff has been called. Informed that his "counsells [are] all laid open" and his "wild conspiracie bound in / With each mans knowledge" (183, 184–85), he is ordered by his peers to leave the city.

Strange as it may seem, the spectators' attitude toward Catiline begins to modulate during this scene. Certainly, he is never to become a sympathetic figure, but he does become less the object of unmitigated disdain as their attention is directed to Caesar and Crassus, fellow conspirators who desert him in order to save themselves. In Act V, in which he speaks only fifty-three lines, he comes closest to a moment of dignity; as John J. Enck is compelled to remark, "Nominally the villain of the piece, he only exudes a kind of glory."[16] Again, it is not sympathy; but, in the context of the arrest of principal supporters (most of whom readily confess their treason in the hope of saving their skin), the promise of material reward to Cicero's spy Curius (originally himself a party to the conspiracy), and Cicero's willingness to compromise his own integrity by refusing to move against the other powerful senators he knows to be guilty, Catiline strikes the spectators as strangely worthy of something akin to respect for his very consistency. Not for a moment in these final scenes does either his courage or his conviction flag. In his oration to his army he again extols the patriotic cause for which they fight. And this time there are neither overt references to material spoils nor covert, cynical asides concerning personal glory to taint the fervor of his words:

> haue your valours, and your soules, about you;
> And thinke, you carrie in your labouring hands
> The things you seeke, glorie, and libertie.
> . . . .
> You might haue liu'd in seruitude, or exile,
> Or safe at *Rome,* depending on the great ones;
> But that you thought those things vnfit for men.
> (392–94, 403–405)

Caught between two armies and suffering from "great want / Of corne, and victuall" (387–88), he has a prescience of defeat but urges his men, if such is their destiny, to sell their lives "at such a price, as may / Vn-doe the world, to buy vs; and make *Fate,* / While shee tempts ours, feare her owne estate" (417–18). Moreover, the opposing general Petreius reports Catiline's fall on a titanic scale. As the conspirator rose, "the day grew black with him; / And *Fate* descended neerer to the earth" (634–35). The

"Furies stood, on hills" (655) and "pietie left the field" (657) as Catiline moved in rage across the plain. "(Arm'd with a glorie, high as his despaire)" (671), he struck "like a Lybian lion,"

> scornefull of our weapons
> Carelesse of wounds, plucking downe liues about him,
> Till he had circled in himselfe with death:
> Then he fell too, t'embrace it where it lay.
>
> (673–76)

Catiline has not changed in the course of the play; he is as intent upon destroying Rome in Act V as he was at the outset, and he is just as careless of human life and the ethical values upon which social harmony is predicated. The spectators' perspective, however, has changed radically. It can hardly be accidental that they see the central figure in a progressively less execrable light. So, for that matter, do his enemies on stage: witness Petreius' account of the final battle and the observation by Cato, his severest critic, concerning his "braue bad death" (678). Clearly, this is a part of Jonson's design to force the spectators to look beyond Catiline to find the ultimate cause of the tragedy which stalks Rome. The arch-conspirator may provoke widespread bloodshed and suffering, and he himself may exemplify the tragic waste of a life whose genuine human potential has gone unrealized. But Catiline's depraved personality is only a portion of the focus; as the audience comes increasingly to realize, tragedy results as well from the flaws of various other significant characters and from a general loss of political integrity and social cohesion.[17]

Complementary to the anomalous treatment of the titular villain are additional fundamental structural features which provoke this broader perspective. The prologue and the choral passages, for example, create a frame for the tragedy, not of a single individual, but of a society. Sylla's spirit invokes Catiline to bring against Rome the combined force of the Gracci, Cinna, Marius, and Hannibal. This new rebel is to pursue no less than "the ruine of [his] countrie" (I, 45), to

> leaue *Romes* blinded walls
> T'embrace lusts, hatreds, slaughters, funeralls,
> And not recouer sight, till their owne flames
> Doe light them to their ruines.
>
> (63–66)

And the blame for this destruction is in Act I placed directly upon
the citizens who revel in opulence: Rome "builds in gold. . . . Her
women weare the spoiles of nations. . . . The men [are] . . . kemb'd,
and bath'd, and rubb'd, and trim'd. . . . They eate on beds of silke,
and gold" (551, 555–56, 560, 561, 565). More importantly, this
disease of excess has destroyed her virtue; ambition has invaded
the state with "auarice, / Riot, and euery other vice" (577–78).
Laws, honors, offices, and the peoples' voices are bought and sold.
Her own "spoiler, and owne prey" (586), Rome will "Be by it
selfe, now, ouer-come" (536). The commentary at the conclusion
of Act II, at the point at which new consuls are being elected, calls
for the public to "make a free, and worthy choice" (II, 373) and
reiterates the dangers of power corrupted by bribery or by envy,
hatred, or fear. Later, when the rebellion is in process, the Chorus
describes the panic gripping the city as each individual struggles to
save himself:

> The priests, and people runne about,
> Each order, age, and sexe amz'd at other;
> And, at the ports, all thronging out,
> As if their safety were to quit their mother.
> (III, 848–51)

Again ambition, the "neere vice / To vertue" (860–61) is the signal
villain; since it is a flaw common to all, its excesses are rarely perceived and acknowledged "till those plagues doe get aboue / The
mountayne of our faults" (856–57). And finally the Chorus laments
the whimsicality of the people, whose support of leadership varies
with their own comfort and fortune. This "euill seed" (887) must
be plucked "Out of our spirits" (888):

> Lest we seeme fallne (if this endures)
> Into those times,
> To loue disease: and brooke the cures
> Worse, then the crimes.
> (891–94)

Obviously, the thrust of this external commentary is to suggest
that the total citizenry must answer to both the causes and the
consequences of Catiline's conspiracy. Additionally, two segments
of the action proper specifically distance the spectators from a
consuming interest in his personal activities. Act II, in fact, bridg-
ing Catiline's machinations and his confrontation with Cicero, is a

satiric inset which serves to symbolize the general vanity and
decadence. Whether one agrees with Dryden that this action is an
unnatural "oleo" of comic and tragic effects[18] or with T. S. Eliot
that it is "the best scene in the body of the play,"[19] the Roman
women function as "alternative symbols of the body politic."[20]
The prostitute Fulvia rails at her slave-girl concerning the jewelry
which best will enhance her attire. Never appearing "two dayes
together, in one dressing" (II, 14), she must outshine those around
her even as she scoffs at the paints, powders, perfumes, and
dentifrices which conceal the decays in her colleagues. Her ac-
quaintance, Lady Sempronia, unwittingly extends the theme of
corruption hidden by superficial ornament as she denounces the
"mushroom" Cicero, who dares stand for office without pedigree,
house, or coat. She would "Hang vertue, where there is no bloud"
(122); now, she insists, Rome's "wealth, / Fortune and ease" will
support them " 'Gainst all new commers: and can neuer faile vs, /
While the succession stayes" (131–32, 134–35). Their sexual
depravity merely accentuates the corruption as Fulvia discusses
her "secret fellows" (166) with strong backs and Sempronia her
affection for young faces and smooth chins. With the entrance of
the Senator Curius and his bartering conspiracy's secrets for lust's
gratification, the scathing social vignette is complete, and against
this background of general corruption Catiline's individual atrocities pale by several degrees. Similarly, the introduction of the
Allobrogian ambassadors in Act IV provides commentary on the
broader scene. Meeting several senators quaking and trembling,
they laugh at the "ridiculous feare" of those whom they once
feared "beyond the *Alpes*"; the Romans now move, not as proud
and courageous conquerors, but "downe-ward all, like beasts, /
Running away from euery flash" (IV, 4, 5, 9–10).

In addition to these particular segments of the action, the
dialogue sporadically turns on the pervasive corruption of the city
at large. Catiline denounces the "giants of the state" (I, 348) who
by turns enjoy and defile the city and the "riches of the world"
which they "powre / Out i' their riots, eating, drinking, building"
(352, 377–78); if his view is admittedly biased, it is nonetheless
consonant with what more objective voices have spoken. Cicero,
for example, from his vantage describes the diseased state of the
commonwealth:

> O *Rome,* in what a sicknesse art thou fall'n!
> How dangerous, and deadly! when thy head

> Is drown'd in sleepe, and all thy body feu'ry!
> No noise, no pulling, no vexation wakes thee,
> Thy *lethargie* is such.
>
> (III, 438–42)

From yet another point of view, Petreius in Act V compares the
present condition of Rome to that of her glorious past. He dedi-
cates the imminent battle to a renewed commitment to the
"labours, counsells, arts, and actions" (V, 9) purchased over so
many years by their "great ancestors." Time and again, in other
words, the spectators are reminded of general corruption which in
part at least is responsible for the tragic actions of any single member of the society.

Certainly, the structural feature most significant in establishing
this societal perspective is the pattern of multiple levels of perception which progressively forces the spectators to bring their own
judgments to bear upon the characters and the events. Specifically,
the action builds on three levels of awareness, each of the first two
subsumed in turn by a more nearly omniscient view as the audience's complex perspective develops. Catiline himself maintains
the primary level only for the first act, 17 percent of the tragedy.
Following his opening soliloquy he shares with Aurelia only so
much as conveniently serves his purpose, persuading her to feign
with him a love of the rabble whom they must use to achieve their
goal: "I must pray my loue, shee will put on / Like habites with
my selfe. I haue to doe / With many men, and many natures" (I,
130–32). In turn, he practices upon every character on stage in the
first act. Claiming to be but "a shaddow" (I, 286) helping to work
out their fortunes, he relentlessly pursues his private design for
power at whatever cost to the city and to its inhabitants. In Act II,
however, Catiline—who never appears—suddenly becomes the
potential victim as his secret intrigue becomes known outside his
circle of conspirators. If the spectators gain a degree of relief in the
probability that his destructive plot will be foiled, they are offered
little moral comfort in the fact that the informant Curius, goaded
by sheer lust, provides the information as the price for a whore's
services. And Fulvia, in turn, reports the sedition to the State, not
for honor and love of country, but for spite rather than be party
to a plot in which Lady Sempronia, her colleague in the behind-
door trade, "should take place of me" (III, 376).

Nonetheless, it is by this means that Cicero in Act III emerges
with the highest level of perception, employing Curius and Fulvia

as spies in the rebel camp and monitoring each phase of Catiline's
activity. Again the spectators might assume that the action is to
be neatly resolved through control exercised by the virtuous consul, who will manipulate the villain into an inescapable position,
destroy him with suitable moral commentary, and project a leadership and a society purged at least temporarily of cruelty and callous ambition. Jonson's, however, is not Elizabethan tragedy, and
the problem of evil is not to be so easily packaged and resolved.
Not only, as we have observed, does the playwright from this point
attempt to temper the spectators' attitude toward Catiline; he also
begins subtly to draw their attention to demeaning, if sometimes
practical, characteristics of the consul.[21] A rather strident touch of
pride, for example, is evident in Cicero's first words in the play as,
following his election as consul, he panegyrizes on the prudence of
the Roman people and his own integrity. He represents the "new
man," "before me, none," without "forged tables / Of long
descents, to boast false honors from" (II, 19, 25, 16–17). His election has

> cut a way, and left it ope for vertue.
> . . . .
> At my first suite, in my iust yeere; preferd
> To all competitors; and from the noblest—
> (21, 26–27)

Similarly, later, he seems almost overly concerned with self as he
observes that it was "my strengths, . . . my aides, my watches" (IV,
251, 258) which prevented Catiline's moving against the city.
Obviously, these are only sporadic moments, but they are sufficient to plant suspicion in the spectators' mind. And such suspicion feeds on Cicero's willingness to bribe those who can serve his
ends—Curius ("What thankes, what titles, what rewards the *Senate* /
Will heape upon you, certaine, for your seruice" [III, 401–402];
"*Rome* / Shall proue a thankfull, and a bounteous mother" [430–
31]); Curius and Fulvia ("They must receiue reward, though't be
not knowne" [IV, 521]); his fellow consul Antonius, who later
admits Cicero has "bought" his favor by "giuing" him land ("I
must with offices, and patience win him; / . . . and bestow / The
prouince on him; which is by the *Senate* / Decreed to me: that
benefit will bind him" [III, 474, 476–78]); the Allobrogian ambassadors, who for their double dealing with Catiline receive a "free
grant, from the state" and a "reward, out of the publike treasure"

(V, 295, 296). Of Fulvia he speaks publicly as Rome's "sauer" for whose "vertue, / I could almost turne louer, againe" (III, 342–43), yet privately brands her a vile thing, a "base / And common strumpet, worthlesse to be nam'd" (450–51). And most disturbing of all is his willingness to compromise principle for security. Though evidence mounts of Caesar's and Crassus' guilt, Cicero refuses to accuse them; "if they be ill men," they are also "mightie ones" (IV, 530, 531), and their conviction "shall not be sought by me" (V, 96). When direct charges are brought against them, Cicero labels the accuser a "lying varlet" and Crassus a "great, and good" citizen (V, 340, 345); the charge against Caesar he will "throw . . . out o' the court" (353); "You shall haue no wrong done you, noble Caesar, / But all contentment" (365–66). Later Cicero suppresses written evidence of Caesar's guilt and prevents his arrest by the praetors: "Hold, friends. . . . No violence. Caesar, be safe" (581, 582).

Again, this evidence is admittedly massed to make a point. Clearly, Cicero is the dominant positive force in the tragedy, and it is through him that judgments are drawn on the obvious villains. At the same time, though, the spectators have seen too much to accept uncritically the consul's assertion that "fortune may forsake me, not my vertue" (IV, 821) or his concluding remark—made at the height of his renown in the full flush of public praise when humility would represent the better part of prudence—that fame "euer is ill got" without conscience (V, 702). They alone, in other words, are in a position fully to comprehend the multiple levels of perception, with each person being manipulated by those who can gain at his expense. Catiline and Cicero are obviously two extremes on the spectrum, but each emerges as a figure whose character and ultimate fate are molded in large part by the actions and expectations of those around him.

The plot, then, opening with Catiline's vow to "dig . . . a seate" in Rome's "stony entrailes" (I, 94, 93) where he will live again the greatest of her "prodigies, and monsters" (96) and concluding with the chilling account of his death in battle, turns superficially on a senator's abortive conspiracy to seize autocratic power and destroy the Roman Republic. The dramatic focus, however, is pitched far beyond Catiline's individual perceptions. Viewing the action simultaneously from both the traitor's prospect and from Cicero's, the spectators' perspective belies the simplistic assumption of Catiline's arrant villainy set against the purity and strength

of the Roman Republic. To the contrary, the viewers are forced to
recognize duplicity within the most influential members of the
senate, whose secret support for the rebellion holds promise of
enormous wealth to be gained from political rapine without the
danger of tainting their good name and public reputation, and the
audience must confront directly the sad spectacle of virtue and integrity compromised by necessity and ambition. In a word, they
witness not so much the tragedy of an individual—Catiline, the
political monster, is after all a creature of unmitigated evil and his
destruction can hardly provoke either a sympathetic or cathartic
response from those who observe it; more profoundly, they witness the tragedy of a society and the human interrelationships
which, in combination with the individual's flaw, impel him to
corruption and destruction. Their knowledge that within a few
brief years the Republic will fall victim to Julius Caesar and in
turn to Octavius, whose purge will strike down Cicero himself,
grimly intensifies the sense of an oppressive and pervasive evil
which the death of a single reprobate—however infamous—is incapable of purging. Jonson, then, is not merely a "pitiless recorder
of vices and vanities" without a moral center, as Ornstein (p. 88)
would have it. Rather, the spectators come away "instructed"
(Knoll, p. 136); suspended "at the brink of chaos for five acts,"
they are turned "back to the disorder of [their] own lives with a
new sense of disquiet and hence of purpose."[22]

Admittedly, the tragedy contains several abortive elements for
which neither critic nor playgoer has ever completely excused the
author. For one thing the use of Sylla's ghost as a prologue figure
to catalog macabre horrors both past and yet to come is simply
too theatrical.[23] The oration establishes both the theme of social
decadence and the theme of Catiline's villainy, to be sure, but
there is never a meaningful connection developed between the
earlier tyrant and the title figure—not even to the extent that
reemergence of such evil could be seen as a cyclic inevitability.
Sylla does not serve as a guiding spirit to Catiline throughout the
action, either in fact or fancy; indeed, he is mentioned only once
following the first seventy-two lines, and Catiline's projected
physical destruction of Rome is not seriously an issue beyond the
first two acts. The ghost, in other words, is essentially a tonal
contrivance. Serious also is the narrative fragmentation occasioned
by the societal perspective. The spectators (and the critics in the
study) who of necessity confront the villain with such private

intensity in Act I understandably expect the focus of the tragedy to explore his development, and they may be excused for a degree of emotional confusion in their perplexed attitude toward him at his death. So, too, Aurelia is introduced as a significant character, partner to Catiline's design; yet she is dropped abruptly following the opening scene. In like fashion the superficial treatment of Fulvia's and Curius' *volte-face* is at best disconcerting to the viewer who might well anticipate exploration of the motives and consequences involved. Cato, Cethegus, Lentulus, and Sempronia are all given strong individualizing traits, but the rich possibilities of their relationships with the leading figures are sacrificed to the rapidly shifting perspective.

More effective is the use of omens and portents, probably suggested by Plutarch, Livy, or Lucan,[24] to reinforce the playwright's presentation of a genuinely ambivalent situation. The sudden darkening, for example, followed by the sound of mysterious groans and the appearance of a fiery light and a bloody arm when the conspirators prepare to take the human sacrament suggest heavenly powers not indifferent to human events—as does the lightning and thunder during the attempt to assassinate Cicero and the darkening of day during Catiline's final battle. Both sides, however, claim to fight with the gods' blessings. The rebels' enterprise is sealed by a cosmic sign (I, 313); they rally behind the "faith of gods" (368) and speak confidently of the will of the gods (III, 120). Their opponents, on the other hand, refer to the "lou'd gods" (79, 211; V, 693) who will protect the city (II, 235, 393, 783; IV, 24, 842) and to whom temples are raised (V, 15) and public prayers must be offered. Such contradictory human counterclaims certainly in a sense express the ambiguity of the human condition, but more importantly they effectively reflect the sheer desperation of individuals consumed by ambition and a lust for power.

This design is obviously committed to breadth, and in its complex features it is dependent on an observer who to some degree at least is able to perceive Jonson's artistic intentions. Well might the author dedicate the piece to the "Reader extraordinary" (p. 432) and appeal to the Earl of Pembroke's "great and singular faculty of judgment" (p. 431), for the role played by the spectators is the key to the drama's power and the significance of its theme. Like *Sejanus* it provides an early example of the Jacobean and Caroline stage worlds which attempt, through the experience of the individual, to give dramatic focus to the tragedy of an entire

society. With the central figure flawed by a passion which renders
him susceptible both to personal error and to manipulation by
those who pursue their own self-interests at his expense and with
no fundamentally virtuous counterforce in whom confidence can
be placed, the spectator perforce becomes the sole objective judge
of the characters who inhabit the stage world. And it is hardly
likely that Jonson's audience would have been oblivious of the
broad analogies with the pervasive ambivalences of contemporary
society—any more than viewers of Beckett and Ionesco fail to see
contemporary analogies. As such figures as Faustus, Tamburlaine,
Hamlet, Othello, Lear, and Macbeth symbolize the tragedy of
individual error in a world of assumed, if ambiguous, metaphysical
presence, so Catiline takes his place in a steady line of figures who
reflect tragedy in a world in which that presence has paled to
insignificance—or at least indifference—in the face of cruelty and
inhumanity inherent to man's unrestrained greed and ambition—a
world closely resembling what Theodore Spencer has called the
"reawakened emphasis on man's bestiality"[25] in the seventeenth
century and to which twentieth-century man uncomfortably must
acknowledge a close affinity.

IV. Tourneur

—THE REVENGER'S TRAGEDY, THE ATHEIST'S TRAGEDY

Chronologically the first Jacobean tragic playwright, Cyril Tourneur is represented by only two extant works, *The Revenger's Tragedy,* acted by the King's Men and printed in 1607, and *The Atheist's Tragedy,* acted in "divers places" and printed in 1611. Tourneur, then, was completing his initial tragedy—for Shakespeare's company—at approximately the same time Shakespeare himself was broadening his focus on the nature of tragedy; and, not surprisingly, *The Revenger's Tragedy* reflects the same fundamental concerns. The critics have advanced various keys to this macabre, yet compelling drama. It has been described as melodrama,[1] as melodramatic farce,[2] as a dance of death,[3] as a combination of revenge play and morality play.[4] Above all, it has been analyzed as "tragic satire"[5]—"satire molded into a revenge play."[6] Certainly, there need be no argument that the satiric qualities of *The Revenger's Tragedy* are both trenchant and vital to the design of the piece. On the other hand, T. B. Tomlinson's recent comment that "few would want to call this play a tragedy" because "no powerful *human* sympathy and energy combine to give us a dominating central character"[7] poses a critical danger. However necessary such a character may be for *effective* tragedy, to make it a *sine qua non* for generic qualification is not only to contradict the term used by the playwright himself but, more seriously, to disregard Tourneur's contributions to the developing societal perspective of Jacobean tragedy.

The most striking characteristic of *The Revenger's Tragedy*[8]—and ultimately the most important—is the multiplicity of the antagonists. Instead of any one person, a progression of individuals through acts either committed or attempted stand in opposition to Vindice and his moral outrage.[9] The events, moreover, are so arranged as to form a crescendo of deceit and decadence which—combined with Vindice's mounting cruelty in his private dispensation of justice— underscores both the pervasive corruption of the stage world and the interrelationship of the hero's flaw with the actions of those who misuse him for selfish gratification.

Clearly, the villain in the opening scenes—as Vindice and the spectators see it—is the old Duke. The act itself which has prompted Vindice to seek vengeance lies in the past, and the Duke is unaware of either the protagonist's anger or his grisly scheme. In fact, the Duke apparently does not even realize that he has wronged Vindice at all. To be sure, he apparently held Vindice's father in general disfavor, and the old lecher had Gloriana poisoned because she would not submit to his designs. But there is nowhere an indication that he knew she was Vindice's beloved—or for that matter that he was or is aware of Vindice's existence. Such a conflict is probably unique in Renaissance tragedy. Lorenzo (*The Spanish Tragedy*), Claudius (*Hamlet*), Montsurry (*The Revenge of Bussy d'Ambois*), Piero of Venice (*Antonio's Revenge*), and Ithocles (*The Broken Heart*), for example, know full well the existence of an adversary who might attempt to gain vengeance for a past murder. Othello may fail to suspect Iago, but at least he knows him through an occupation which involves daily contact. If Duke Pietro Jacomo is unaware of Malevole's true identity, he certainly realizes that he has egregiously wronged Duke Giovanni Altofronto. Although Hoffman moves furtively, the execution of his father for piracy was a public affair; all know of the son's existence, and Otho—along with other members of the ducal family—perceive clearly the villainous revenger's motive. By comparison, this unilateral struggle between Vindice and the Duke is no conflict at all. The spectators observe the construction of the trap to which the unsuspecting culprit is almost certain to fall victim; and, if on the one hand they are perturbed by a protagonist who will stoop to such wily calculations, they on the other hand can take comfort of a sort in the fact that it is the Duke's continuing acts of lechery which make him vulnerable. In any case the Duke for the initial lines of the play is the sole villain against whom Vindice directs his schemes.

In line 80, however, the Duke's son, Lussurioso, emerges as a second antagonist. He, too, is totally unaware of Vindice, and at first his fault is simply the decadent desire to have a man as his lackey-panderer who is "for evil only good." Vindice determines to take such employment, disguised as Piato, in order to ingratiate himself with those in the court circle and thereby gain an opportunity for moving against the old Duke. Lussurioso's flaw suddenly becomes personal to Vindice two scenes later when, admitting that he is "past [his] depth in lust" (iii, 88) and that his "desires / Are levell'd at a virgin not far from court" (89–90), the son orders Piato to "bewitch" a certain Castiza's "ears, and cozen her of all grace" (112). Infuriated with the youth's audacity and horrified that his sister's honor is to be tried, he swears inwardly to dispatch the villain even as he assures Lussurioso that he will assault her with fine words, finer gifts, and finest promises of advancement.

These scenes (i, iii) which establish the Duke and his son as the primary objects of Vindice's hatred are flanked by scenes (ii, iv) which introduce additional characters bent on using others to their own advantage. If Vindice is not centrally involved in these matters—indeed, in some instances not even aware of them—they help to form the spectators' perspective, the focus of which begins to shift from Vindice's particular quarrels to the decadence which touches every corner of Tourneur's society. In scene ii, for instance, one of the Duchess' sons, Junior Brother, is charged before the Duke with raping Lord Antonio's wife. Nor does the culprit deny his moment of sadistic pleasure: moved to it by "flesh and blood" (47), he would be well pleased to do it again (60–61). In the face of such palpable guilt, the father-in-law listens to the decrees of the judges on the one hand and the pleas of the mother on the other. The tension exposes true colors on every hand. The Duke's bastard son, Spurio, indicates in asides his "hope [Junior Brother] shall die,— . . . / Would all the court were turn'd into a corse" (34–36). And, if the Duke disappoints Spurio with his whimsical defiance of justice in delaying sentence upon the accused, he does not thereby please his Duchess. Furious in soliloquy that he with "one of his single words" failed to free her "youngest, dearest son" (102, 103), she pledges to "kill him in his forehead. . . . That wound is deepest, though it never bleed" (108, 109). To this end she prompts Spurio to sexual response, encouraging him in this manner to gain vengeance for his bastardy. Each in aside voices the further ends his lustful pleasure will serve. Spurio shall

> be reveng'd for all; now hate begin,
> I'll call foul incest but a venial sin. . . .
> Duke, on thou brow I'll draw my bastardy
> For indeed a bastard by nature should make cuckolds,
> Because he is the son of a cuckold-maker.
> (170–71, 202–204)

And the Duchess, who finds this act sweeter than dispatching her husband with poison, avers that now her "vengeance shall reach high; I'll arm thy brow with woman's heraldry" (176–77).

The fourth scene underscores both the tragedy and the frustration of subjects ruled by one who is a law unto himself and his own lust. In failing to sentence Junior Brother, the Duke has raped the law just as surely as his son-in-law has raped Antonio's wife, and in such a society those who would find relief must look beyond the established order. For Antonio's wife, her "honor forc'd" (45), death alone can furnish adequate recompense; she "deem'd it a nobler dowry for her name / To die with poison than to live with shame" (46–47). Antonio himself, holding his dead wife in his arms, at least tacitly endorses Hippolito's suggestion that they take the law into their own hands and proceed to execution of the guilty party even in the face of those who stand above the law and use their power to protect him.

In the first act, then, Vindice provides the dramatic center for opposition to the sexual license which characterizes the entire stage world. But the corruption, far more extensive than the two particular objects of his indignation, wells up in such proportion that only the spectators' perspective can encompass it. Thus the spectators are drawn significantly into the action as they observe Vindice's private struggle against the Duke and his son Lussurioso. While certainly they are not able to condone the methods by which the protagonist achieves vengeance, they nonetheless can comprehend his desire to destroy them; indeed, their judgments on him are temporized further by their exclusive realization of the extent of the pride and lust which surround him and which specifically lead others to attempt to corrupt him for their own foul purposes. Not only, in other words, is the antagonist doubled for Vindice; it emerges as a multiplicity of individuals for the spectators, and the conflict of values exists simultaneously on Vindice's private level and on the audience's more nearly omniscient level.

Certainly, Acts II and III continue to expand the circle of villainy within the play. In II, i, for example, Gratiana proves to have her price. For the "comfortable shine" (127) upon her "poor estate" (109) she will prostitute her own daughter. She will convince Castiza to "leave those childish haviours, / And understand [her] time. Fortunes flow to [her]" (170–71). The various sons at court also reveal their true nature as they begin frantically to parry for position. Not only, for example, does Spurio fully plan to proceed with his sexual assignation with his mother-in-law, he also, learning of Lussurioso's intended tryst with Castiza, intends to strike down the Duke's legitimate son in the act: "I'll damn you at your pleasure—precious deed; / After your lust, O, 'twill be fine to bleed" (II, ii, 127–28). Similarly, following Lussurioso's arrest by the Duke, the stepsons Ambitioso and Supervacuo desperately urge their "brother's" death under the guise of pleas for mercy; their "hate and love [are] woven / So subtilly together, that in speaking / One word for his life, [they] make three for his death" (iii, 61–63). Even as they labor jointly to achieve his death, however, each in aside reveals his determination to eliminate his ally as well. Supervacuo observes that, once Lussurioso is out of the way, he has a pin to prick Ambitioso's bladder (III, i, 13–15); and Ambitioso in turn quips that he next will seize "upon thy neck, kind brother. / The falling of one head lifts up another" (27–28). And, when plans backfire and Junior Brother is mistakenly—albeit deservedly—led to execution, he too reveals his foul nature, offering no token of repentance—no tears which he hates "worse than any citizen's son / Can hate salt water" (III, iv, 57–58)—only curses upon his brothers' soul for their perjury (75–77). Meanwhile, the old Duke, who has seen through their ploy and again has violated all sense of justice by freeing Lussurioso though he assumes him to be guilty, reveals in soliloquy the full extent of his own depravity:

> It well becomes that judge to nod at crimes,
> That does commit greater himself and live;
> I may forgive a disobedient error,
> That expect pardon for adultery,
> And in my old days am a youth in lust!
> Many a beauty have I turn'd to poison
> In the denial, covetous of all:
> Age hot is like a monster to be seen;
> My hairs are white, and yet my sins are green.
> (II, iii, 124–32)

Even as he falls victim to Vindice's macabre scheme, threats against his life arise from another direction; in their lascivious embraces the Duchess would "poison" him (III, v, 214), and Spurio would "add murder to adultery, / And with [his] sword give up his years to death" (218–19).

In the last two acts the primary antagonistic force is Lussurioso, whom Vindice envisions as the next victim of his righteous indignation. Again, however, the spectators perceive far more than the

protagonist. Lussurioso in soliloquy notes his intentions of employing Vindice to "kill / That other slave [Piato], that did abuse my
spleen" (IV, i, 61–62):

> Slaves are but nails, to drive out one another.
> He being of black condition, suitable
> To want and ill content, hope of preferment
> Will grind him to an edge.
>
> (68–71)

So later, after approaching Hippolito's brother with his scheme and
with the money which lends substance to the temptation, he quips
in asides that Vindice "has wit enough / To murder any man, and
I'll give him means" (ii, 106–107). A few lines later he attempts to
intensify Vindice's commitment with the palpable lie that Piato encouraged him to corrupt the virgin sister Castiza with jewels (133–
36). When his father's murder is subsequently discovered, Lussurioso, after privately revealing his delight with the "sweet titles"
(V, 1, 143) which come his way, orders revels for the occasion. He
indicates further in an aside that, in order to capture popular support, he will "begin dukedome" by banishing his mother-in-law,
who is "suspected foully bent" (167). Neither does he intend to
allow to live long the other members of the ducal family, his
potential rivals for power:

> The bastard shall not live. After these revels
> I'll begin strange ones; he and the stepsons
> Shall pay their lives for the first subsidies.
> We must not frown so soon, else 't had been now.
>
> (ii, 8–11)

Although the focus is on Lussurioso, however, the multiple
antagonists continue to be much in evidence. Both stepsons and
bastard son, for instance, inwardly gloat over the old Duke's
murder, the latter thanking the fates for the occasion. And all
three shortly turn in secret to plans for Lussurioso's destruction.
Spurio will not "miss his heart" (173); Supervacuo, vowing that
the new Duke "shall not live, his hair shall not grow much longer"
(177), "shall dispossess him, then we're mighty" (180); Ambitioso,
in turn, will set his mark upon Supervacuo: "And do you think to
be duke then, kind brother? / I'll see fair play; drop one, and there
lies t'other" (184–85). In the final scene each is as good as his
word. Supervacuo, discovering the slain Lussurioso, proclaims him-

self duke, and is murdered by Ambitioso, who in turn is struck down by Spurio. With Spurio's destruction by an unidentified nobleman, the entire nest of maggots has been purged.

Thus throughout the tragedy Tourneur strips bare for the spectators eight characters actively engaged in the moral corruption to which Vindice stands opposed. Their thoughts, voiced privately through nine soliloquies and twenty-nine asides (totaling one hundred fifty-seven lines) provide the only complete view of the teeming decadence and create the perspective through which the spectators must sit in ultimate judgment upon the actions both of the protagonist and of those whom he opposes. As a frame of reference for such judgment Tourneur establishes a value structure so firm that many critics have claimed a "missionary tone" and a "moral fervor"[10] which creates "in literature the pattern (in this instance, the moral pattern) missing in life."[11] For one thing, Tourneur's characters are forever referring to God or to some aspect of the Christian tradition. Antonio's ravished wife, for example, dies with "a prayer-book the pillow to her cheek" (I, iv, 13); her assailant, claims Hippolito, is clearly guilty in heaven (64). Castiza comments on the temptations which produce a profusion of sinners (II, i, 1–8); Vindice counsels Gratiana to "forget heaven" (121) in persuading her daughter to lie with the Duke's son, but privately invokes "Troops of celestial soldiers" (140) and angels (245) to guard Castiza's honor; Heaven itself should "turn black" and "frown" upon a mother who would sacrifice her daughter for secular advancement (254). Later, Vindice and Hippolito must "conjur that base devil out of [their] mother" (IV, iii, 226); her tears of repentance are a gift from heaven showering the "fruitful grounds and meadows of her soul" (iv, 55, 47). Night graces the sin of the Duchess' incest (II, ii, 135), which Spurio describes as sweet, if sinful (III, v, 208). The Duke would not be slain before his "penitential heaves" can atone for his "great sins" (II, iii, 12, 11); Lussurioso later would have Piato stabbed in his drunkenness so that straightway he will "reel to hell" (V, i, 49). Junior Brother, advised to "Lift up [his] eyes to heaven" as he approaches his execution (III, iv, 70), responds with oaths "in the stead of prayer" (III, vi, 47). "Just is the law above" (V, iii, 91), Antonio observes, that has revenged his wife's rape and placed the crown on his head.

Not only do the verbal references to God and heavenly decree occur with furious frequency; the virtuous characters—unlike their counterparts in Webster—survive for some sort of presumed happiness. Castiza, for example, preserves both her life and her virginity; Gratiana repents her dishonor; and Antonio lives to see his wife's tragedy avenged and the crown passed to his head. Moreover, signs and portents suggest a metaphysical presence cognizant of the earthly events.[12] A comet blazing across the sky strikes at least a momentary fear in Lussurioso as he assumes ducal authority. Likewise, thunder seems a response to Vindice's assertion that Lussurioso's wickedness "provokes the almighty patience" (IV, ii, 194).

Since the spectators never perceive a moral sensitivity within Vindice which lends immediate credence to the teleological frame, it is easy enough to brand all of this as the mere trappings of morality.[13] Certainly, Vindice in this respect does not satisfy those critics searching for a naturalistic protagonist who is a microcosmic focus of the conflicting values in the stage world. Quite probably, however, realizing that detachment keys the spectators' perception and judgment both of the evil which pervades the stage world and also of the multiple causes of tragedy, Tourneur was consciously avoiding the amblyopia which could result from an intensely introspective central figure. For one thing, the complex turns of plot prevent an anticipation of the action, and the natural consequence is to absorb the spectators' interest in the events rather than the characters—in what is going to happen rather than how a character is affected by or involved in such events. More specifically, Vindice at the outset asserts his determination to achieve vengeance against the Duke. The concern is not for the general corruption in the ducal family but solely for the old lecher who previously has poisoned Vindice's mistress for her refusal to cater to his palsy lust (I, i, 34). Vindice's "abused heart strings [are turned] into fret" (13) as he proclaims sternly that revenge, "murder's quit-rent" (39), will have her due. The spectators can only assume that the action of the play will focus essentially on Vindice's private struggle and his ultimate confrontation with this adversary. And, indeed, the first act firmly supports the assumption. He questions his brother about the "bald Madame, Opportunity" (55) and seizes upon the suggestion that he serve Lussurioso in disguise as the "Occasion" or small "advantage [to] fatten . . . wronged men" (98). A few lines later the grounds for his personal hatred are intensified by the spectators' discovery that his life has been "unnatural" (120) since his worthy father died, both materially and spiritually crushed by this same Duke.

Yet, strangely, Act I concludes, not with Vindice's establishing his scheme for either immediate or eventual dispatch of the Duke, but with Hippolito's binding certain lords with oaths before heaven to revenge the ravishment and death of Antonio's virtuous wife. And Act II confuses the issue even further. To be sure, nothing seems to come of Hippolito's concern for Antonio's wife, and the focus shifts back upon Vindice's intrigues in the disguise of Piato. But the Duke he seems utterly to have forgotten. Now his concern—in no way related to his earlier mission of vengeance—is to test the integrity of his mother and his sister and to vent his abhorrence of Lussurioso, who is bent on seducing Castiza. Throughout this act personal responses arise directly from the threat against his family honor. He is delighted, for example, that his "most constant sister" (II, i, 45) flatly refuses to entertain the temptation. Conversely, he is appalled beyond measure that the promise of wealth and social position can so easily lead his mother to agree to prostitute her daughter. When she promises ultimately to sway Castiza to Lussurioso's desire, he privately denounces gold and women as the sole cause of damnation; were it not for them, "Hell would look like a lord's great kitchen without fire in't" (258-59). In scene ii the spectators see him in hot passion drawing his sword to strike Lussurioso down, only to decide to await a more opportune moment. Within forty lines, he is on yet a different tack as he overhears the plans for Spurio's incestuous relationship with the Duchess.

Act II, then, scatters the plot, setting in motion several additional layers of Vindice's intrigues but failing even to mention what the spectators in the first act saw as the dominant motif of the tragedy. Suddenly in III, v (Vindice's first appearance in the act), the avenger is not only once more set on dispatching the Duke; he also has established the scheme by which he will do it. With no advance notice whatever, the spectators hear him suddenly report the macabre device to Hippolito: having received orders (in the disguise of Piato) to supply the old Duke a woman to slake his lust, he will place a mask on the skull of his mistress, provide proper feminine attire for the body, and apply a deadly poison to the skull's teeth so that the Duke in stealing a kiss will be lethally infected. Again, however, the spectator is sadly mistaken if he assumes that the intrigues and delays in effecting this elaborate plan will spin out the remainder of the action. For within *this very* scene the Duke arrives at the prearranged trysting place, falls victim to the trap, is poisoned, and dies. Thus by the middle of Act III the basic intrigue of the drama is settled and the antagonist dead. This revenge Vindice has effected in such a manner as to be entirely above suspicion; only by accident—through his involvement with subsequent murders—is his role in the Duke's death discovered.

Tourneur, in a word, establishes a basic theme and an anticipated pattern of action in Act I, ignores that theme in Act II, then reaffirms it—and for all intents and purposes resolves it—in Act III. With such plotting, then, by its very nature demanding the spectators' primary attention, there is little tendency to become introspectively involved with the protagonist. Moreover, Vindice is notably lacking in the kind of philosophic depth we have come to expect in the central tragic figures. Never once prior to the Duke's death does he explicitly or implicitly refer to himself as God's agent; nor does he once betray the least suggestion that, failing such absolute conviction, he is subject to the slightest moral qualms.

Tourneur, nevertheless, is careful to establish and to maintain Vindice as the focus for interest and concern. For one thing, the spectators certainly come to know him more intimately than anyone else in the stage world. Vindice delivers seven soliloquies and forty asides for a total of two hundred and one lines, just nineteen fewer than Hamlet. And, despite the fact that these private lines are concentrated most heavily in the first two acts, Vindice shares his private observations with the spectators to some degree throughout the entire drama. Consequently, even though there is no reflection of a mind torn by conflicting values, the playwright builds a compelling fascination for this Machiavellian schemer bent on vengeance in kind.[14] In the first act, for example, Vindice speaks two lengthy soliloquies, one at the outset of the action and one at the conclusion of scene iii. The initial passage of forty-nine lines serves in effect as a chorus providing both the narrative and emotional exposition. While he verbally introduces the audience to the bastard son begotten in evil and the Duchess willing to copulate with the devil, the adulterous Duke is Vindice's obsession as he beckons for infernal fires to be kindled within the spendthrift veins of the "parch'd and juiceless luxur" (9). Fondling the skull of his beloved, Vindice recalls the beauty of a face beyond compare with "any woman's bought complexion" (22). The grotesque scene, coupled with his specific comparison of the "shell of death" (15) to a "Once . . . bright face" (16) and the "unsightly rings" (20) to sparkling eyes set like "two heaven-pointed diamonds" (19), points up the diseased nature of his passion. After relating that his mistress was poisoned by the old Duke because her "purer part would not consent / Unto his palsy-lust" (33–34), he vows vengeance; though there be merriment, ease, and laughter, murder will not go unpaid. His passionate fury is even more in evidence in the later soliloquy in which he reacts to Lussurioso's suggestion that he—as Piato—act as pander to his sister. Observing grimly that he will burst from the "noble poison" (iii, 169) which he has eaten, he swears that his sword shall "dis-heir" the Duke's son.

Not only is Vindice totally oblivious of the ethical dimensions of his actions, he clearly considers himself to be above the moral quagmire which engulfs all members of the royal family. Indeed, his two soliloquies and fourteen asides in Act II reveal how swiftly and unilaterally he can impose moral judgment on all around him. When Castiza sternly repudiates the disguised brother's prurient innuendoes on Lussurioso's behalf, she stands "approv'd for ever in [his] thoughts. / It is not in the power of words to taint [her]" (II, i, 48–49). Approaching his mother with equally firm confidence that no "siren's tongue could . . . bewitch her so" (53), he is horrified at her malleability, and he pours out his ex-cathedra judgments in ten asides within the space of one hundred and forty-one lines. His "spirit turns edge" (110) as he cries for the "precious side / Of both [his] eyeballs [to be turned] inward, not to see [himself]" (130–31). In bitter vituperation against his mother in a subsequent soliloquy, he brands her uncivil and unnatural, man's damnation, the "hooks to catch at man" (261). So distorted is his moral sensibility that he can beg heaven's forgiveness for calling his mother wicked in the same breath that he—blind to the paradox—can proclaim that, since his sword "was never a back-biter" (ii, 91), he will pierce Lussurioso to his face; "He shall die looking upon me: / Thy veins are swell'd with lust, this shall unfill 'em" (93–94).

Vindice's twenty-four asides scattered through the final three acts consistently reflect his delight as his macabre schemes take their toll. His comments ("O happiness! . . . He strives to make sure work on 't. . . . Have at all! [III, v, 127, 132, 139]) are gleeful, for instance, as the Duke—by ordering complete privacy for his supposed romantic tryst—creates the opportune moment for assassination. Similarly, his perverse choric comments in the final act cast an added pall over the proceedings. While Lussurioso views his murdered father whom he assumes to be the drunken Piato,

Vindice quips tnat it is a "good child" who "calls his father slave" (i, 39); similarly, he delights in Lussurioso's assumption that this dead "slave" has paid well for the injury and the insult. His vindictiveness culminates in the remark that it is the token of the wit of a deep revenger to be far from suspicion when the murder is known and in his grim satisfaction in allowing Lussurioso to sentence an innocent nobleman to death for the Duke's murder ("Who would not lie, when men are hang'd for truth?" [132]). This invidious callousness is reiterated in his final asides, spoken over the body of the dying Lussurioso as courtiers enter the room—"Heart, does he breathe so long? . . . A vengeance throttle him" (iii, 59, 63).

Throughout the tragedy, then, the spectators' interest is literally riveted on the protagonist. To be sure, there being no trace of conflicting emotions in the soliloquies, Tourneur makes no effort to reflect a moral progression in Vindice. The character who can strike down Lussurioso and three of his nobles in cold blood and then brag about it is not essentially different in kind from the character who—skull in hand—can vow vengeance for his once beautiful mistress or who can calmly spread poison over the teeth of the skull and deck out a body for the Duke's femme fatale. Never, though, does Tourneur permit Vindice to become totally repellent. The spectators may well have reservations about him at the outset, but their judgment is tempered by the rank corruption which previously destroyed his betrothed and now threatens to touch his sister. And while they certainly cannot condone his sadistic violence in Act III, neither can they deny the poetic justice of the murder of the lecherous old Duke whose desires are still green and whose power of office is prostituted to self-gratification. Vindice's murderous act, moreover, gains a kind of moral credence from the scenes of mounting depravity which precede it: Spurio's lying in wait to slay Lussurioso during his presumed sexual assignation with Castiza, Supervacuo's and Ambitioso's plotting to expedite the execution of their elder brother, and the bastard son's involvement in an "incestuous" relationship with the Duchess. In a word, Tourneur has methodically established a context in which the spectators, despite their personal or religious revulsions, are forced at least momentarily to sense a degree of moral justification for the murder. Even when Vindice leads the maskers to Lussurioso's grisly murder in the final act, it seems the lesser evil compared to the lurid activities of the ducal family—with Lussurioso plotting

the death of his servant Piato and with the remaining sons chopping
down each other in their final lunge for power and wealth. Tourneur,
then, carefully modulates the spectators' attitude toward Vindice;
if at no point they are able to experience a full measure of sympathy for him, they likewise are never provided the opportunity
for shifting their primary interest and concern to a second character. Again the difference between Vindice and characters like Barabas and Richard III is essentially one of focus. In earlier plays
dominant emphasis is upon the ambitions and the machinations of
the central figure. From the audience's perspective the surrounding
figures—whether virtuous or corrupt—serve a primary function as
victims of his mounting cruelties; the impetus for destructive action
in both instances originates with the single figure. Vindice, on the
other hand, is responding to action initiated by another, and the
spectators' attention is constantly upon this surrounding corruption.

Equally important, despite Vindice's morally static quality, the
increasing complexity and sophistication of his revenge techniques
suggest a protagonist who develops markedly in the course of the
action. At the outset he grieves in private, having bitterly thirsted
for vengeance for nine years (III, v, 123), but having had no opportunity to strike and no specific plan of action. From this point
his scheme evolves in three increasingly intricate stages. In the
initial phase, he arranges his disguise as Piato (a "knave," "a man o'
th' time," a "strange-composed fellow" [I, i, 93, 94, 95]). Carefully
guarding his plan from his mother and sister, to whom he announces
intentions to travel, he is employed by Lussurioso as pander to
gratify his lust. When the old Duke engages him for a similar purpose, the opportunity has arrived to gain an eye for an eye. The
same lust which earlier destroyed Vindice's mistress now is the
precious method for dispatching the Duke, as he kisses the poisoned
skull prepared by the protagonist. And the vengeance is made the
sweeter as Vindice, with Hippolito's aid, forces the Duke to view
the adulterous relationship of his wife and his bastard son even as
he dies a victim of his own lechery.

Through involvement of his brother, then, Vindice has accomplished the vengeance which obsessed him at the beginning of the
drama. In the second stage his net is also cast for the son Lussurioso, whose death he sees as the only fit punishment for the
attempted seduction of his sister. Since Lussurioso has come to
distrust his confidant, his disguise as Piato is no longer effective.

Consequently, in his own person he offers to serve the heir apparent as one who for discontent and want is the "best clay to mould a villain of" (IV, i, 48). Whereas in his first disguise he was familiar and voluble, now he is a taciturn individual "in whom much melancholy dwells" (55). In this role through which he leads Lussurioso to assume that Piato has murdered the Duke, he shares his confidence with his mother as well as with Hippolito. While she is not apprised of the entire scheme, he does reveal his earlier disguise and his knowledge of her willingness to sacrifice her own integrity and Castiza's virginity for wealth and social prominence. His bitter contempt provokes a shame leading to genuine contrition as her tears ("salt enough to tast of grace" [IV, iv, 53]) remove the infectious spot from her soul.

In the third stage, involving yet another disguise—that of a masker celebrating the new Duke's revels—Vindice devises the scheme for Lussurioso's actual murder. Here for the first time he moves outside his immediate family circle as he invokes the aid of others whose detestation of the decadence of the ducal family renders them tractable. Specifically, for example, he charges Piero and an unnamed nobleman to stab home their discontents and "blast this villainous dukedom, / Vex'd with sin" (V, i, 4, 6). Moments before the murder he exults in the irony that Lussurioso and his associates, just when they "think their pleasure sweet and good, / In midst of all their joys, . . . shall sigh blood" (V, ii, 21–22).

Like Iago, Vindice fascinates the spectators through the evolving complexity of his machinations coupled with his increasing audacity and self-confidence. Following the murder, he is totally free of suspicion and needs only to remain quiet. Yet, it is precisely here that his disregard of the ethical values upon which civil cohesion is constructed turns into hubris. Motivated essentially by ego and self-righteousness, not by the least touch of doubt, remorse, or repentance, he proclaims his responsibility for the royal massacre, nonchalantly damning his brother with the same words:

> We may be bold to speak it now; 'twas somewhat witty carried,
> though we say it. 'Twas we two murdered him. . . .
> 'twas well managed.
>
> (V, iii, 96–98, 100)

His subsequent arrest and the peremptory order for execution provoke a brief moment of haughty indignation: "Heart, was 't not for your good, my lord?" (103), after which he assumes the posture of almost sublime indifference, quipping that it is time to die when such friends turn foes. With a discernible touch of arrogance, he observes that the murder might have "slept in tongueless brass, / But for ourselves, and the world died an ass" (113–14). In his final words he accepts his fate stoically; "we have enough, i' faith; / We're well, our mother turn'd, our sister true; / We die after a nest of dukes. Adieu" (123–25).

Here, certainly, is not the fundamentally good character who has been tainted and destroyed by pressures both external and internal. The Vindice we see—whatever he might have been prior to Gloriana's death—is a man committed to vengeful murder, and he never commands more than a semblance of genuine sympathetic rapport. Certainly, too, he is not a character in whom the spectators—blocked from the agony of moral choice which is central to the most profound dramatic perceptions of the human condition—can find a satisfactory emotional center for the tragedy. It is not surprising, then, that the critics have not been generally kind to Tourneur. While a few plead special cases for symbolic characters and emblematic scenes, most assert that his principals are devoid of conflict and thus lacking in human interest; and, while many would grant his trenchant ability to depict a vicious and decadent society, they would at the same time denounce his failure to produce a tragedy of revenge which engages the full sensibilities of the spectators.

In the creation of just such a figure, however, Tourneur plays a vital role in the general dramaturgical movement toward a societal perspective of tragedy. No matter how much the spectators come to abhor the Duke, Lussurioso, and the entire ducal family, their perspectives can never be identical with that of Vindice. Through him their emotions of hatred find an outlet, to be sure; but they also must sit in constant moral judgment upon his actions as well as upon those of his enemies. Tourneur's perspective, then, constructed on multiple levels of awareness, qualitatively differs from Shakespeare's, which is predicated on moral involvement with the character. In a detached position involving at times satiric revulsion and at times compassionate sensibility, Tourneur's spectators are able neither to embrace Vindice fully nor to find a point of emotional reference in the society which has produced him. Thus they are forced to view tragedy as a social cancer, the seeds of which grow from the juxtaposition of the protagonist's own

diseased personality with the misdeeds of those around him and
the ultimate effects of which reach far beyond the destruction and
the spiritual mutilation of the single individual.

Equally significant, the anagnorisis of the tragedy—reminiscent
of the final moments of *The Jew of Malta, Richard III,* and *Macbeth*—
occurs essentially within the spectators, not within the character
Vindice. Unlike Coriolanus, Antony, and Vittoria, he achieves no
significant insights prior to his death either about himself in particular
or human nature in general. Nor does his experience profoundly
affect a second character such as Aufidius, Cleopatra, Flamineo, or
Bosola. The only character to share the ordeal is his brother Hippolito,
whose lone comment following Vindice's unexpected confession
to Antonio ("'Sfoot, brother, you begun" [V, iii, 106]) suggests
nothing beyond sheer exasperation. And nowhere does Antonio,
who strives to pick up the pieces of the shattered social order, indicate the least sympathy for, or perception of, what Vindice unquestioningly views as justifiable purgation of the evil at the center
of the court. The old lord's peremptory order to lay hands upon
the villains Vindice and Hippolito and bear them to speedy execution signals that he regards them as little more than heartless
murderers.[15] Moreover, Antonio's final words ("how subtilly was
that murder clos'd; bear up / Those tragic bodies; 'tis a heavy
season. / Pray heaven their blood may wash away all treason"
[126–28]) invite the spectators' attention, not to the prime
mover of the piece (who is already off stage), but to the victims
whose decadence seems swallowed up and forgotten in their
deaths. The spectators, in other words, must look beyond even
Vindice's jaundiced view to the full extent of tragic waste and
desolation; they alone can envision the best hope for mankind in
their own purgation arising from their perceptions of evil and the
suffering caused by it.

The Atheist's Tragedy, probably written some four years later, is
cut from the same cloth as *The Revenger's Tragedy,* but in a sense
it exploits both the best and the worst of the earlier work. The
carefully modulated devices produce an undeniably more powerful
vision of the pervasive social decadence than the delineation of the
festering moral decay in the surrounding characters who in large
part create Vindice's tragic dilemma through willful manipulation
of him to their own material and emotional ends. But, as protagonists, Vindice and Charlemont are poles apart. Vindice may lack
the moral sensitivity necessary to engage the spectators, and he

may never experience the anagnorisis which in the most powerful tragedies of the period provides a metaphysical rationale for the suffering and waste. He may even be oblivious of the full extent of the corruption which pervades the court circle. His presence, however, is clearly dominant; and in his persistent opposition to the lust and treachery of those around him, however questionable his means, he functions actively as the protagonist of the piece. Charlemont, on the other hand, is free of the least semblance of character flaw, and he is aloof from the potential corruption of the most outrageous of external circumstances. His blandness, however, is apparently intentional, a part of Tourneur's effort to cast the primary focus upon the antagonist of the piece.

The consequence, no one would dispute, is a noticeable lack of genuine conflict within the stage world of *The Atheist's Tragedy,* but Tourneur's experimentation in structure forms a significant link between Shakespeare's final tragedies and those of John Webster.[16] Certainly, few stage worlds so effectively capture the tone of a general decadence which constantly threatens to consume all who comprise the society.[17] That the spectators view the stage world through the eyes and machinations of a villain bent on usurpation of his brother's estate is of paramount importance. D'Amville, like Richard III, juxtaposes the Renaissance world of power politics with the medieval world of chivalric order. The only dynamic force in the play, he engages in a flagrant annihilation of Old World values, despising friends, kin, and beauty in his determination to build an estate which, through his children, will embrace posterity itself. By comparison the surrounding characters appear pallid, impotent, and unimaginative; and, despite the sense of moral outrage, the audience cannot block their mounting fascination with his single-minded brutality. Committed to self-aggrandizement at any cost and perversely delighted that through his cunning he is able to manipulate and destroy those in his way, he swerves only momentarily from his aims when terrified by what he assumes to be Montferrers' ghost.

In the opening moments both his philosophy and his ultimate goals, if not his precise methodology, are abundantly clear. The syllogistic reasoning in his opening dialogue with Borachio is reminiscent of Faustus' decision to renounce Divinity as useless and fallacious since (a) the reward of sin is death and (b) no man is without sin. In similar fashion D'Amville asserts that (a) man, like the beast, is subject to the law of nature—the cycle of birth, growth, and decay—and that (b) man is distinguished from the beast only in his capacity to develop his "full and free" (I, i, 11),[18] nature by getting that which pleases him in great abundance. It follows, then, that wealth—which can purchase pleasure—is the *sine qua non,* the "lord / Of all felicity" (30–31).[19] It follows further that, since hedonism is man's highest good, the honest man must first practice charity upon himself. And his children, as extensions of himself, multiply both his dimension and his needs. If the logic is specious, the firm commitment to family is not devoid of emotional appeal, and Irving Ribner has commented on the "quality of intimacy as we are taken into [D'Amville's] confidence and participate in the easy fellowship of his household."[20] The point is reiterated a few lines later when he greets his sons as his "eternity" through whose succession his life "shall for ever live" (124, 125); so long as he for them can increase his "gain," he would have "all men lose" and "have no feeling of another's pain" (128–29).

Through these comments to Borachio, then, D'Amville establishes for the spectators the scale of values upon which his goals are predicated. The actual scheme, however, must develop as time, circumstance, and audacity permit. In fact, the key to the fascination of D'Amville's character is that, like Iago, he steadily grows in villainy through three distinct stages before he is plunged into despair in the final act. The cleverness of the intrigues is stressed as much as the horror of the crimes in what Henry W. Wells has aptly described as "picaresque drama."[21] In the first five scenes (I, i–II, i) D'Amville operates essentially through insinuation, enlisting those to his cause who can lay the proper groundwork for bolder action later. First, for example, as he carefully explains to his henchman, he must remove Charlemont so as to be able more easily to manipulate Montferrers, the father who is "ready ev'n / To drop into his grave" (I, i, 113–14). To this end, in the name of family honor and heroic manhood, he urges Charlemont "to set forward to the world" (63), offering a thousand crowns to support his nephew's military "maintenance" as a "witness only of [his] love" (98). Shortly thereafter Borachio, disguised as a lame soldier, is employed to report Charlemont's death at the Battle of Ostend, vowing to wear his scarf forever as "the end remembrance of his life" (II, i, 106). At the same time, D'Amville with a diamond ring bribes Snuffe to act on his behalf in arranging a marriage between Rousard and Castabella which will "join the houses of Belforest and D'Amville into a noble alliance" (I, ii, 181–83). Although the

chaplain moments earlier agreed to stand as surety for the love of
Charlemont and Castabella during Charlemont's absence, his struggle between integrity and lucre is no contest, and two scenes later
he is urging Belforest to wed his daughter to Rousard, indeed to
counter her protestations by forcing immediate nuptials: "Dis-
obedience doth not become a child. It proceedeth from an un-
sanctified liberty. You will be accessory to your own dishonour if
you suffer it" (iv, 15–17). Similarly, he informs Castabella that
Charlemont's love is "frivolous and vain," that the military jaunt
is but an excuse to gain separation from her (45–56). And, later,
when the old father is staggered by news of his son's death, he is
prompt to counsel Montferrers to redraw his will—obviously in
favor of D'Amville, the only remaining immediate family: "You
know not how soon you may be deprived of the benefit of sense.
. . . You shall do well . . . to set your state in present order" (II,
i, 133–36).

Since at this point D'Amville is obviously uncertain of success
and somewhat timorous of method, he chooses minimal risk by
manipulating his subordinates from behind the scenes. In the second stage (II, ii–III, iv) both his confidence and his involvement
increase. To be sure, he continues to operate behind the façade of
friendship and moral impeccability, still in part accomplishing his
ends through the will of others. He urges the servants, for example,
to "drown their brains i' the flood" (II, ii, 24) of drink, then
prompts them to argument, individually encouraging them to attack each other with their torches as they walk through the fields.
Thus assured of darkness when the torches are extinguished,[22] he
insists on seeing his guests Montferrers and Belforest home from
the wedding festivities. Then at the appropriate moment he shoves
Montferrers into a gravel pit where Borachio, poised with a rock,
quickly dispatches him. With both nephew and brother now out of
the way, D'Amville—to secure Montferrers' estate—must play a
more overt role. Feigning despair that "malicious nature" (II, iv,
28) would permit the destruction of "a man of such a native goodness" (65), he is comforted by Belforest: "Recollect yourself. /
Lament him not. . . . For wisdom's sake, let reason fortify / This
weakness" (43–44, 72–73). So, too, he is now committed to public
action. In full panoply he conducts the funeral rites of both Montferrers and Charlemont, delivering before the assembled throng an
impressive epitaph for each kinsman as three volleys give pious
voice to his grief. Then, too, he is twice publicly confronted by the

secretly returned Charlemont. On the first occasion, with superb presence of mind he feigns fear of Charlemont as a ghost, then commits him to prison with a harsh reprimand for bursting in with such a display of violence. On the second, confronted by a Charlemont freed from prison by Sebastian and with sword in hand, D'Amville realizes that force cannot save him. Consequently, proffering forgiveness and friendship to the nephew whose rashness surely must be understood in light of the loss of father and inheritance, D'Amville asserts that he

> will not be
> Your dispossessor, but your guardian.
> I will supply your father's vacant place,
> To guide your green improvidence of youth
> And make you ripe for your inheritance.
> (III, iv, 49–53)

Thus a dissembled histrionic embrace which "confirm[s] / The eternal bond of our concluded love" (74–75) produces at least a temporary solution to a situation which might have cost D'Amville his life or at least his mask of innocence. The calculating intriguer has come far indeed from the point at which he depended on others to give physical shape to his thoughts. In possessions as well, ostensibly reconciled with the nephew who by all rights should be his bitter enemy, and the father of two sons through whom to perpetuate his line, D'Amville at the end of Act III is understandably confident that all in due time will work to his benefit.

In his final stage of development (IV–V) D'Amville, unwilling to await nature's course, becomes obsessed with the instantaneous fruition of his schemes and, in his hubristic self-confidence, blind to the possible consequences. Without hesitation he commissions Borachio to murder Charlemont posthaste. Then, determined to have progeny to inherit the estate he is amassing and nettled by Rousard's inability to consummate the marriage with Belforest's daughter, he concludes that he must play father to his own grandchild. To this end, he entices Castabella to walk with him in the churchyard. Caught in the act of the attempted rape of his daughter-in-law by a nephew wrapped in a sheet and wearing false hair and beard, D'Amville is traumatically shocked. He races from the scene, returning moments later babbling of the death's head before him "vex[ing his] conscience" (213); he would have the sky cover with darkness both his murder and the "loathsome hor-

ror and [his] sin" of lechery (224); Montferrers' ghost he sees
"climbing yond' lofty mountains / To complain to Heav'n" (231–
32); and, terrified by Languebeau's cry of "murder," he would
have his "body circumvolv'd / Within that cloud, that when the
thunder tears / His passage open, it might scatter [him] / To nothing in the air" (248–51).

Admittedly, the distraction is momentary, but it serves as a
prelude to D'Amville's final moments. When his "brains" have
"put themselves in order" (280), he oversees the arrest and imprisonment of both Charlemont and Castabella and once more
rests secure in his success. Indeed, his hubris reaches monstrous
proportions as—like a Volpone set in tragedy—he does obeisance
before his gold chests. Comparing the sound of the coins to a
"melodious touch / Like angels' voices" (V, i, 8–9), he proclaims
them the "stars" which determine the "fortunes and the destinies
of men" (15), the "ministers of fate" subordinant to "man's high
wisdom" (24, 25). He is unperturbed even by the appearance of
Montferrers' ghost, boasting of his "prosp'rous judgment" and
"secure success" (35) and mocking those who worship a "fantastic
providence" while his "real wisdom has rais'd up a state / That
shall eternize [his] posterity" (44, 46–47).

From the rush of events in the next minute, though, he never
recovers—the report of one son's murder, the death of the other
before his eyes, the doctor's insistence on a "superior power to
Nature" (114). D'Amville is able to say only that he is "ridiculous"
and Nature is "a traitor to [his] soul" (115, 116). In the final
scene, he seizes the axe from the executioner, insisting that he
alone shall perform the deed on Charlemont. Dashing his own
brains, he proclaims that God "commanded it / To tell [them] that
man's wisdom is a fool" (247–48); "Nature is a fool. There is a
power / Above her that hath overthrown the pride / Of all my projects and posterity" (258–60).

From first to last, then, the spectators' attention is focused upon
the antagonist. An Iago moved to center stage for the entire play,
D'Amville creates the plot through his ambitions, his schemes to
secure power and fortune, and the subsequent disaster which over-
takes him. The effect is the more macabre since there are essentially three levels of perception—that of the individual practiced upon,
such as Castabella and Charlemont; that of Borachio and D'Amville as the servant is employed for specific acts of villainy; and that
of D'Amville himself, as he shares his private perceptions with the

spectators alone. His four soliloquies and six asides totaling 105
lines occur in every act after the first, for one thing providing narrative coherence through the establishment of the frame of events
which the spectators are led to anticipate. For another, they reflect
not a morally divided soul, but an unholy delight in his ability to
manipulate others to his own profit and a callous indifference to
the pain and misery which he provokes. In II, i, for instance, D'Amville quips that he honors Fortune: "My plot still rises / According
to the model of mine own desires" (29–30).[23] He assures the
audience with a chuckle that Montferrers will never live to revise
his will (50–51) and revels in the mental dexterity which renders
those around him pawns to his mounting ambition: "Who can but
strike wants wisdom to maintain; / He that strikes safe and sure
has heart and brain" (53–54). So, also, following Montferrers' actual
and Charlemont's presumed funeral rites, he gloats that "fair ac-
compliments" have made "foul / Deeds gracious" (III, i, 49–50);
the grave holds Charlemont's "living hopes" and his "dead father's
bones" (52). Again in the final act he fondles his gold, gleeful that
through the methodic elimination of his kin he has "seal[ed] up
[his] assurance," "confirm[ed / His] absolute possession," and
"eternize[d his] posterity" (i, 41–42, 47). Until the final moments
of the play, even those rare occasions which in soliloquy reveal
D'Amville's vulnerability fail to minimize either his sense of self-
sufficiency or his energy of resolve. In IV, ii, for example, he notes
that the sickliness of his elder son and the "boldly dangerous" spirit
of his younger may well prevent the issue which will ensure the
posterity of the family; quickly, however, he buries his fear in the
determination to use his own body so as "not . . . to lose [his]
labour / For want of issue" (42–43). In similar fashion, his momentary terror in IV, iii, at what he assumes to be Montferrers'
ghost, is rapidly transformed into disgust that his blood so easily
turns to water and that the "trembling motion / Of an aspen leaf"
makes him "lie shaking under 't" (237–38, 239). He would at such
a moment commit murder anew, if only to "drink the fresh warm
blood of him / I murder'd, to supply the want and weakness" of
his own (241–42). In a word, Tourneur utilizes the devices of internalization not to create metaphysical depths but to underscore the
horror of villainy which combines a relish for the macabre with a
steadfastly lethal determination.

Throughout the tragedy, to repeat, it is D'Amville who stands at
the forefront primarily because he shares with the spectators a

practice upon all other characters in the stage world. To be sure, there are moments when the audience know more than the antagonist—what in the graveyard D'Amville takes to be Montferrers' ghost in IV, iii, they know to be Charlemont, and they know why he is draped in a sheet; so also, moments before D'Amville, they know of Charlemont's return from the wars, of his release from prison in III, iii, and of Borachio's unsuccessful attempt to murder him in IV, iii. For the most part, though, his level of perception is one with that of the spectators as he establishes his goals, privately informs them of his grisly schemes, and shares with them his malicious delight in their accomplishment.

This villain stage-center creates an atmosphere in which passive virtue and naïveté seem equally defenseless in the face of relentless Machiavellian ambition. As if to underscore the social malaise, Tourneur anticipates Webster in minor characters abandoned to depravity who, "like an antimasque of yahoos,"[24] form a "spirited, saturnalian parallel to the main plot."[25] Borachio, D'Amville's tool, has no apparent will of his own; "Wealth," to him, "is lord / Of all felicity" (I, i, 30–31); and, for the promise of the "reward" which "shall parallel [his] worth" (120), he unquestioningly functions as prime mover in the villain's most atrocious schemes. Among the surrounding characters, Belforest too quickly leaps to wed his daughter for material gain, and Rousard—sick and impotent—plays out his pathetic newly-wed role for the same reason. Far more blatant is "Snuffe the tallow-chandler" turned self-styled Puritan chaplain, whose religion stretches only so far as his profit and whose morals are fitted to the fashion. Not only is he quick to betray Charlemont's love for Castabella, selling his support to Rousard for D'Amville's present diamond and promised benefit; in Act II no less than Borachio he is D'Amville's paid instrument in his brazen advice both to Belforest and to Montferrers. It can little surprise the spectators to discover in Act IV his sexual depravity as well. Lusting after Soquette ("The very contemplation o' the thing makes the spirit of the flesh begin to wriggle in my blood" [i, 74–76]), he assures her his body "is not every day drawn dry" (iii, 44) and, protected by a disguise, would have her at once: "I will try how I can kiss in this beard.—O, fie, fie, fie. I will put it off, and then kiss, and then put it on. I can do the rest without kissing" (67–69). Levidulcia, Belforest's wife, is also obsessed with lechery. She informs Castabella that the "sweet possession of a man" is woman's "greatest pleasure" (I, iv, 80, 92) and quips to Rousard on his wedding night, "Please her hardly, and you please her best" (II, ii, 148). In soliloquy she observes that her passion, like "snow rubb'd through an active hand does make / The flesh to burn, by agitation is / Inflam'd!" (iii, 41–43). When Sebastian "set[s her] blood a-boiling i' [her] veins," she would "clasp [her] waist and try" (48), and she promises in "the compass of two sheets" to give "a testimony" of her love to Sebastian (63, 77). No less prurient is Madame Cataplasma, employer of both Soquette and Fresco for her "behind-door work." Having arranged a tryst between Levidulcia and Sebastian, she properly prepares him through an elaborate double entendre in the disguise of a "lesson o' the lute":

> Dost not see *mi* between the two crochets?
> Strike me full there. So—forward.—This is a
> sweet strain, and thou finger'st it beastly. *Mi*
> is a large there, and the prick that stands before
> *mi* a long; always halve your note. Now—run your
> division pleasingly with those quavers. Observe all
> your graces i' the touch. Here's a sweet close—
> strike it full; it sets off your music delicately.
>
> (IV, i, 49-56)

Later she urges her customer Levidulcia to "enjoy [her] pleasure . . . without fear" (v, 25), cautioning her not "to let consideration of the sin / Molest [her] conscience" (28–29).

Throughout the play, then, the members of the supporting cast live in hedonistic dedication to their passion, whether of the purse or the placket. Devoid of conscience, they may be less potent than D'Amville and consequently subject to his manipulation, but they lend significant emphasis to the pervasive Hobbesian tone of a stage world in which tragedy must be perceived as much in terms of what is done to the protagonist as what he does. A more trenchant delineation of pervasive human depravity than the Egyptian putrescence surrounding Antony, this stage world points directly to Webster's settings in Padua, Rome, Amalfi, and Milan.

There is no argument, of course, that Tourneur's drama is less profound tragedy than either Shakespeare's or Webster's if one is seeking for a central figure humanized by a struggle between opposing values and capable of enlisting the spectators' emotional interest in a conflict taking shape either within the character or in his overt relationship with the principal adversary of the piece. Actually, whereas Tourneur created multiple antagonists in *The*

Revenger's Tragedy, here he establishes three individuals in opposition to the villain, and each character reflects different aspects of the manner in which the external or societal evil poses a vital part of the tragic dilemma. Sebastian, specifically, is first to counter D'Amville's will, proclaiming the forced marriage of Rousard and Castabella a "rape, . . . since it forces her to lie / With him she would not" (I, iv, 128, 130–31). Branded a "disobedient villain" by his father, Sebastian in soliloquy calls for Castabella to cuckold Rousard without mercy. In the same spirit Sebastian in III, ii, frees Charlemont from prison in defiance of his father's orders, noting in soliloquy that he will "bestow [his] abilities to honest purposes" (60). Yet, to the contrary, he responds willingly to Levidulcia's coquetry in II, iii, and two scenes later only Belforest's sudden arrival prevents physical consummation. The two do indeed retire to a private closet in Madame Cataplasma's house in Act IV, and it is this assignation which provokes the fight between husband and lover in which both are slain. Since his objection to D'Amville's perverse values is sporadic and lacking clear motivation, Sebastian's role assumes no protagonistic pattern, and it is blurred further by his flagrant disposition to lechery. Castabella, too, stands in firm opposition to the antagonist. But, whether in fending off Rousard's sickly advances, importuning her father to respect her pledge of fidelity, reaffirming her love for Charlemont, reacting in stark revulsion to D'Amville's incestuous advances, or falsely proclaiming her guilt in order to die with Charlemont, she is a totally simplistic character. Never tempted by the thought of a profitable marriage of convenience, never terrified into thoughts of submission, she is a pawn of prelapsarian virtue whose virginity and life are saved by external turns of event rather than by any action or influence on her part. Again, then, she is a character in whom the spectators can perceive no potential tragic conflict.

Clearly the protagonist as Tourneur envisioned the action is Charlemont, who like Hieronimo, Hamlet, or Vindice suddenly must confront the loss of a loved one—in terms of both personal grief and reaction to those responsible for the murder. It could be a classic tragic dilemma, of course, since the spectators' reaction would inevitably be ambivalent, condoning the protagonist's desire for justice—even to a degree appreciating his thirst for vengeance—but condemning the social and moral anarchy which his actions may encompass. Yet, Charlemont displays no emotions through which the spectators can develop a concern for his physical or

psychic well-being.[26] Doubtless Tourneur intended to block an
emotional rapport in order to keep the spectators' objective attention in part upon the external tragic forces. And certainly the
deeds and misdeeds of others loom large in Charlemont's tragedy—
D'Amville's acts of murder and disinheritance, Borachio's attempt
to murder him, Snuffe's betrayal of trust concerning Castabella,
Belforest's peremptory disregard of his love for Castabella. Charlemont, however, always stands above the situation, never tempted
to a passionate response by adverse circumstance. In a word, while
the external flaw is graphically portrayed, the protagonist lacks
even the slightest touch of a humanizing internal flaw which, by
establishing the opposing values for the conflict of conscience and
the agony of indecision, would both make him interesting as a
character in the individual play and lend him a degree of uni-
versality through which the spectators might emotionally share his
experience.

Two factors are primarily responsible for this one-dimensional
quality—the unequivocal nature of the mandate of Montferrers'
ghost and Charlemont's willing acceptance of the role of passive
revenger. When, for example, the spirit accompanied by thunder
and lightening first appears at an army outpost, it informs Charlemont of his father's death and his own disinheritance and orders
him to return to France. Instead of a call for revenge, however,
this "mere mechanical survival . . . of an old tradition"[27] orders
him to "attend with patience the success of things, / But leave
revenge unto the King of Kings" (II, vi, 22-23). Two scenes later,
as the returned son grapples with D'Amville and Sebastian, the
spirit—apparently visible only to Charlemont—again cautions that
revenge must be left to Heaven: "Hold, Charlemont! / Let him
revenge my murder and thy wrong / To whom the justice of
revenge belongs" (III, ii, 32-34). In the only other appearance of
the ghost, to D'Amville in the final act, instead of a desire for
retaliation in kind, there is a decided note of pity and pathos:

> D'Amville, with all thy wisdom th' art a fool,
> Not like those fools that we term innocent,
> But a most wretched miserable fool,
> Which instantly, to the confusion of
> Thy projects, with despair thou shalt behold.
>   (i, 27-31)

Charlemont is no less strangely imperturbable. He is a son whose "strongest purpose" is turned by his father's "weakest sigh," whose "resolution" is melted to "soft / Obedience" by his "softest tear" (I, i, 9 ff.). Yet, in the face of such a father's murder, he does not thirst for vengeance; indeed, his reaction is so aloof and dispassion-ate that the spectator is momentarily tempted—despite the vicious crimes involved—to respond with confused approval to D'Amville's intense familial allegiance. Upon first hearing of Montferrers' death, Charlemont's concern is not the substance of the ghost's message but rather what conditions might have provoked his fearful dream (II, vi, 24 ff.). Later in France he in soliloquy before his father's grave calls for "understanding" to relieve his "confounded and tormented mind," asserting that his uncle's wrongs are more than the "strongest patience can endure to bear" (III, i, 135, 136, 145); yet in the next scene when cautioned against physical action by the ghost, he utters only two lines ("You torture me between the passion of / My blood and the religion of my soul"), after which he with stoic passivity challenges his uncle to "do / [His] worst" (35-36, 48-49). To put it bluntly, if in soliloquy he might pro-claim that God imposes unrealistic limits upon human conduct in the face of undeserved suffering (iii, 4-11), there are no significant symptoms to suggest that his true passion is constrained by any such limits. His ready answer to Sebastian is that he possesses a "fortitude" necessary to what "Fate is pleas'd to have me suffer. . . . My passions are / My subjects, and I can command them last, / Whilst thou dost tickle 'em to death with misery" (iii, 35-36, 45-47). In the following scene he makes a shockingly easy peace, em-bracing his father's murderer and apologizing for his rashness (38-40). No less incredible, when in self-defense he murders Borachio and saves Castabella from rape by D'Amville, he would deliver himself over to his uncle's law without struggle or remorse:

> My life he seeks. I would he had it, since
> He has depriv'd me of those blessings that
> Should make me love it. Come, I'll give it him.
> (191-93)

In the trial scene he faces criminal charges utterly without emotion, desirous not of "remission" but of the death which can release him from the "stormy troubles of this life" (V, ii, 125). With "peace of conscience," he praises his "native courage" which "lead'st [him] soberly to undertake / This great hard work of magnanimity" (160, 216, 217-18).

Charlemont, in brief, seems drawn more from homiletic illustration than from theatrical tradition; a character without flesh and blood, his motivation far exceeds his actions. With no real temptation, let alone a flaw in deed, there can hardly be illumination or insight gained through suffering either for the character or for the spectators. Thus Charlemont's experience, the "Honest Man's Revenge," provides the audience no philosophic coherence for the welter of disastrous events. That in his passivity he emerges with life, love, and happiness is the result of only the most fortuitous of events. If Heaven would rule in this guise, man need have no will or emotion of its own; and drama based upon human conflict disappears.

It is D'Amville with his awesome energy and determination to succeed who holds the spectators' attention. And he, too, like Vindice is a static figure. Admittedly he dies repudiating the God of Nature under whose aegis he has lived by the standard of survival and gain through force and cunning. But it is equally true that he is not repentant; he never comes to terms with the God of Charlemont and Castabella whose benevolence and justice are so firmly established that they can face man's greatest inhumanities with a serene and robot-like passivity. More serious, as an anagnorisis D'Amville's final moments are dreadfully abortive, both for himself and for the spectators. His questions raised in agonizing despair never receive answers either logical or emotional. Bewildered in the face of the sudden death of his sons (the "two pillars" on which "stood the stately frame / And architecture of [his] lofty house" [V, i, 77–78]), he frantically implores the physician to "inspire new life / Into their bodies" (89–90). This passion is the strongest emotion in the tragedy, and he implores the judges to explain the logic or the rationale of the destruction of his progeny and of his labor on their behalf (ii, 69–83). He would know the source of Charlemont's "peace of conscience" and courage; he would comprehend his nephew's philosophy of life, "the efficient cause of a contented mind" (167). But this insight he never achieves. His statements of God's power suggest little more than a realization of his human limitations and vulnerability; they imply no spiritual illumination, no genuine insight into the realities of experience or human relationships which alone can glean value commensurate with personal waste and loss. As Robert Ornstein has observed, he is no "hero-villain of Faustian proportions" but "a Jacobean parvenu with a criminal appetite for wealth and status,"[28] "too much of a caricature to reveal the imagination and the emotional grasp of his own infamy."[29] Indeed, soliloquies through which to verbalize such spiritual perceptions are noticeably absent in this critical scene. Most disturbing in the long run, the deaths of the sons Sebastian and Rousard which shock D'Amville into submission are in no way occasioned by D'Amville's vices. Given the machinery of Montferrers' spirit and the various displays of thunder and lightening signaling a cognizant heavenly power, the spectators can attribute their deaths only to an implacable suprahuman force striking down D'Amville and in the process destroying a more viable human relationship than any resulting spiritual illumination replaces.

Because the experiences of a central figure fail to yield full tragic potential, it is easy to write off *The Atheist's Tragedy* as melodramatic hack work exploiting the forms of theatrical tradition without providing the intellectual substance. Similar cries have been raised, of course, against *The Revenger's Tragedy,* with its protagonist-revenger devoid of the internal polarities between which the human beast and the human spirit play out man's universal tragedy. By this particular standard, both plays do fail at this central point; the protagonist does not emotionally engage the spectators in ambivalence forcing them simultaneously to share and to judge his decisions and his actions.

To an important degree, however, both plays succeed, a degree most closely appreciated when Tourneur's work is considered in the context of the work of his contemporaries and the general dramaturgical movement toward a societal perspective of tragedy. The multiple antagonists in *The Revenger's Tragedy* and the multiple protagonists in *The Atheist's Tragedy*—by broadening the plot line itself to involve a greater number of individuals, by creating the possibility through such parallel figures of effective variation upon the tragic theme, and above all by diffusing the intensely individual and internal focus of earlier tragedy and thereby provoking the spectators to a greater alertness to the diverse components which produce tragedy—help to sharpen the spectators' perception of the external forces which contribute directly to the corruption of the individual. To the same end through the sheer entanglements of plot which draw attention to the action itself and through a protagonist in the one whose commitment to vengeance is no less implacable than his lack of moral sensibility and an antagonist in the other bent on advancement quite literally at whatever cost, he minimizes emotional involvement with the character and thus creates a more detached view of the extensive social ramifications of tragedy. Consequently, in both tragedies the spectators must judge simultaneously the individual and the corrosive society to which he is both victim and tormentor. For this complex design in which tragedy encompasses the scope of satire, Tourneur attempts to provide dramatic unity through a central figure whose frequent soliloquies and asides in conjunction with the increasing intricacies of his vengeful scheme make him the firm center of the spectators' attention.

V. Webster

—THE WHITE DEVIL, THE DUCHESS OF MALFI

The enigma of John Webster's tragedies still looms large. No one now accuses him of being an "insufferable bungler . . . and dullard"[1] who "revelled in 'violent delights' for their own sake";[2] conversely, few shower him with unqualified encomiums as a dramatist with "never-withering bays"[3] who, "beyond the imagination of ordinary poets,"[4] "attains the utmost limit and rounds the final goal of tragedy."[5] Nevertheless, twentieth-century scholars have continued to debate where his mark truly lies. As John Russell Brown observed, "It has proved possible to talk of him as an old fashioned moralist, as a sensationalist, as a social dramatist, as an imagist or dramatic symphonist, as a man fascinated by death, or a man halting between his inherited and his individual values."[6] Perhaps the most vigorous point of contention is the moral quality of his two surviving tragedies. Ian Jack, for example, attacks what he terms Webster's "moral flaw,"[7] and James R. Hurt accuses the playwright of parodying "the Christian ethical system";[8] to the contrary, E. E. Stoll praises his "stern, true moral sense,"[9] and Irving Ribner describes his "agonized search for moral order in the uncertain and chaotic world of Jacobean skepticism."[10] Only slightly less volatile is the disagreement concerning the structural coherence of his work. What one group brand "mere sensationalism,"[11] an oppressively monotonous tragedy[12] "uncertain what its pattern is to be,"[13] another group praise as a "mixing [of] unrealistic conventions with psychological-realistic representation"[14] to produce effectively a "satiric voice coequal with the tragic,"[15] the "finest villain play of the period."[16]

Such diversity of opinion emphatically underscores the need for further consideration of the nature of the tragic perspective Webster was attempting to achieve. Like Tourneur and like Shakespeare in his final tragedies, Webster depicts a pervasively ambivalent world in which the protagonist faces choices or alternate paths of action which defy clear moral judgment. A woman takes the center stage

for the first time, but the dramatic focus again falls in large measure upon the surrounding characters who eagerly abuse her for
their own emotional or material profit.

In *The White Devil,* more specifically, Webster achieves this
societal perspective by utilizing the major antagonists (like D'Amville) as the central characters of internalization, by methodically
and consecutively emphasizing the corruption of other significant
characters surrounding Vittoria and the pitiful impotence of the
few with moral integrity, and by limiting the tragic experience of
Vittoria so as to block the spectators' consuming interest in the
protagonist and thus force their attention to the broader issues.

Of first importance, the spectators from first to last view the
stage world through the eyes of characters whose single and obsessive concern is the gratification of self-interest. In large part they
see the events of the first three acts through Flamineo's eyes as he
manipulates those around him to achieve his goals of wealth and
position.[17] Ironically, he will accomplish neither; his own villainy
will ultimately prove incapable of protecting him from the "rare
trickes" (V, iii, 196)[18] of an even more cunning Machiavel. But the
early scenes are his as in soliloquy he describes his "ingag[ement]
to mischiefe," comparing the "winding and indirect" "waies" of
his "policy" to the circuitous stream bent on finding the ocean or
the mountain path which winds deviously to the top (I, ii, 240-48).
In the opening act he serves as pander to his own sister and encourages the lustful Brachiano to see in her "coynesse" and "blush"
the "superficies of lust" (18-19). At the same time he tricks her
naïve husband Camillo into refraining from sex and sleeping apart
from her on this night so that the "silkworme" can "spin . . . the
better" on the following evening (170-71). Staging virtually a scene
within a scene, he argues Camillo's case to Vittoria in tones sufficiently loud for the husband to hear, yet in undertones to his
sister mocks him unmercifully as a "capon," a "lousy slave . . . that
hath an itch in 's hams, which like the fier at the glasse house hath
not gone out this seaven yeares" (126, 127, 133-35). He chuckles
in an aside at the old fool who "intanglest [himself] in [his] owne
worke like a silke-worme" (186-87) and beams on the "most happie
union" (205) of the adulterous lovers with a pleasure compounded
of the lechery of a voyeur and the anticipation of the petitioner ex-
pecting to profit from a sister's preferment. When censured by his
mother for the immorality of his conduct, he flatly denounces her
honesty as the cause of his family's poverty; for the "meanes" of

reward he will blink at morality and "arme" his face "'gainst shame and blushing" (308, 324, 325).

His control of the action reaches its apex in Act II. By goading Brachiano to the murder of Isabella and Camillo, he assumes that he can strengthen his sister's liaison with the Duke. To this end, following Isabella's unsuccessful attempt at reconciliation, he whispers to Brachiano that it will be simple enough to "compound a medicine . . . deadlier then stibium" (II, i, 284-85). If the doctor can make sure of Isabella, Flamineo promises to dispatch Camillo this very night "by such a polliticke straine, / Men shall suppose him by's owne engine slaine" (312-13). And, indeed, in the next scene the spectators see the villain pull Camillo from a vaulting horse, break his neck, and leave him as if killed in a fatal accident.

The first two acts, then, the spectators have viewed essentially as Flamineo's machinations; he has both anticipated the events and participated in their fulfillment. From this point, however, even though as Vittoria's brother and Brachiano's confidant his position and power seem secure, his fortunes decline and his acts become defensive. While being led to Vittoria's trial, for example, he informs the spectators that he is putting on a "feigned Garbe of mirth, / To gull suspition" (III, i, 30-31). Later, mistakenly assuming that Monticelso's reference to Vittoria's bawd is to him rather than to Zanche, his asides betray a private moment of terror (ii, 274-75). In the following scene, he "fain[s] a madde humor for the disgrace of [his] sister" in order to "keepe off idle questions" (316-17), railing distractedly at the cruel fortune which has placed him in a position of service to a lustful man.

The spectators' vision in Acts IV and V totally outgrows that of Flamineo. Again he strives earnestly to reunite Brachiano and Vittoria; he would have Brachiano "stop her mouth, with a sweet kisse" that they might "couple together with as deepe a silence, / As did the Grecians in their wooden horse" (IV, ii, 195, 202). When the Duke helps Vittoria to escape her imprisonment and rushes to Padua to make her his wife, Flamineo once more assumes that his fortune is made, smugly proclaiming that "this mariage / Confirmes [him] happy" (V, i, 203). So blatantly confident of his power is he that he strikes down his brother in cold blood and seems to fear no consequences. Throughout the last two acts, however, the spectators have become fully aware that Flamineo's every action renders him more completely the dupe of Francisco. In urging the reconciliation and marriage of Vittoria and Brachiano

and later in befriending the Moor and the Hungarian noblemen
(Francisco and his fellow conspirators), Flamineo unwittingly per-
forms those very deeds that ensure the destruction of all for which
he has labored. Thus the arch villain at the outset of the drama has
come full circle; in a stage world emphasizing the ever increasing
number of individuals whose actions in the name of self-interest
produce Vittoria's tragedy, the manipulator becomes the manipulated. His overt dedication to policy and self-advancement afford
him no protection against those who mask their true intentions behind the disguise of the holy frock.

Francisco emerges as this consummate manipulator in Act IV,
and Webster through the devices of internalization immediately
establishes a private level of perception with the spectators.
Francisco's first soliloquy indicates that he will not, as Monticelso
suggests, give open expression to his grief and anger concerning
Isabella's death; he will trust no one; the Cardinal can "not reach
what [he] intend[s] to act" (IV, i, 43). "Fashion[ing his] revenge
more seriously" (102) in a second soliloquy, he drafts a feigned
love note to Vittoria, then instructs a servant to pass it to her when
some of Brachiano's followers are nearby to take note of it. And
in a third soliloquy he observes that—with "bold Count *Lodowicke*"
as the "engine for [his] busines"—he is now "fit" for the crucial
encounter with Ursini (137, 140). After sending Lodovico one
thousand ducats in Monticelso's name and thus persuading him
that Brachiano's murder has the blessing of the Church, Francisco
methodically plans the Duke's grotesque poisoning, his strangulation by the disguised Capuchins, and the brutal murder of Vittoria,
Flamineo, and Zanche.

Through the devices of internalization, then, the spectators come
to know most intimately the principal antagonists of the piece. The
soliloquies are utilized, not to reflect physical suffering, the agony
of a divided mind, or a spirit in conflict with itself, but rather to
establish the tunnel-visioned egocentricity of the Machiavels' judgments and to signal the schemes which the spectators can subsequently expect to view in execution. Most significant to the structure of the play, Flamineo's callous amorality in manipulating his
sister's conduct and Francisco's bestial obsession for revenge against
Brachiano and all associated with him converge to form the backdrop for Vittoria's personal tragedy. From them the corruption
extends even to the minor figures—to Zanche, for example, whose
lust drives her to the court favorite of the moment, or to Lodovico,

who by defying banishment for murder can kill again by official commission.

Webster further emphasizes this pervasive external corruption through the hapless destruction of the few virtuous characters of the piece. Like Flavius, Timon's faithful steward, or Virgilia, Coriolanus' timid wife who detests the grand heroics of martial butchery, these characters simply cannot cope with the machinations which surround them. Isabella, for example, journeys from Padua to Rome to "freely pardon" (II, i, 13) her husband; with her arms she will "charme his poyson" (17) and effect a reconciliation. When Brachiano, provoked by Francisco and Monticelso, curses their wedding and swears an irrevocable divorce from her bed, she turns the other cheek, and offers privately to be the ostensible cause of their separation:

> I will make
> My self the author of your cursed vow.
> I have some cause to do it, you have none.
> . . . let the fault
> Remaine with my supposed jealousy.
> (219-21, 224-25)

Silently she suffers the recriminations of her brother and the Cardinal, who assume that she is a "foolish, mad, / And jealous woman" who "deserves" her horns (266-67, 270). Only in an aside can she utter that such "killing greifes which dare not speake" are breaking her "poore heart" (278, 279). Even more pathetic, grotesque murder is her reward for sacrificial love as following her evening prayers she thrice kisses her husband's poisoned picture. Moreover, both Isabella and Brachiano presumably carry to their graves knowledge of the vicarious assumption of her husband's guilt; her name is never cleared of the blemish of the shrewish harridan who refused marital reconciliation and goaded her husband into more extreme commitments. The spectators alone, in other words, are in a position at the end of the play to realize just how cruel fate can be in such a world to a passive creature whose values are based solely on selfless love.

The situations of Cornelia and Marcello are different only in degree. Both function as active voices of conventional morality driven to distraction or silenced for their convictions. The aged mother must suffer not only the agony of a family fallen to moral disrepute; "The curse of children," as she remarks of Flamineo's panderism and Vittoria's adultery, "make[s her] brow bend to the earth" (I, ii, 269, 270). She must also endure a son who totally repudiates her affection as well as her principles, a son who to escape poverty would have "the common'st Courtezan in *Rome*" to be his "mother rather than thy selfe" (328, 329); those who enjoy a "plurality of fathers . . . shall not want" (332, 333). Like Isabella a voice of conventional morality, Cornelia (the first character to speak in an aside) observes that "violent lust" will lead her house "to ruine" (208, 210); she berates Vittoria for "dishonour-[ing her] husbands bed" (288) and proclaims that Duke Brachiano's life should move like a dial "whose regular example is so strong, / They make the times by them go right or wrong" (280-81). Her fate, too, revealed in two scenes late in the play, is pitiful. In V, ii, she must bear the full horror of Flamineo's fratricide; reminiscent of Lear she calls for a looking glass or a feather to place upon Marcello's lips in a desperate assertion that he still lives. When, moments later she rushes at Flamineo with a dagger, she cannot bring herself to slay her only living son: "One arrow's graz'd all-ready; it were vaine / T'lose this: for that will nere bee found againe" (V, ii, 67-68). In V, iv, sorrow has converted to madness as the "reverend mother," now "growne a very old woman in two howers," intones "a solemne melodie" while placing the winding sheet on Marcello's corpse (V, iv, 47, 48, 50). Ophelia-like, she distributes flowers to those nearby; her final song—punctuated by vague references to her dead son—describes the various animals that befriend man in his grave and warns of the wolf who will dig up the body.

Marcello's fate, of course, is inextricably bound with that of Cornelia. A foil to his brother, he counsels "love of vertue" and "an honest heart" (III, i, 60). He would have "cleft [his sister's] heart" with his own "daggers point" had he known she would prostitute herself to Brachiano, and he brands the lustful Zanche his brother's "shame," a "devill" who "haunts," "a strumpet [who] brags that you shall marry her" (V, i, 85, 91, 182, 186). When he threatens to "cut her throate" if she comes near and to "whip / This folly" hence (191, 192-93), Flamineo accuses him of bastardy —a charge which provokes him to challenge his brother to a duel and to send his sword so that his opponent can "fit the length on't" (204). Flamineo's response, under pretense of returning the weapon, is to run him through without warning. This murder is the more bizarre because—unrelated to the action of the play—it is so senseless.

Vittoria, through subsequent comments and reactions, indicates
her painful cognizance of the murders of Isabella and Camillo;
similarly Flamineo is not unaffected by the madness of Cornelia.
These horrors assume a kind of value in the insights which the
sister and brother gain moments before their own deaths. In
contrast, Vittoria is never even informed of Marcello's death, and
Flamineo never seems to give his fratricide a second thought.
Webster, then, both through the atrocity itself and more sharply
through the absence of a resolution of any sort, underscores again
the vicious and animalistic nature of his stage world.

Not only, however, are those with obvious moral standards impotent and thus destroyed; those who occupy positions of prominence and power are methodically stripped of values which could
provide a positive frame of reference for the horrors of the stage
world. This experience is all the more disillusioning for the spectators because they have been encouraged to accept these individuals as men of principle. Cardinal Monticelso, more specifically, in
his initial entrance is to all appearances the voice of moderation
which allays the passion of both Brachiano and Francisco. Indeed,
his first words caution Brachiano to "forego all passion" in the
interest of frank and "free discourse" (II, i, 24–25), and a few
moments later his stern rebuke ("My Lords, you shall not word it
any further / Without a milder limit" [83–84]) prevents an open
altercation between Brachiano and Francisco. Rather than leveling
insulting charges concerning Brachiano's adultery, he points out
the larger political implications of the Duke's conduct and urges
him to be a "patterne" for his son: "It is a more direct and even
way / To traine to vertue those of Princely Bloud, / By examples
then by precepts" (105–107). It is notable also that later the
Cardinal avoids a passionate response when it appears that Isabella
has refused reconciliation with her husband. While Francisco rails
in fury (266 ff.), Monticelso utters not one word; presumably his
expression should register his supreme disappointment—not his
anger.

Even when his dispassionate council fails to correct the situation,
he continues to reflect a quality of self-control predicated on
ostensibly moral grounds. He urges Camillo to "change the aire"
for a time; while the husband is away, Monticelso will "bee [his]
ranger" and possibly can "blast [his] *Cornucopia*" (353, 360, 354)
by shaming Brachiano through public exposure of the adulterous
relationship with Vittoria. To the spectators, this is the full extent

of the "revenge" of which he speaks, whereby he would attempt to aid one who, "wrong'd, durst not avenge himselfe" (388, 389).

Throughout Act II, in a word, Cardinal Monticelso—and by implication the institution which he represents—provides a strong moral undercurrent in a world of sexual depravity and murderous violence. He is, it would appear, a man of reason, self-control, and moral principle. There is little wonder, then, that the spectators are disillusioned when this Cardinal emerges as a scheming machinator determined to impose judgment whatever the legal consequences. The hint that his intention is to secure judgment against Vittoria at any price is registered at the outset of Act III. Since, as he himself admits, there is "naught but circumstances / To charge her with, about her husbands death," he has "discreetly" assembled the lieger ambassadors to hear his "proofes / Of her blacke lust" (III, i, 4-5, 1, 6-7); if he can but establish that she and Brachiano have "kist one another," insinuations and innuendoes can "make her infamous / To all our neighbouring Kingdomes" (20, 7-8). Content at first to sit in quiet dignity as presiding judge while a lawyer uses the Latin tongue to protect her reputation by hiding her shameful conduct from the common folk—content even to let the lawyer establish the charges in equally recondite vernacular jargon, he leaps to "play the lawier" (III, ii, 63, 64) when it becomes clear that she will not permit the obscurity of charge to imply the assumption of guilt. "Paint[ing her] folies in . . . red and white" (54-55), he brands her a "whore" (59), "soote and ashes" (70) fit only for "*Sodom* and *Gomora*" (68); her rooms blaze forth with light as she carouses in "musicke banquets and most ryotous surfets" (79). Guilty also of her husband's murder, she is a true picture of the "devill" (224) and a "notorious strumpet" (252) who brought her husband neither dowry nor honor.

The scene is shot through with emotion, and the Cardinal to be sure attacks with passionate intensity. In the final analysis, though, his evidence is at best circumstantial. Moreover, his most flagrant act of tyranny is still to come in squelching her attempt to respond in self defense: "Nay heare me, / You shall have time to prate" (254-55); yet, within twelve lines—and without permitting her to utter another word, he sentences her to confinement in "a house of convertites" (273). Well might she scream that he has "ravisht justice" (285) as he turns off her further attempts to respond with "Away with her. / Take her hence. . . . fy shee's mad—. . . . She's turn'd fury" (283-84, 286, 289).

Despite Vittoria's guilt, then, Webster forces the spectators to see Monticelso's actions, not as the ultimate endurance of moral values, but as the brute use of position and power to achieve familial vengeance.[19] The shock is not that it should be so, but that—in a world overfilled with decadence and violence—the one character of both presumed moral strength and social position should partake of that decadence. On the heels of Isabella's senseless death, the development is doubly depressing.

Webster persistently pursues the same effect in Act IV by darkening the character of Francisco. Certainly, the Duke of Florence is not without flaw in the earlier scenes; everything the spectators have seen of him suggests a white hot temper which bursts forth with the slightest provocation. He is furious with Brachiano for neglecting Isabella's marriage bed, and he loses no opportunity during their initial conversation to goad his brother-in-law unmercifully: Brachiano is "soar[ing] high" in "lustfull ease" (II, i, 51); Vittoria, who wears "cloth of Tissue," though her husband is "of a poore fortune," is his "Strumpet"; he is sure to be found "'Bout moulting time" (56, 57, 60, 93). Francisco, in fact, is quite ready to "end this with the Cannon" (76), but his anger abates almost as rapidly as it rises. Moments later he is willing to use the boy Giovanni to effect a reconciliation between husband and wife; even when this fails, he is content to "have the Duke *Brachiano* run / Into [such] notorious scandale" that nothing can "repaire his name" (382-83, 384).

Francisco, then, is a volatile individual, but throughout the early acts there is no suggestion of a festering and aberrant animosity; he, in fact, during the trial cautions the Cardinal not to press beyond reason the charges of Vittoria's responsibility for the murder of Camillo:

> . . . there's great suspition of the murder,
> But no sound proofe who did it: for my part
> I do not thinke she hath a soule so blacke
> To act a deed so bloudy.
>
> (III, ii, 189-92)

When he learns of Isabella's death, his seven short responses to Giovanni within thirty lines reflect both his shock and his attempt to comfort the distraught boy. His grief and anguish seem sincere; there is no trace of any thought whatever of either murderer or vengeance.

Again, then, the spectators are understandably stunned at Francisco's sudden emergence in Act IV as a full-blown Machiavellian intriguer. And, again, the effect in a stage world already rife with corruption and villainy is to apply one final thrust of corrosive evil. With the murder of Isabella in Act II, the emerging duplicity of Cardinal Monticelso in Act III, the sudden exposure of Francisco's Machiavellianism in Act IV, and the murder of Marcello coupled with Cornelia's madness in Act V, the horror and depression are cumulative as all traces of virtue are either extinguished or destroyed. Admittedly, this sensationalism is achieved in part by dramatic sleight of hand; rather than being led to anticipate the sudden developments in the Cardinal and the Duke of Florence, the spectators are surprised by the turns of character; and, as noted earlier, Marcello's murder and Cornelia's madness are never effectively integrated into the major action. Clearly, though, Webster has been methodic in his efforts to depict a stage world dominated, not by the sense of a hostile or indifferent fate, but by a thoroughly human depravity which vitiates every segment of society.

Against this grim, carefully modulated background occurs the tragedy of Vittoria Corombona. The depiction of this protagonist most clearly reveals the perspective by which Webster focuses the spectators' attention upon the external as well as the internal causes of tragedy. Vittoria's experience lends unity and meaning to the events of the stage world; yet she appears in fewer than one-third of the scenes (five of sixteen), and she speaks fewer than one-tenth of the lines (322 out of 3,480). Since she speaks not a single word of aside or soliloquy, the spectators gain no insight into the moral anguish which could provoke a strong emotional rapport. Indeed, for nine-tenths of the play she gives virtually no indication that there is an internal moral struggle; her commitment to passion has occurred antecedent to the action, and rarely indeed does a thought cross her mind concerning the immorality of her position or its consequences to herself or to others. At the outset she is a mistress and an adulteress, quite capable with no qualms whatever of suggesting double murder as the most expedient means of removing any impediments which might bar her continued liaison. On the other hand, in the final scene moments before her death, she expresses a sense of value and responsibility which, achieved in the face of adversity and pain, provokes a tragic response from the spectators. The courtesan without principle now recognizes that her blood now pays for her great sin (V, vi, 240).

Webster's most significant artistry lies in his ability to impart this tragic dignity to Vittoria Corombona through a role which lacks even a moment of internalization and which is minor by comparison with that of several other characters. Her particular sin—provoked in part by Flamineo and Brachiano—is the catalyst for a chain of corrupt events ultimately costing seven lives; yet for most of the play the emphasis is not on her growing moral awareness but on the emerging decadence and corruption in those around her. Thus at the same time Webster underscores the evil in the surrounding characters which contributes to the tragedy of the individual, he methodically strips away all vestiges of virtue in those characters with whom the spectators might sympathize. Meanwhile, Vittoria in the middle acts displays remarkable fortitude and self-control in the face of Monticelso's public charges in Act III and Brachiano's false charges of infidelity in Act IV. The result is that, even though she does not develop a complete emotional rapport with the spectators, a kind of sympathetic interest begins to develop in part because—for her courage if not for her morals—she is the only principal worthy of such concern.

Vittoria's action, in other words, gives the impression that there is a progressive growth in the development of her character. In her initial appearance, though her silence to Flamineo might suggest disapproval of his scheme and though her reaction to her mother's comments does indeed suggest that she is not insensitive to moral rebuke, the emphasis is upon her sensuality as she totally controls the situation through her beauty; Brachiano lusts after her and complies with her every wish, even the temptation to murder. When she next appears four scenes later, her character has not changed, but her situation has been so drastically altered as to make it appear so. Now she is totally the victim of those around her, haled to trial for adultery and for the murder of a husband whose death she claims ignorance of until the arraignment itself. Certainly, Vittoria is not innocent. But just as certainly she is not guilty of the full charges; nor does she deserve the peremptory treatment which makes a mockery of the legal proceedings. The spectators at the very least must respect her courage to fight what she considers the injustice of the trial. And they realize full well that her exclamations during the trial ("If you be my accuser / Pray cease to be my Judge. . . . A rape, a rape! . . . You have ravisht justice" [III, ii, 233–34, 285]) carry more than a modicum of truth. In the face of it all, moreover, she refuses to lose her composure; she will not weep or "call up one poore teare / To fawn [on his] justice" (III, ii, 296–97).

This scene (III, ii) contains more than one-third of Vittoria's total lines in the drama, and clearly she is the emotional victor in the trial, though actually she has admitted nothing—not even the guilt which the spectators have observed directly—and has in no way responded to the moral issues involved. This same inflexible spirit she displays again in Act IV. Instead of dissolving in feminine tears before Brachiano's charge that she is Francisco's "statelie and advanced whore" (IV, ii, 77) and a "devill in christall" (89) yoked to his political enemy, she firmly maintains that there is "some treacherous plot" (85). More than that, she fires back that she has gained nothing from him but "infamie" and a stain upon the "spotlesse honour of [her] house" (109, 110); his "high preferment" is but a "house of penitent whores" (119, 116); were she able, she would make him "full Executor / To all [her] sinnes" (126–27):

> I had a limbe corrupted to an ulcer,
> But I have cut it off: and now Ile go
> Weeping to heaven on crutches.
>   (122–24)

Since the spectators know full well that Vittoria is innocent of the specific charges Brachiano levels against her, their sympathetic response is more immediate. Then, too, here is the first indication that she is willing to measure her previous actions against the moral standard she has so long neglected. As an admission of error it is admittedly like confession without penance; she would still have the best of both the spiritual and the secular worlds in her tacit acceptance of the opportunity to live as Brachiano's duchess in Padua.

Vittoria's most significant tragic action occurs in the final act, but even here her development is carefully limited. For one thing, she is still not above the use of deceit to save her life; she leaps at Zanche's suggestion to feign compliance with Flamineo's suicide pact in order by trickery to gun him down. To this end, she at one moment swears to Flamineo that she readily will "sacrifice heart and all" (V, vi, 87) to Brachiano's memory, yet, assuming Flamineo is fatally wounded, she at the next moment brands her brother a "most cursed devill" (124) justly caught in his own engine. For another thing, the dominant emphasis is again on her remarkable fortitude rather than her moral sensitivity. After enduring the macabre and torturous poisoning of her husband, she refuses to

panic before either Flamineo or Lodovico. In the face of certain
death for herself, Zanche, and Flamineo, she offers her breast first:
"I will be waited on in death" (218). She will "meete [the] weapon
halfe way," welcoming death "as Princes do some great Embassa-
dors" (222, 221). And again there will be no show of feminine
emotion: "I will not in my death shed one base teare, / Or if looke
pale, for want of blood, not feare" (226–27). After being stabbed,
she asserts that her life's blood is just payment for her sin of passion; her soul, "like to a ship in a blacke storme, / Is driven [she]
know[s] not whither" (248–49).[20] Whether this moment is convincing as genuine moral insight for Vittoria herself is irrelevant;
the impact upon the spectators is unmistakable. Dorothea C. Krook
has well reminded us in her study that "in spite of what our post-
Shakespearean preconceptions lead us to believe," the anagnorisis
"need not involve or issue in self-knowledge. . . . The necessary
condition to be satisfied is that the *spectacle of suffering* [italics
mine] shall yield knowledge of the human condition, or some fundamental aspect of it, not necessarily to the tragic hero but to us, the
readers or audience."[21]

Vittoria's tragic experience, in the final analysis, never provokes
the spectators to a full emotional commitment. Nevertheless, the
structure of the piece does command profound admiration of her
courage and her perseverance in the face of a dilemma from which
her inability to escape becomes ever more certain. Throughout her
struggle this structure maintains a progressively intensifying focus
on the developing corruption of those around her who contribute
to her dilemma—Flamineo, Brachiano, Monticelso, Francisco,
Zanche. Each acting in his own self-interest has produced a viciously decadent society to which Webster gives artistic coherence
through the fortunes of a single famous courtesan. She never repents in the full sense of the word, but within their broader context
the spectators accept her acknowledgment of the moral justice of
her fate. Appropriately, her dying words are not merely the conventional rhyming couplet to signal the conclusion of her role;
they also recall the larger context in which her tragedy has un-
folded: "O happy they that never saw the Court, / Nor ever knew
great Man but by report" (261–62).

In his treatment of Vittoria's anagnorisis, Webster seems, at least
in a general way, to follow Shakespeare's lead in *Timon, Coriolanus,*
and *Antony and Cleopatra.* In each of these plays Shakespeare is
concerned with a second character who is integrally involved in the

final insights gained by the tragic protagonist. Two significant purposes are served by such a transfer of the anagnorisis. For one thing, it reduces the necessity of extensive internalization of the protagonist, a significant factor if the playwright wishes to limit the emotional identification with the spectators in order to emphasize the characters surrounding the protagonist who contribute to his tragedy. Equally important, through the insights gained by a second character the dramatist can reflect that, just as others share the responsibility for tragedy, so also they can share the durable insight into certain realities of human experience which emerge from it. Thus whether in the decision to commit oneself to love at the expense of empire, the reestablishment of civil peace, or the exercise of mercy to a besieged city, Cleopatra and Aufidius, and less successfully Alcibiades, are profoundly altered by what the principal learns through the suffering leading to death.

Webster achieves much the same effect by transferring the anagnorisis in part to the villain Flamineo. An early indication that Flamineo's "conscience is active" may well occur, as Thomas Stroup maintains, in III, ii, where Savoy's statement ("You must have comfort") reminds him of the liturgy and stings his unrepentant mind.[22] That he possesses "Compassion" and a "conscience in [his] brest" is certainly clear in V, iv, as—following his mother's madness— he admits that he has "liv'd / Riotously ill" (109, 115, 112–13). His most significant comments, however, come in response to Vittoria's courage and her admission of guilt. He "love[s her] now," praising the "masculine vertue" (V, vi, 242, 245) by which she has been able to hide her faults and endure their consequences. At the moment of her death he asserts that "there's some goodnesse in [his] death" since his "life was a blacke charnell" (269, 270). And for a flickering moment he senses the stark horror of a world in which each creature is obsessed with self-interest: "Prosperity doth bewitch men. . . . Wee cease to greive, cease to be fortunes slaves, / Nay cease to dye by dying. . . . This busie trade of life appeares most vaine, / Since rest breeds rest, where all seeke paine by paine" (250, 252–53, 273–74).

In a penetrating insight into the essence of tragedy, Richard Sewall observes that the tragic vision "impels the man of action to fight against his destiny": his hubris is not sin, but "the mysterious dynamic of all tragic action"; the tragedy of Oedipus extols above all "man's freedom and his capacity to learn"; Lear's agonizing experience reflects "an affirmation in the face of the most appalling

contradictions."[23] Yet these observations set in the context of
Webster's stage world fail to assure and persuade. Vittoria's last
moments constitute a brilliant display of courage, to be sure, but
they hardly seem, as Lear's do, to seek out an affinity with a
dimension of human love which has forever asserted its power in
the very face of life's limitation. It is precisely that dimension of
shared belief—whether expressed in terms of a teleological cosmos,
in terms of human potential in such a universe, or in terms of a
mutual human capacity for compassion and affection—which lends
a degree of coherence to suffering and pain, even to death. And it
is through a stage world devoid of such a dimension that the
Jacobean playwrights project their vision of a society struggling
between two faiths and their pessimistic appraisal of a world in
which man is his own measure. If coherence is possible at all, it
must be found in the individual's will or determination; however
much he himself is flawed, he must engage in his separate war
against the greater human depravities which surround him.

Webster's particular contribution in *The White Devil* lies in the
intensity of the societal tragic perspective. His stage world, viewed
primarily through its Machiavellian intriguers, is unrelieved by a
Cleopatra whose love comes to transcend the corruption around
her. To the contrary, every human relationship is characterized by
tumescent sex, from Camillo's description of the nights when a
great "flaw" (I, ii, 56) rose between him and his wife, to Brachiano's
panting desire for Vittoria to "weare [his] Jewell lower" (217), to
Flamineo's voyeurism, to Lodovico's pursuit of Isabella "with hot
lust" (IV, iii, 15), to Zanche's prurient agitation for the Moor;
Vittoria herself, whether as mistress or as wife, never once suggests
an affection for Brachiano beyond her blood. No Flavius or Virgilia
is left to express genuine human grief. The only characters capable
of experiencing sincere remorse have long since been driven to
destruction or distraction. No Alcibiades or Aufidius remains who—
however tainted—can provide leadership conditioned by the wisdom
of human nature he has shared with the protagonist. In Webster
both the central figure and the character who shares her insight die
simultaneously. While Shakespeare's protagonists through a second
character can assume a future wisdom built on the human frailties
of the past, Webster's figures seem capable only of a flickering
moment of dignity and integrity before the darkness closes upon
them and whatever insights their anguish has generated for themselves, and, of course, for the spectators. Following the bloodletting

no Alcibiades stands by to restore civil order, only the boy Giovanni whose tender age would probably suggest only a period of
continued unrest and instability to an English audience with even
a short memory. P. B. Murray aptly reminds us that "evil is still
very much in command in the world, for Monticelso is Pope and
Francisco is still the great Duke of Florence."[24] While such an observation suggests a too rigidly moralistic standard for tragedy, the
fact remains that those who have selfishly manipulated and
destroyed Vittoria and others remain alive, passionately uncon-
scionable, and socially powerful.

Webster's tragedy, in a word, is carefully structured to emphasize the pervasive corruption and bestiality in a society in which
passion reigns supreme. At the same time, through the delineation
of Vittoria as the lone figure among Webster's characters who in
her admission of guilt reveals a mind at least aware of the conflict
between passion and a higher scale of values—and through the
delineation of Flamineo as the single character capable of perceiv-
ing the desolation to which unchecked passion ultimately leads,
such tragedy for the spectators projects the best hope of the race
in the individual's ability to develop through suffering the self-
knowledge which constitutes his best protection against the inhumanities of the human world.

In *The Duchess of Malfi,* presumably composed within two years
of his first independent production, Webster relentlessly pursues
this same tragic vision. Again, to be sure, the stage world is replete
with the macabre trimmings which so often first come to mind
when Webster is mentioned—a nose bleed presaging disaster, a
child's nativity chart prophesying "short life" (II, iii, 78) and "a
violent death" (80), a dream about a coronet of pearls signifying
tears of anguish, waxen duplications of human bodies and dis-
membered hands, a grotesque chorus of madmen, a cave which
echoes fragmented warnings of destruction. Fundamentally, however, the playwright is concerned with more than the horror of the
grotesque and the shock of the sensational. Building in various
ways upon his experience in *The White Devil*—he in this play once
more creates a tragic vision which extends beyond the private experience of the individual.

Webster utilizes several specific structural devices to emphasize
this societal perspective. Most obvious is the opening scene in
which more than two hundred lines establish the general decadence
in Italy, the treachery, poison, and slow corruption working in

individuals and in the state. A similar scene of eighty lines in *The White Devil* finds Lodovico—justly banished for his profligacy and his crimes—asserting that he is no worse than those who remain behind, great men like Duke Brachiano with his base attempts to prostitute the honor of Vittoria. *The Duchess* even more forcefully directs the spectators' attention to the social corruption through Antonio, who—having just returned from an extended visit—describes the perfection of the French court as the precise opposite of what is to be found in the Italian court. The "juditious King" of France "begins at home" in "seeking to reduce both State and People / To a fix'd Order" (I, i, 6–7); he rids his court of "flattring Sicophants, of dissolute, / And infamous persons" (9–10); mindful that the court is like a fountain at the center of the kingdom from which must flow "pure silver-droppes in generall," he rules through a "most provident Councell, who dare freely / Informe him [of] the corruption of the times" (18–19).

In stark comparison, the fountain of the Italian court, the leaders of both Church and State, is rankly polluted. The Cardinal and the Duke are "like Plum-trees (that grow crooked over standing-pooles) they are rich, and ore-laden with Fruite, but none but Crowes, Pyes, and Catter-pillers feede on them" (50–53). In such a court which caters to "flattring Panders," "places . . . are but [like] beds in a hospitall, where this mans head lies at that mans foote, and so lower, and lower" (53, 67–69). The Cardinal, who is suspected of "suborn[ing]" a murder, "were able to possesse the greatest Divell, and make him worse" (72, 47–48); he is a "mellancholly" and "jealous" churchman not above using "Flatter[er]s, Panders, Intelligencers, Atheists, and a thousand such politicall Monsters" to effect his "plots" (158, 160, 162–63). Similarly the Duke, of "a most perverse, and turbulent Nature" (169), would have his courtiers be his "touch-wood, take fire when [he] give[s] fire; that is, laugh when [he] laugh[s], were the subject never so witty" (125–26).

Such complaints are also registered in Act IV, where two pilgrims to the Shrine of Loretto witness the banishment of the Duchess by the Church and by the State of Ancona. They observe that the "Cardinall / Beares himselfe much too cruell," vowing to "sacrifice" her wedding ring "to his revenge" (III, iv, 27–28, 42–43), and that the Pope, acting only on the Cardinal's "instigation," "hath seaz'd into th' protection of the Church / The Dukedome, which she held as dowager" (34–35). Various passages additionally underscore the

general social corruption—the obsession to hide the reality of
motive and physical mien behind a fair façade—which emanates
outward from such a poisoned fountain. Bosola informs Castruccio, who would "faine be taken" for an eminent courtier, that the
prime requisites are large ears and arrant hypocrisy in criminal
causes along with an ability to "twirle the strings of [his] band"
and to "hum, three, or foure times" at the end of each sentence
(II, i, 1, 5, 7); he can be certain he is considered "an eminent fellow" if the people curse him when he reports that he "lie[s]
a-dying" (18, 19–20). An old lady painting her face in an attempt
to retain court preferment prompts Bosola to exclaim against the
human's concern for "outward forme" (47). Though the "rotten
and dead body" is riddled with diseases such as "the most ulcerous
Woolfe, and swinish Meazeall" and though it is "eaten up of lice,
and wormes," the courtly creature "delight[s] / To hide it in rich
tissew" (59, 56, 57, 59–60). And while some such women "give
entertainment for pure love," far more do so for "precious reward"
(II, ii, 14–15). The canker of court favoritism is evident again in
the conversation among the officers which follows Antonio's banishment on the false charge that he has dealt falsely in his accounts
with the Duchess. The flattering rogues who earlier "waited on his
fortune" and "would have prostituted their daughters, to his Lust"
now brand him "scurvy prowd," an "hermophrodite" who "stop'd
his eares with blacke wooll . . . (to those [who] came to him for
money)" (III, ii, 269, 272, 263, 261, 259–60). In the final act the
Marquis of Pescara refuses to bestow upon Delio the Citadel of St.
Bennet, formerly owned by Antonio; yet he readily grants it to
Julia at the Cardinal's request. His explanation further attests to
the sickness which grips the kingdom:

> It was *Antonios* land: not forfeyted
> By course of lawe; but ravish'd from his throate
> By the Cardinals entreaty: it were not fit
> I should bestow so maine a peece of wrong
> Upon my friend. . . .
>   I am glad
> This land, (ta'ne from the owner by such wrong)
> Returnes again unto so fowle a use,
> As Salary for his Lust.
>   (V, i, 47–51, 55–58)

As in *The White Devil*, the minor roles in *The Duchess of Malfi*
clearly reflect either the virtuous or the depraved, and this simplistic

configuration of characters further darkens the stage world through
its emphasis upon the hapless victimization of those whose innocence or naïveté renders them easy prey to the social monsters surrounding them. The children of the Duchess, for instance, are
created solely to be brutally butchered on stage; their fate, like that
of Macduff's children, reveals the hideously irrational forces which
men's passion looses upon those whose only guilt is the societal
stain of kinship. Only slightly less pathetic is Cariola. If she secretly
harbors the news of the Duchess' marriage, she does so in the name
of loyalty and devotion; if she is incapable of meeting death without screaming that she is pregnant and will discover treason to the
Duke, the lies provoked by terror do not render her murder
justifiable by any stretch of poetic justice. Appearing in six scenes,
she is the domestic confidante—witnessing the marriage, announc-
ing to Antonio the birth of his son, bantering lovingly with her
master and mistress, ominously cautioning the Duchess to go to
the baths at Lucca rather than to the Shrine of Loretto, accompany-
ing the family in banishment. Nowhere is there a touch either of
personal ambition or of the sexual lust which characterizes her
counterpart Zanche in *The White Devil.* Like the children she is
guilty only by association, and her death serves to intensify the
horror of a society in which a ruler's vendetta is synonymous with
the law of the land.

    Paralleling the guiltless characters are Julia and Count Malatesti,
corrupted figures who reflect the libertinism and the sycophancy
of such a court. With no thought for her husband Castruccio, the
"rutting bitch"[25] Julia prostitutes herself to the Cardinal for the
gifts which he can bestow, dallies coyly with Delio—an old suitor
who desires her as his mistress, and lusts madly after the "excellent
shape" (V, ii, 125) of Bosola. She has a "paine" for Bosola and
would have him "kill [her] longing" (166, 168):

> We that are great women of pleasure, use to cut off
> These uncertaine wishes, and unquiet longings,
> And in an instant joyne the sweete delight
> And the pritty excuse together.

>   (202-205)

While sensuality eventually precipitates her destruction by provoking the suspicions of the Cardinal, Malateste—like Castruccio—is
tailor-made for survival in Calabria. To be sure, he is recognized by
the Duchess as "a meere sticke of sugar-candy [whom one] may

looke quite thorough" (III, i, 51–52). He is also mocked by Delio
and Silvio as a braggadoccio who wears "gun-powder, in 's hollow
tooth, For the tooth-ache" (iii, 19–20); by the almanac, he would
select his good days for battle, then run from it to protect his
mistress' scarf. But with no conviction of his own, he is the "touch-
wood"; his predilections are dictated by the prevailing political
wind. He laughs only when the Duke laughs; at Ferdinand's suggestion he is a willing candidate for marriage to the Duchess; praise
for the Cardinal rolls easily from his lips as he reports the Emperor's
commission. The Count, in a word, is an obsequious fawner in a
society in which such servility provides a measure of protection.

   The general decadence and hostility, then, are carefully and
firmly drawn as a backdrop for the central figures. Concerned with
what James Calderwood describes as the "relationship between
individual impulses and societal norms,"[26] the tragedy sketches a
society dominated by the values of "Machiavellian" policy in which
man loses his sense of direction—a society confronting a "loss of
faith" in its transition "from a feudal to a capitalistic economy."[27]
Whereas in *The White Devil* the depravity of the leaders of Church
and State, Monticelso and Francisco, becomes apparent only grad-
ually, *The Duchess of Malfi* sharply depicts at the outset the corruption of those in positions of social prominence. Furthermore,
objective commentators (such as Antonio, Delio, Silvio, and the
pilgrims) are positioned throughout the tragedy to draw the spectators' constant attention to the general condition. Also central to
this perspective is the characterization of the protagonist. In *The
White Devil* Vittoria is depicted as a creature of passion who shares
fully the corruption of her society. The spectators' sympathy for
her in the middle portion of the play is constructed upon her brutal
mistreatment by those in positions of social and spiritual authority.
The methods by which her accusers provoke the ignominy of public repudiation force the viewers to admire her courage, if not her
morals; moreover, her suffering does lead to at least brief flashes of
self-knowledge just prior to her death. Admittedly, then, Webster
depicts a protagonist who—like Coriolanus or Antony—is deeply
flawed and thus in large part is herself responsible for her situation;
but, at the same time, he emphasizes the societal aspects of an
individual's tragedy by dramatically accentuating the actions of
those around Vittoria who contribute to her dilemma and by
eliminating the moments of soliloquy and aside through which the
spectators confront firsthand the agony of any spiritual struggle.

The result is a delicately balanced dual focus upon both the external and the internal causes of tragedy. To the contrary, the protagonist in *The Duchess of Malfi* is stained, not by moral aberration, but by indiscretion.[28] Moreover, she is essentially a static character; with no significant internalization, her private desires and anxieties are never revealed to the spectators. Whatever naïveté she possesses in the early stages of the play obtains also at the moment of her strangulation; at least she never displays the least remorse for her attempts to deceive her brothers, and she never suggests an awareness that her lack of foresight has rendered her so vulnerable to their hatred. Since she is an individual sinned against far more seriously than she sins, she clearly does not seem to deserve her predicament. Thus, the emphasis all the more sharply falls upon the societal or external causes of tragedy, and the Duchess' suffering and death stand as a powerful indictment of those willing to manipulate and destroy others for their own benefit.

Despite her static quality and her relative innocence, though, Webster is able to achieve a remarkable degree of interest in this central figure. "Different sides of her character are disclosed," as Gunnar Boklund has noted, "causing the audience to hesitate and waver between different possible reactions."[29] More specifically, the juxtaposition of Antonio's idealistic description with her initial actions on stage projects an ambiguity of character which serves effectively to catch the spectators' close attention. Antonio—following the discussion of the morally vicious qualities of both Ferdinand and the Cardinal—sets forth the Duchess as a paragon of perfection. She is "right noble," her discourse "full of Rapture," her looks "sweete," and her countenance "divine" (I, i, 191, 194, 199, 203). "Practis'd in such noble vertue" that "all sweet Ladies [should] breake their flattring Glasses, / And dresse themselves in her" (205, 208–209), she—in a word—"staines the time past: lights the time to come" (214). Such hyperboles whet the imagination, and the spectators are understandably disquieted to observe that her conduct toward her brothers hardly justifies the praise. To their advice that she not consider marriage again, her ready response is, "I'll never marry. . . . This is terrible good Councell" (334, 346). Yet the moment they depart, she asserts that neither "frights" not "threatnings, will assay / This dangerous venture" (388–89):

> If all my royall kindred
> Lay in my way unto this marriage:
> I'll 'd make them my low foote-steps.
> (382–84)

Since Webster provides no mention of the issues which had led the Duchess to her resolve and since there is no suggestion of internal struggle, the conflict remains on the surface. The spectators confront will pitted against will; if they have been told in no uncertain terms that the one is vicious and corrupt, they see the other practicing duplicity despite the glowing accounts of her character. With Cariola they might well ask whether "the spirit of greatness, or of woman / Raigne most in her" (576–79).

Obviously, the Duchess is not guilty of any flagrantly cruel and unnatural act, but neither at this point are the Duke and the Cardinal; the spectators have almost as little reason to sympathize with her sudden inclination to marriage (in fact, the issue seems also to catch Antonio by total surprise) as they have reason to oppose her brothers' determination to prevent it. To be sure, the stylization of the brothers' arguments "enables us to observe a schism between the form and content of their objections"[30] and suggests, as Boklund (p. 84) has noted, an almost "sinister undertone to the advice they proceed to give her." But not until later can the spectators suspect an incestuous passion on Ferdinand's part, and not until the end of Act IV does the Duke state his ostensible motive, that "Had she continu'd widow" he would have "gain'd / An infinite masse of Treasure by her death" (ii, 303–304). Moreover, the dramatist for the first half of the tragedy focuses upon the Duchess' least admirable traits. With no attempt whatever to convey her desire to her brothers, she seems rather arrogantly to disregard their predilections against marriage. While doctrinally she may be sound in her wedding *"per verba* [de] *presenti"* ("What can the Church force more? . . . How can the Church build faster? / We now are man, and wife, and 'tis the Church / That must but eccho this" [I, i, 548, 558–60]), she almost flippantly disregards the significance of public ritual which attaches to her social position. Moreover, she never once seems to consider the danger to which she is exposing Antonio through choosing him as a mate;[31] nor does she later express even a private concern that she must slander his reputation by accusing him of false dealing as her steward. Certainly, too, she is mindless of her own sound reputation. Her "loose-bodied gowne" "contrary to . . . *Italian* fashion" (II, i, 164, 169) suggests how easily she believes she can hide pregnancy—as well as ugly rumours, since she is still assumed to be a widow. Ferdinand's concern, if not his passionate rage, is understandable when he hears that she has given birth to a child. He brands her "loose i' th' hilts," a "notorious Strumpet" (II, v, 5-6); "cunning baudes . . . serve [the] turne" of the "hyenna" with in-fected blood (13, 53); he would "have hewed" to pieces both the "strong-thigh'd Bargeman" "who leapes [his] sister" and the whore who has given birth to the bastard (42, 57, 99). Even when she later implores Ferdinand to realize that she is married, he responds that her loss of reputation is irrevocable. And indeed Antonio him-self admits to Delio that the "common-rable, do directly say / She is a Strumpet" (i, 29-30).

Of course, since the spectators are fully informed of the true situation, they never completely lose sympathy for the Duchess, especially in light of the emerging villainy of Bosola and the desperate fury of Ferdinand. Even so, through the early acts they must observe her naïveté at virtually every turn. It seems incredible, for example, that she could so dimly perceive the ferocity of her brothers' opposition to her marriage. When Antonio raises the point following their private ceremony, the Duchess almost non-chalantly responds, "Do not thinke of them. . . . Should they know it, time will easily / Scatter the tempest" (I, i, 536, 539-40). This same credulity blinds her two acts later to Ferdinand's true motive in suggesting Count Malateste as a prospective husband. Again she chooses to conceal her marriage and to feign utter innocence; when her brother all too easily pretends to accept her protestations at face value, she ingenuously exclaims in aside, "Oh bless'd comfort– / This deadly aire is purg'd" (III, i, 66-67). And how ominously her blatant imperception colors the following scene a few lines later as with Antonio and Cariola she listens to bawdy pleasantries about her "Lord of Misse-rule" and her "labouring" man who is the "sprawlingst bedfellow" (III, ii, 9, 23, 17)—even while the Duke gains secret access to her quarters! Most preposterous of all is her gullibility to Bosola. Both Antonio and Delio report in Act I that Bosola is infamous, a suspected murderer known to have his price. It is strange enough that she would accept him as a retainer in her household, despite the Duke's urging. That she should confide in him concerning Antonio as her husband is arrantly stupid; she may be desperate for counsel and comfort, but her alacrity to reveal all to Bosola in return for his words of seeming praise for Antonio hardly seems consistent with the woman with whom both marriage and children have been such a well-kept secret for several years. Webster, moreover, underscores this gullibility by juxtaposing the scene with additional conversation in III, iii, which registers again the commonplace knowledge of Bosola's present business and his past reputation.

In brief, even though the Duchess is not morally flawed, her actions throughout the first half of the play constantly force the spectators to question her good judgment. Her final scenes, in contrast, focus upon another facet of her personality—her courage and her dignity in the face of overwhelming opposition and brutally inhumane treatment. In this manner, then, despite the static quality of her character, Webster is able to evoke a powerful sympathy in the scenes leading to her destruction. The crucial scene is at the Shrine of Loretto where, though she does not speak a word, the spectators see the full force of Church and State set against the defenseless woman and her family; certainly it would be impossible for the spectators to miss the bitter irony in the Cardinal's banishing the Duchess for her secret marriage and her pilgrimage which, in his words, "make religion her riding hood" (III, iii, 72), even while he cloaks his adulterous relationship with Julia behind his clerical frock. The Duchess' reaction in the two following scenes borders on hysteria. She laments that this "poore remainder" of her train "puts [her] in minde of death" (v, 5, 11); the "birds, that live i' th field . . . live / Happier than [she]; for they may choose their Mates" (25–27). Not so foolish as to believe Bosola's good wishes for a second time, she counsels Antonio to fly towards Milan with the eldest son; to her the husband's cold kiss presages both permanent separation and death. Convinced in IV, i, that he is dead, she too desires only death, whether by starvation or, like Portia, by swallowing fire—thereby "reviv[ing] the rare, and almost dead example / Of a loving wife" (85–86). "Account[ing] this world a tedious Theatre . . . [where she] play[s] a part . . . 'gainst [her] will" (99–100), she curses the stars and calls for the world to return to chaos, for plagues and tyrants to torment mankind. Through these darkest moments, however, emerge the fortitude and strength to face her brothers' ultimate cruelties without fear and without despair. She refuses, for example, to denounce Antonio (presumably to save her life) as a "base, low-fellow . . . of no Birth" (III, v, 140, 143), stating that she is "arm'd 'gainst misery" and that "men oft are valued high, when th'are most wretch[e]d" (167, 166). Her tone is similar a few lines earlier when she asserts to Antonio that the "heavy hand" of Heaven is instrumental in her misery; "naught made me ere / Go right, but Heavens scourge-sticke" (92, 94–95).

While the Duchess' insight through suffering is never developed beyond these random remarks, the stage is now set for her final heroic posture. Confronted by a chorus of madmen, she proclaims, "Necessity makes me suffer constantly, / And custome makes it easie. . . . let them loose when you please, / For I am chain'd to endure all your tyranny" (IV, ii, 31–32, 63–64). So, too, she refuses to panic in the face of Bosola's disguise as a tomb-maker, his ravings about the body's being "weaker than those paper prisons boyes use to keepe flies in" (135–36), and his ghastly intro- duction of the executioners. Her affirmation, "I am the Duchesse of *Malfy* still" (139), flies in the very teeth of the worst her fellow- men can do to her. Nor does death any longer frighten her. She requests Cariola to give her boy syrup for his cold and to let her girl say her prayers. Calmly, then, she forgives her executioners and kneels, anxious to meet the "excellent company / In th' other world" and aware that "they that enter there / Must go upon their knees" (217–18, 240–41). The dignity of her death, underscored by Cariola's murder amidst futile struggling and screaming seconds later, she establishes in her final message to her brothers that she "perceive[s] death, (now [she is] well awake) / Best guift . . . they can give or [she] can take" (230–31).

All things considered, then, the Duchess does not fundamentally change in the course of the action. Only by stretching the material can one perceive any kind of fundamental development of charac- ter. If, however, she is naïvely guileless and unsuspecting in the early acts, the thrust of the tragedy is not to force her to realize that she is insufficiently alert to the machinations of those in the court circle; it is to confront her with the need for courageous dignity in the face of man's grossest inhumanities, a quality which presumably she possesses from the outset when she refuses to be terrorized by her brothers' threats. Unlike Vittoria, then, she is without moral flaw, even though Webster creates the semblance of development by manipulating the spectators' view first to her credulity and imperceptiveness then to her courage and moral convictions. Like Vittoria, however, she forms the center of a tragedy upon whom the cruelties of others converge. Each woman is surrounded by adversaries wielding the power of both Church and State, and each faces a Machiavel of policy who is a vicious social riser in the body politic.

Indeed, the most important structural comparison of the two tragedies involves this Machiavellian machinator as the principal

character of internalization. Again in *The Duchess of Malfi* the
spectators experience the drama primarily through the eyes of the
antagonist rather than the protagonist, and again the perspective is
especially effective as a structural device for focusing upon the evil
which dominates the stage world. The analogy, however, is not so
significant as the extent to which Webster is able to develop the
technique in this play. Whereas two roles are involved in *The White
Devil* (the schemes which Flamineo shares with the spectators in
the first three acts give place to the villainy of Francisco in Acts
IV–V), Bosola is the single character of significant internalization
in this play.[32] Consequently, the impact of this sinister intelligencer
upon the audience is more profound. His development in the final
acts is also extensive, and the spectators are provoked to a far more
powerful emotional response to Bosola than to Flamineo.

Certainly, there can be no question about Bosola's commitment
to policy at the outset. Antonio observes that he is a "Court-Gall"
whose "rayling" is entirely self-interested:

> Indeede he rayles at those things which he wants,
> Would be as leacherous, covetous, or proud,
> Bloody, or envious, as any man,
> If he had meanes to be so.
>
> (I, i, 26–29)

Having served seven years in the galleys "for a notorious murther"
(71), he is spurned by the Cardinal, and this neglect and denial have
confirmed him as a "blacke male-content . . . [who,] / (Like mothes
in cloath) . . . hurt[s] for want of wearing" (82, 83). Actually the
Cardinal, intent upon maintaining a seeming innocence, well knows
the value of an informer with no moral scruples; and he works behind the scene to convince Ferdinand to employ Bosola for his
intelligence. Bosola himself has no illusions about the proffered
job of "Provisor-ship o' th' horse" for the Duchess, which will
make him "a very quaint invisible Divell, in flesh," a "corrupter,"
and an "impudent traitor" (I, i, 291, 280, 287). Agreeing to be
Ferdinand's creature, he fully realizes that, in order "to avoid
ingratitude / For the good deed [the Duke has] done [him, he]
must doe / All the ill man can invent" (297–99).

From this point the intelligencer is the moving force of the play;
the progress of Ferdinand's disease and of his actions against his
sister are directly related to the information which Bosola supplies.
And from this point Webster establishes a private level of perception

which leads the spectators to anticipate the incidents of the plot
and provides them a perspective through which morally to evaluate
the Duchess' fate and Bosola's reaction to it. More specifically,
Bosola delivers ten soliloquies and eight asides for a total of one
hundred thirty-four lines. These internal moments are utilized in
Acts II and III entirely to establish a pattern of anticipated action
and to reveal his malefic delight in his ability to outwit the
Duchess. In the final acts, however, the soliloquies both chart the
events to come and provide the machinery for developing a transfer of anagnorisis which effectively rivals that of Shakespeare's
Antony and Cleopatra. Bosola's spiritual transformation coupled
with his vengeance in the name of justice and compassion brings
him full circle from his position of Machiavellian egocentricity at
the beginning of the tragedy; he emerges, in C. G. Thayer's words,
"from a kind of moral and intellectual disguise early in the play,
to a genuine understanding of his true identity at the end of IV, ii,
to a final personal redemption at the end of the play."[33]

Four soliloquies and five asides in Act II firmly establish Bosola's
intimate relationship with the spectators. Since they are fully informed of the Duchess' marriage and of her potential pregnancy,
their level of awareness is for a time superior to his. This knowledge
serves to sharpen their admiration for Bosola's ingenuity as he
methodically works to uncover the facts of which all else in the
court are apparently totally oblivious. He informs the spectators,
for example, of his suspicions concerning the Duchess' seething
stomach, fattening flanks, and loose-bodied gown, after which he
prepares them for a "pretty" "tricke"—some early spring apricots—
which "may chance discover" the truth (II, i, 71, 72). When she
complains that she is "troubled / With the mother" (hysteria,
thought of as a disease arising from the womb), he snidely quips in
an aside, "I feare to[o] much" (playing on the meaning of maternal
affection or responsibility) (118-19, 120); and, when he offers her
the fruit, his asides persistently refer to the "young spring-hall
cutting a caper in her belly" (166): "Good; her colour rises" (140);
"how greedily she eats them" (162); "Nay, you are too much
swell'd already" (172). On hearing that the Duchess is suddenly
taken ill, he has momentary fears that the fruit might have been
poisoned without his knowledge. He is now convinced, however,
that her "teatchi[n]es" and "vulterous eating" are "signes of breeding" (ii, 1, 2-3). A "woman['s] shreike . . . From the Dutchesse'
lodgings" in the following scene he assumes to be the sounds of

labor as he observes that he must defy the order confining everyone to his quarters lest his "intelligence . . . freize" (iii, 1, 3, 6). Again the spectators are ahead of him, having been informed earlier of the birth of a son, but Antonio becomes so flustered at Bosola's effrontery that he drops the child's nativity chart. The intelligencer now has his proof; while his assumptions that the Duchess is a creature of lust and Antonio is her bawd are erroneous, his news—to be sent "I' th morning poasts to Rome"—will be sufficient to "make her brothers Galls / Ore-flowe their Livours" (89, 90–91). He also clearly sets as his next goal the discovery of the father of the child.

Act II in large part, then, consists of a series of private comments by Bosola as he seeks to discover what the spectators already know. Again, in Act III their prior knowledge focuses a keener interest, not on what he discovers, but the method by which he does it. And, however ineffective the chronological compression may make him seem to the armchair readers—with passage of sufficient time between acts for birth of "two children more, a sonne, and daughter" (III, i, 7), he appears doggedly persistent to the audience. In the early lines he fires Ferdinand to renewed passion with the suggestion that "some Sorcery [has been] / Us'd on the Duchesse" (77–78), and he is quick to establish his strategy when the crisis occurs between brother and sister prompting the Duke to depart in the middle of the night with the threat that she is undone. His reaction in an aside ("this is cunning" [ii, 206]) immediately registers his suspicion concerning the Duchess' charge that Antonio has been a dishonest steward. Reward for such suspicion is immediate as his unqualified praise of the man completely dupes her and prompts her confidential admission that Antonio is her husband. Now possessed of the facts and commanding her full trust as well, his control of the action reaches its height at the same time his level of perception becomes equal to that of the spectators. With his advice that the entire family "faigne a Pilgrimage / To our Lady of *Loretto*" (353–54), he is now—as he observes in soliloquy—in a position to "reveale / All to [his] Lord" and reap his "gaine, or commendation: / Now for this act, I am certaine to be rais'd" (374–75, 377–78). With this information the Duchess' fate is sealed. Notably, Webster does not dramatize the scenes in which Bosola conveys his intelligence to the Duke; the result is that, although Ferdinand possesses the power and the authority which ultimately destroy her, Bosola is clearly the dramatic antagonist whose conflict with the Duchess gives shape to the tragedy.

The richly complex character of this antagonist appears for the first time in Act IV. To this point a single-minded creature of policy, here he displays a spirit not untouched by the suffering and fortitude of the Duchess. This sensitivity, developing in three successively stronger waves but mixed throughout with a determined commitment to self, creates a curious incongruity not to be resolved until the final act. The first hint of compassion, for example, occurs early in the act with Bosola's description to Ferdinand of the Duchess' behavior in imprisonment. He is impressed by her "behaviour so noble, / As gives a majestie to adversitie" (i, 6–7); her loveliness appears "more perfect, in her teares than in her smiles" (9). The moment passes quickly, however, and Bosola is soon ready to act again as the Duke's agent in arranging the macabre conference in which artificial figures are used to convince the Duchess that her husband and children are dead. Moments later the intelligencer proves to be as vulnerable to her despair as he was previously to her stoic fortitude. Reacting with "pitty" (103), he urges her to take comfort, to "remember / [She is] a Christian" (87–88); indeed, he vows to "save [her] life" (101), and he subsequently urges Ferdinand to "go no farther in your cruelty. . . . when you send me next, / The businesse shalbe comfort" (142, 163–64). But Bosola at this point is still a creature of price, and the next scene finds him playing a central role in his master's grotesque scheme to provide the Duchess a serenade of madmen and then at the height of her terror to execute her by strangulation.[34] Bosola's function is presumably to build her hysteria to a fever pitch. Dressed as an old man, he introduces himself as "a tombe-maker . . . [with] a present from [her] Princely brothers" which will bring "last benefit, last sorrow" (ii, 145, 164, 166); he is the "common Bell-man, . . . sent to condemn'd persons" whose intent is to bring her "by degrees to mortification" (173, 174, 179). When these antics fail to render her distraught, he is perplexed that the "manner of [her] death" has not "afflict[ed]" her, that the "cord" has not "terrif[ied]" her (220, 221). Moments after the murder of mother and children, his humanity surfaces again in his assertion that she suffers beyond reason; "murther shreikes out: . . . blood flies upwards and bedewes the Heavens" (278–80). And Ferdinand's peremptory refusal to grant the promised reward provokes Bosola to reiterate his repugnance toward his deeds in a protracted soliloquy during which the Duchess momentarily recovers consciousness. Admitting that he has hitherto played the true servant rather than the honest man, he now swears that he would not change "peace of conscience / For all the wealth of Europe" (366–67). When the Duchess stirs and opens her eyes, he declares that heaven itself seems to be offering him mercy. This hope dashed with her death moments later, he compares her "sacred Innocence" (383) to his "guilty conscience" (384), and tears which "never grew / In [his] Mothers Milke" flow like "penitent fountaines" (390–91, 392). Finally, he rouses himself to action in her behalf, indicating that he will convey her body to some good women for its "reverend dispose" (399) and vowing that he will "poast to *Millaine*" (401) for an apparent act of vengeance "worth [his] dejection" (403).

Bosola's sense of human compassion and the recognition of his own moral aberrance, then, have developed in three successive waves, and his final words in Act IV imply a permanent and profound transformation of values. Admittedly, however, the assumption of personal gain has twice suppressed his conscience, and total repudiation of his previous actions has come only with Ferdinand's failure to reward his villainy. By removing the Duchess at this point Webster has set the stage for powerful development of the transfer of the anagnorisis. Bosola obviously develops the necessary human sensitivity to be convincingly affected by the Duchess' tragic death; now will come the crucial test of his values in Act V as he confronts the proffered monetary reward to which previously his life has been so totally committed. Structurally, the dramatic situation is a duplication of that in *Antony and Cleopatra.* At the end of Act IV the protagonist Antony lies dead; Cleopatra has sworn that, with the "garland of the war" fallen, she will never be reconciled with Caesar, that instead she will "make death proud to take" her as a token of her fidelity to Antony. On the other hand, consistency has not previously been a matter of great concern to the Egyptian queen; time and again the spectators have observed her resort to trickery and deceit as a matter of self-interest. In the final act the extensive testing of her transformation, like Bosola's, provides the basis for registering effectively the social impact of tragedy; just as individuals surrounding the central figure can directly contribute to his destruction, so also they can share the insights which his suffering and tragic death provoke.

Webster psychologically prepares the spectators for Bosola's full transformation by establishing the villainous nature of the Cardinal in the opening lines of Act V before Bosola reenters; thus a new antagonist is created to receive the spectators' scorn at the very moment they must begin to develop a guarded sympathy for Bosola as they observe his spiritual anguish. The Cardinal's true colors have been obvious since the first scene, to be sure. But his actions have remained subordinate to those of Ferdinand, who has grown increasingly frenetic in his determination to spy upon the Duchess, to discover the father of her children, and then to take his full revenge upon all of them. Indeed, on one occasion in Act II the Cardinal pits himself directly against his brother's vengeful fury, accusing the "starke mad" Duke of flying beyond his reason with "rage," "violent whirle-windes," and "intemperate noyce" (II, v, 86, 65, 67): "there is not in nature / A thing, that makes man so deform'd, so beastly, / As doth intemperate anger" (74–76). Later in Act III the spectators assume that the Cardinal has done his worst when he banishes the Duchess and Antonio, especially in light of the fact that he neither appears nor is mentioned in Act IV as Ferdinand through Bosola directs his scheme against the pair to grisly fruition.

In Act V the Cardinal's role darkens with dramatic suddenness. Not only does Pescara describe the Cardinal's ravishing the land from Antonio; the Cardinal himself admits in soliloquy that he "counsell'd" (V, ii, 108) the Duchess' death but that he is determined to cast the full blame upon Duke Ferdinand, who now suffers constant distraction in the advanced stages of lycanthropia. A part of that scheme is to feign ignorance of the Duchess' death; hence, when Bosola enters, the Cardinal urges him to kill Antonio so that another marriage can be arranged for her. Although Bosola readily accepts the commission, he immediately informs the spectators in soliloquy that he is aware of the duplicity and in his "cunning" is simply "follow[ing the Cardinal's] example" in an attempt to discover the actual guilt for the mass murders of the previous act. When—with the aid of the doting Julia—he verifies that the Duchess and two of her children were strangled "by [the Cardinal's] appointment" (291), he seizes the initiative and confronts the cleric with his information. The moment is crucial, for now the terrified Cardinal offers Bosola "a fortune" (333) to remain loyal; "I have honors in store for thee" (336). Bosola once more appears to capitulate, reaffirming his willingness to murder Antonio. Again, however, in soliloquy twenty lines later he vows to seek out the good Antonio:

and all my care shall be
To put thee into safety from the reach
Of these most cruell biters, that have got
Some of thy blood already.

(374–77)

Motivated not by money but by the "sword of justice" (380) and his own "Penitence" (382), he suggests, moreover, that he will join with Antonio "in a most just revenge" (378).

It is Bosola's tragic blunder to strike down Antonio, "the man [he] would have sav'de 'bove [his] owne life" (iv, 62), thinking he is murdering the Cardinal; so also he momentarily falters in his fatalistic assumptions that "We are meerely the Starres tennys-balls (strooke, and banded / Which way please them)" (63–64). But his despair is short-lived, and he quickly determines that he will openly confront the Cardinal and "bring him to th' hammer" (93). In the climactic moments the Cardinal not unexpectedly again tempts his would-be assassin with wealth; indeed he in desperation would "faithfully devide / Revenewes with [him]" (v, 16–17). The trans- formed antagonist is now resolute, however: "Thy prayers, and proffers / Are both unseasonable" (18–19). And there is no trace of a Hieronimo-like struggle of conscience concerning the fact that Bosola has become both judge and jury for the corrupt clergyman: "when thou kill'dst thy sister, / Thou tookst from Justice her most equall ballance, / And left her naught but her sword" (52–54). In the struggle which ensues, Bosola, the Cardinal, and the Duke all receive death wounds. Bosola, however, dies in his finest hour. He avers that "the last part of [his] life, / Hath done [him] best service" (82–83); and, as the officers close around them, he pub- licly proclaims the guilt of the "*Aragonian* brethren" (103) and defends his actions as just "revenge, for the Duchess of *Malfi*, . . . for *Antonio*, . . . for lustfull *Julia*, . . . and lastly, for [himself]" (102–105).

Bosola's final words ("Let worthy mindes nere stagger in distrust / To suffer death, or shame, for what is just" [127–28]) may well sound aphoristic. But, on this point a comparison is salutary be- tween Bosola, whose transformation has been put into action, and his counterpart Flamineo, whose response to Vittoria's death reaches only the articulation of such maxims. In underscoring once again the transformation in spiritual and social values which lead Bosola in Act V to act in behalf of the Duchess and what she morally represents in the play, these words confirm the profound

social ramifications which the Duchess' tragic end have provoked;
more powerfully than in *The White Devil* the dramatic emphasis
concerning the insights gained by suffering is registered externally
on those around the protagonist rather than internally as a flash
of illumination on the central figure preceding her death. In the
final analysis it is the combined deaths of Antony and Cleopatra
which so strongly impress the spectators and Caesar, influencing
him to do them homage in death (albeit in part for the sake of his
own glory); similarly it is the combined deaths of the Duchess and
of Bosola, in conjunction with his scheme for vengeance destroying
both Ferdinand and the Cardinal, which purges the kingdom of the
cancer at the center and leads Delio to proclaim that "integrity of
life, is fames best friend, / Which noblely (beyond Death) shall
crowne the end" (145–46). The conclusion to be sure is not
utopian. The canker of evil remains, and the contemporary English
audience would see in the "yong hopefull Gentleman" (137) who
assumes rulership, as in Giovanni in the earlier play, a disturbingly
dangerous situation. Given this realistic caution, however, the
"great ruine," (136) put to "noble use" (135), provides the opportunity for the audience and for the entire society of the stage
world to profit from the tragic experience which takes focus on
the Duchess.

VI. Middleton

—WOMEN BEWARE WOMEN, THE CHANGELING

A prolific writer who worked both independently and in collaboration, Thomas Middleton composed five tragedies and some eighteen comedies and tragicomedies. His three extant tragedies are all plays of lust and intrigue. *The Mayor of Queenborough or Hengist, King of Kent,* presumably the earliest, is set in a post-Roman Britain not yet conquered by the Saxons. It relates the grisly tale of Vortiger's usurpation of Constantius' throne, his poisoning of his own wife Castiza in order to wed Roxena, daughter of his Saxon henchman Hengist, and his subsequent cuckolding by his close friend Hersus. After Hengist assumes virtual royal prerogatives, the British attack and burn Vortiger's castle, killing Vortiger, Roxena, and Hersus. In a comic subplot Simon the tanner becomes Mayor of Queenborough, and his pride and petty tyranny are no doubt intended to parallel Vortiger's actions. The tragedy is not without moments of power, to be sure, and its appraisal of human life is consistent with that of his later plays, but it is generally uneven and fails to sustain emotional power and to achieve unity of purpose.

More certain is his dispassionate and realistic observation of a viciously corrupt society in *Women Beware Women* and *The Changeling,* the latter in collaboration with William Rowley. Since neither play was printed during Middleton's lifetime (indeed the earliest reference to *Women Beware Women* is 1653, the year of the first printing of both pieces)[1] precise dating is virtually impossible. Both, however, clearly represent relatively late Jacobean contributions. Arguments for the date of *Women Beware Women,* more specifically, have ranged from 1613 to 1623. Whether chronologically nearer to the work of Webster or of Ford, it shares the vision of life which binds the two together. Like both writers he epitomizes an age of dubiety and unscrupulous individualism, a mercenary world in which morality has its price and violence is the rule rather than the exception. And, like both, with human disaster —psychological and physical—occasioned by the individual's flaw

and his manipulation by others to their own selfish advantage, he
projects a broad view of tragedy which indicts not only the single
figure but also society at large.

The world of *Women Beware Women* in particular is characterized by a general abandonment to passion. Involving both aristocratic and mercantile classes in its web of intrigue, it is one of the
most extensively decadent societies in the entire range of Jacobean-
Caroline tragedy. The focus, similar to that of *The Revenger's
Tragedy,* is exclusively upon sexual depravity, concerning both the
lechery and lust which seek physical gratification at whatever cost
to another and the avarice which barters flesh for position and
wealth. No fewer than five sexual relationships form the basis for
the action, only one of which—and that one only for a period of
days—is morally sound.

Such a sexual scene provides perhaps the most graphic manner
of depicting one's manipulation and use of another to self-advantage or satisfaction.[2] Indeed virtually the entire cast of characters
is made up of those who either practice against others or are practiced upon. Brancha and Isabella, for example, are pawns whose
fate is determined in large part by those who move against them.[3]
Lured into the back rooms of Livia's home, Brancha is helpless in
confronting the lustful Duke who spied her in an upper window
during a ceremonial procession and immediately moved to slake
his sexual appetite without regard for her feelings, family, or
marital status.[4] When, proclaiming "treachery to honor" (II, i,
376),[5] she struggles physically to escape, he firmly informs her
that she has no recourse against him:

> strive not to seek
> Thy liberty, and keep me still in prison.
> 'Yfaith you shall not out, till I'm relest now.
> . . . .
> I am not here in vain. . . .
> Take warning I beseech thee. . . .
> I should be sorry the least force should lay
> An unkinde touch upon thee.
> (386-88, 393, 403-404)

Her submission, to the contrary, will bring wealth, honor, provision,
and shelter (437, 450, 451). Without the slightest moral qualm he
sees it as a fair exchange and peremptorily calls a halt to further
dialogue: "We'll walk together, / And shew a thankful joy for both

our fortunes" (454–55). A prime agent in the arrangement is
Guardiano, who five times within five hundred lines (II, ii) acknowledges the advancement which his success as procurer will guarantee.
Worth much in "wealth and favor" (24), the Duke's satisfaction
will bring "riches or advancement" (32); "good Fortune . . . will
spring from't" (48).[6] He sneers in an aside at the fine "snares for
womens honesties / That are devis'd in these days," noting how he
weakened her resistance by showing her "naked pictures by the
way" (467–68, 473). And in response to her deep curse of his
"smooth brow'd treachery," he scoffs, "Well, so the Duke love me, /
I fare not much amiss then" (518–19).

Similarly, Isabella, who at the outset envisions honest love as
"next to Angels, the most blest estate" (I, ii, 202), is manipulated
from two separate points. Her father Fabritio, on the one hand,
determines that she "shall love" (I, ii, 2) the rich Ward; if the
"gentleman is somewhat simple, . . . he's rich; / The fool's hid
under Bushels" (91, 94). As Fabritio observes after the two young
people have been officially introduced, "Marry him she shall then,
/ Let her agree upon love afterwards" (161–62). Later he un-
abashedly suggests that the Ward dance with her so that he can see
"what y'have for your money, / Without fraud or imposture" (III,
ii, 199–200). The dilemma, for Isabella, is genuine; she would
"honor and obey" her father, yet she would not "marry a Fool!"
(I, ii, 187, 183). On the other hand, Hippolito and Livia, her uncle
and aunt, combine to promote a sin which renders her consternation inconsequential. Livia, on her brother's behalf, agrees to use
her "craft t'undo a Maidenhead" (II, i, 203). As long as Isabella
believes Hippolito to be her uncle, she refuses his protestations of
love with an almost holy zeal. Informed falsely by Livia that she is
actually the daughter of "that fam'd *Spaniard*, / Marquess of *Coria*"
(II, i, 166–67), she opens her arms to her uncle and agrees to use
her marriage bed with the Ward as a convenient front for their
assignation.

Obviously, neither Brancha nor Isabella is without fault. Both, in
fact, are peculiarly void of moral stamina when faced with a
dilemma. Brancha may protest vigorously to the Duke; when he
releases her, having satisfied his lust, she may even lament in an
aside the "Leprosie" of her beauty and call her ravishment a murder
whose "weight is deadly" (II, ii, 498, 508). But from this point she
seems morally atrophied, never again voicing either regret for or

moral judgment on the few moments which so drastically altered
her life. Since she lacks any kind of firm spiritual commitment, as
Charles A. Hallett has observed, "She finds nothing to prevent her
from spiraling downward in her continuous need to adjust to
deteriorating circumstances, until she hits rock bottom."[7] Argu-
mentative with her mother-in-law and calculatingly shrewd with
her husband, she obeys the Duke's next summons with open
alacrity; and soon the spectators and Leantio observe her kissing
him publicly while he offers material compensation to the
cuckolded husband. If she has another introspective moment, it
comes in a later soliloquy in which she muses over the irony of her
present life despite her overprotected childhood: "Restraint breeds
wand'ring thoughts. . . . I'll nev'r use any Girl of mine so strictly, /
Howev'r they're kept, their fortunes finde 'em out" (IV, i, 37, 39–
40). This is not regret, however, and from this point of adultery
she moves with apparent ease to thoughts of banishment for a
complaining husband (124) and murder for a chastising Cardinal
(V, ii, 24). Isabella, too, seems a strange paradox. If she is the
epitome of chastity in recoiling against the horror of incest, she
almost too readily enters a private relationship once assured it will
not bear that brand, and from that moment forward she offers not
one word of protest against a public marriage to a fool. When she
later discovers that Hippolito is indeed her uncle, her reaction is
equally extreme. She has committed "sin enough to make a whole
world perish" (IV, ii, 144) and would readily repent (147); yet in
virtually the same breath she considers the means of her "revenge"
by which to practice "cruel cunning" upon Livia's life (157, 158).

Admittedly the two women, both intellectually and sprititually
shallow, share lustful affinities with the other inhabitants of
Middleton's Florence. Clearly, however, since they are first set in a
path of corruption through the actions of others who seek self-
gratification, forces both external and internal converge to produce
their tragedy. The same is true of Leantio, whose murder is the
result of an assignation provoked by his wife's infidelity and thus
ultimately by the Duke's thoughtless imposition of self-will. In
him the chain of evil emphasizing the external human interaction
of tragedy assumes its most obvious pattern, a tragic perspective
reversing the dramatic focus upon Hamlet's or Othello's private
hell beside which external action pales to relative insignificance.
Appearing in six of the thirteen scenes the factor is the most

extensively developed character in the play, his final repudiation of
Brancha shortly before his murder building through three progressively emotional stages.

In Act I he is a veritable idealist. Although he may be guilty of a
serious breach of ethics in eloping with a young Venetian gentle-
woman and he may be both naïve and ill-advised in his determination to hide her from Florentine society, he is blinded by the assumption that their love is both permanent and true; and to
consider his marriage a "theft . . . vitiated at its very source"[8] has
the same effect as laying the cause of Othello's fall to his choice of
wife and manner of marriage. His new wife is "the most unvaluedst
purchase" (i, 13), his "masterpeece" (43) who is "contented" (55),
skilled in "obedience" (81), and "loves her husband" (96). Though
the secret marriage costs them her dowry, theirs is an "innocent"
(55) and "honest love" (101) which will mock poverty (102).
While parting from her the next morning to attend his business is a
difficult task, he realizes that a successful marriage is predicated on
both the reality of work and the bliss of physical pleasure:

> As fitting is a Government in Love,
> As in a Kingdome; when 'tis all near Lust,
> 'Tis like an insurrection in the people
> That raised in self-wil, wars against all Reason:
> But, Love that is respective for increase,
> Is like a good King, that keeps all in peace,
>
> (45–50)

Not surprisingly such sublime confidence in the integrity of his
mate converts to utter disillusionment when the marriage quickly
collapses. Puzzled by the studied coolness with which she receives
him on his return home and by her irascible complaints concerning
the poverty of her surroundings, he is dumbfounded at her prompt
response to the Duke's invitation to dinner. The honey of matri-
mony is now gall, and he denounces wedlock as "the ripe time of
man's misery" (III, i, 307). Better far is the satisfaction found in a
strumpet's arms than the transient bliss of a wife purchased with
"fears, shames, jealousies, costs and troubles" (329). At the
banquet in the following scene he quips cynically in asides of their
bold adultery (40) and of his whorish wife (140). "Damnation has
taught" her the wisdom of taking gifts (156); her "good is common" (194), and her "cool pride" reflects the "glory of her sin"
(260, 261). Judgmental pronouncements meliorate to disconso-

lation as he reflects upon their "whole nights together" when they "kiss'd as if [their] lips had grown together" (294, 302). Having lost her forever, he would gladly welcome death (370); his only recourse is to hate her as extremely as he previously loved her (387). Partially no doubt in retaliation for his emotional pain, he first accepts the Duke's offer of "the Captainship / Of *Rouans* Cittadel" (44–45)—direct earnest for his cuckoldery—then responds willingly to Livia's sexual advancements in order to gain compensation in kind.

A sense of moral revulsion overwhelms Leantio in his final scenes. Even though he himself is hopelessly compromised, reaping both the profit of his wife's infidelity and the pleasure of his own, he scathingly condemns her prostitute state, mocking her "sumptuous lodging" and her "brave life" and branding her "An impudent spiteful strumpet" (IV, i, 59, 70, 78). Then, in his most furious moment he directly threatens her life, swearing that he will find the time to drive "her course of sins / To their eternal Kennels" (101–102), at which time "Thunder shall seem soft musick to that tempest" (106). Without a conscience and possessed of sin as dark as death, she is a creature of "blind pride," and her "perjur'd soul" shall feel his "revenge and anger" (121, 117). Moments before his death his mind is still obsessed with the "glistring Whore [who] shines like a Serpent" (ii, 21); and, after Hippolito has served him a lethal blow, his final words reflect the strange combination of pathos and fury with which his personality has been inextricably bound: "Rise strumpet by my fall, thy Lust may raign now; / My heart-string, and the marriage knot that ty'd thee, / Breaks both together" (48–50).

Though clearly able to judge Brancha's conduct for what it is, Leantio, admittedly, is never able to acknowledge his own stain and guilt.[9] Consequently, the turning of his tragic wheel never brings him to a moment of self-knowledge, and his experience as a tragic protagonist is abortive. Again, though, his wheel—like that of Brancha and of Isabella—in large measure is turned by those who abuse him for self-gratification. Against each of them is arraigned the combined passions of the Duke, Hippolito, Livia, Guardiano, and Fabrito. Middleton, in other words, does not focus predominantly on the experiences of any single individual; indeed he seems consciously to avoid the internalization which encourages the spectators' close emotional involvement. Instead, by interweaving the double plots of Brancha and Leantio (each involved in an adulterous affair) and of Isabella and the Ward (with Hippolito as her furtive lover), he depicts a stage world literally teeming with decadence and effectively broadens his tragic perspective.

At least four additional features of the plot seem designed to contribute directly to the sense of pervasive corruption. Of relatively minor significance is Isabella's song at the Duke's banquet. The *carpe diem* theme, suggesting that only a mother of fools will bestow her affection without material benefits, is appropriate reinforcement for a scene triply reeking with bartered sex as Hippolito gazes on the singer, the Duke and Brancha gaze on each other, and Fabritio calls the Ward's attention to the delightful breasts of his potential wife. Similar thematic reinforcement is provided by the chess game engaged in by Livia and the Widow while Brancha is being raped by the Duke.[10] The conversation, stressing Livia's cunning as she uses a Duke to "strike a sure stroke" while her "pawn" is unable to "relieve it selfe" (II, ii, 350, 351), forms a prurient running commentary on the sexual attack. The Duke fetches her over; he "has bestirr'd himself" and is responsible for "all the mischief in this Game" (456, 486, 487). The constant *double entendre* on the one hand thrusts the act itself vividly into the spectators' imagination; at the same time it dramatically underscores an individual's susceptibility to manipulation whether by physical force or by deception.

More significant are the Ward's marital arrangements which lend sporadic emphasis to the marketability of human flesh. For one thing his readiness to marry is based solely on his urgent need for sexual encounter:

> I feel my self after any exercise
> Horribly prone: Let me but ride, I'm lusty,
> A Cock-horse straight y'faith.
> . . . .
>   If my hot blood
> Be not took down in time, sure 'twill crow shortly.
>   (I, ii, 138–140, 144–45)

For another, he would select a wife as one might select a horse, examining her parts one by one; ideally he would examine her naked so as to determine her physical fitness (II, ii, 114–41). At the Duke's banquet the plot strands merge as the Ward critically examines Isabella like chattel: "the Ape's so little, / I shall scarce feel her. . . . See how she suffers it" (III, ii, 77–78, 80). And in IV,

ii, when the match is drawn, the Ward with the aid of his man
Sordido checks her against a literal catalogue of feminine faults:
"But at which end shall I begin? . . . And is that hair your own?
. . . 'Tis a good hearing. . . . Does her eyes stand well? . . . What
qualities have you beside singing and dancing? . . . I have fair hope
of her teeth. . . . I'ld feign mark how she goes. . . . Will it please
you walk? . . . 'Tis enough forsooth" (43, 64, 66, 67, 82–83, 100,
105, 115, 126). The antics of the doltish Ward, certainly the most
humorous moments in the play, do indeed provide comic release.
But, thematically akin to the developing strands of tragic action,
it is humor which intensifies rather than lessens the pervading sense
of human bestiality and impending doom.

Clearly, the most significant structural feature in setting a broad
focus on this oppressively hellish society is Act V. By all rights, if
Middleton had wished to focus on the decadence of a society
totally unperturbed by the fate of the individual figure it has been
responsible in large part for destroying, the play might well have
ended with IV, iii. Leantio is dead, yet his death provokes no positive response in the surrounding figures, least of all in Livia. Moreover, there is no move whatever to apprehend Hippolito for the
murder to which he freely confesses. If Brancha's sexual liaison
stands condemned, the Duke has successfully contravened the
Cardinal's moral castigation by arranging to marry Brancha virtually while Leantio's murdered body is still warm. In a word, this
society inhabited by "moral idiots" has managed to extirpate any
semblance either of positive spiritual value or of basic human
decency.

The fifth act, however, projects an even more startling vision of
human depravity through a calculated exercise in violence which
seems to prefigure the total annihilation of society by unrestrained
passion. In this final explosion of horror the entire nest of maggots
is eliminated through a web of intricate intrigues in which three
separate revengers work at cross purposes, yet each incredibly
accomplishes his mission. Each death, as J. B. Batchelor has noted,
"is a moral emblem, a carefully worked out model of appropriate
retribution seen from the perspective of orthodox Christian
dualism."[11] Livia, deprived of her lover, is the primary revenger,
joining with Guardiano to present an entertainment for the Duke's
nuptials during which Hippolito will be dispatched by being
dropped on steel spikes and Isabella will be killed by a flaming
substance cast upon her from above.[12] Isabella too wants

vengeance, however, for Livia's lie which prompted her to an
incestuous relationship with her uncle, and to this end she prepares
a deadly incense to offer to Livia during the pageant. Meanwhile,
Brancha arranges a deadly potion to be offered the Cardinal for his
effrontery in opposing her relationship with the Duke. With the
poison mistakenly drunk by the Duke instead, Brancha almost
eagerly commits suicide by kissing his lips and quaffing the remains
of the poisoned cup. Combined with the death of Guardiano, who
accidentally falls into his own spiked snare, and the death of Hippolito by poisoned arrows, the various revenges create macabre
carnage as three women lie strewn about the stage. The final act,
then, provides a frightening culmination of the numerous strands
of passion in the play, leaving a sense of utter exhaustion in a
society in which the fundamental moral principles of harmony and
cohesion have been destroyed by Hobbesian self-gratification.

   In preparing the spectators for this sense of exhaustion Middleton establishes a conventional moral framework through three
separate characters—Leantio, the Duke, and the Cardinal—in each
case vitiating their objectivity and integrity with the result that,
while the values are not repudiated, they fail to provide convincing
moral justification for the suffering and waste which infest the stage
world. Consider, similarly, how figures like Arruntius in *Sejanus* or
Friar Bonaventura in *'Tis Pity She's a Whore* provide specific moral
standards, but the value structure is undercut either by conflicting
counterforces which lay equal claim to the spectators' basic sympathies or by the relative ineffectiveness, insignificance, or manifest
duplicity of the characters who are spokesmen for conventional
morality. The latter is clearly the case with Leantio and the Duke,
while the Cardinal is simply not in a position to be able to pro-
nounce effective judgment on the welter of events.

   Leantio, as we noted earlier, is the first to speak of the sinfulness
of adultery in contrast with the bliss of his marriage, which is
"seal'd from Heaven" (I, i, 29, 47); he now can "go to Church"
free of the "Devil" of sexual temptation (33, 181). Once Brancha
has violated the marriage bed, his dialogue is peppered with the
vocabulary of Christian theology and his judgment is rigidly dog-
matic. "Lust" and "Adultery" (III, ii, 40) will reap "damnation"
(156); the Duke's soul is black (III, ii, 190), and Brancha is as difficult to retrieve from him as the "redemption of a soul from Hell"
(376). The strumpet and her "Devil," sinning with "nev'r a conscience put to't," perjure their souls; "A plague will come" (93, 96,

109, 121). Yet, as the spectators realize full well, Leantio all this while enjoys both the wealth and the physical pleasure derived from his own private affair with Livia, and the double moral standard he would impose, despite Brancha's being the initial sinner, can hardly carry conviction.

Through the Duke's action in IV, i, Middleton even more obviously undermines the spectators' easy confidence in the efficacy of Christian morality. In the face of the Cardinal's fervid remonstrations against the sinfulness of his brother's sexual escapades, the Duke is abjectly penitent, and in the absence of asides to the contrary the spectators have every reason to assume he is sincere.

> Brother of spotless honor, let me weep
> The first of my repentance in thy bosome,
> And shewe the blest fruits of a thankful spirit;
> And if I ere keep woman more unlawfully,
> May I want penitence, at my greatest need.
> And wisemen know there is no barren place,
> Threatens more famine, then a dearth in grace.
>
> (292-98)

When the Cardinal praises "Heaven" for a "conversion" for which "The powers of darkness groan" and all Hell is sorry and for which is sung "a Himn in Heaven" (299-302 *et passim*), a moral force seems to be active once again and to have achieved for the ruler the "peace of a fair Soul" (306). It can only be disconcerting that, moments after the Cardinal's departure, the Duke is again oblivious of all ramifications; his lust will now simply await the legal union predicated on her husband's murder. Morality clearly must be the servant, not the master.

The moral frame of the tragedy must, of course, rise or fall on the role of the Cardinal, who is demonstrably the spokesman for the standards of human conduct espoused by established religion. Appearing in three of the last five scenes (IV, i, iii; V, ii), he vigorously opposes the immorality in the court. The Duke's "great sin" will provoke a "veng'ance" through his "eternal death" (IV, i, 231, 232, 239). In the Duke's position of public responsibility "Ev'ry sin thou commit'st, shews like a flame" (248). If eminent persons through virtue set a positive example for others, theirs is "the greater glory after death" (263); conversely, they who set a "light up to shew men to Hell" will face the full "height of torments" (267, 265). No less furious when he learns of the Duke's intended marriage, he brands the projected nuptials "Religions honors done to sin" which "will pull / Heavens thunder down upon *Florence*"(IV, iii, 1, 3). His "hot lust" and "worship done to Devils" would but "take sanctuary in marriage" (18, 19, 38). Such sanctuary might protect his body but not his "guilty soul" (45). Again, as the tragedy moves toward its conclusion, the moral structure which will provide the standards for evaluating the final actions of the principals appears firm. Yet, inexplicably, all traces of this zealous opposition have disappeared in the final scene. Without the least hint of judgment the Cardinal now proclaims that he professes peace and is content (V, ii, 16); both the Duke and Brancha "shall have all [they] wish" (18). He does not speak again for almost two hundred lines at which time he describes the multiple deaths as the "greatest sorrow and astonishment" (216)—not, as one might expect, the greatest judgment or vengeance of God—that ever struck Florence. And it is he who is left on stage to deliver the final observations. He draws a moral on "these ruins," to be sure, but it is so limited in its focus that it seems both insufficient and inappropriate. It may well be that a "King" ruled by lust "cannot raign long" (246)—that a mind ruled by passion will destroy reason and obviate moral standards—but the cleric gives no indication of genuinely realizing the full scope of the corruption and destruction. Providing no view which would lend some degree of coherence to the multiple strands of action, the comment simply attests to the pitiful inability of that society to come to grips with the cancer which vitiates its moral structure.

At the same time, Middleton's fundamental design for the play is firm. In the absence on stage of a dominant and consistent moral force, whose presence would dilute the sense of moral evisceration, he develops a perspective which forces the spectators to become active participants in the play and thus to provide the judgment of which the Cardinal is incapable.[13] Normally, tragedy centers on the experience of a single dominant figure or on the struggle between the protagonist and the antagonist. The audience possesses an omniscient view, but the principal's level of knowledge at times closely approximates this view; indeed a significant portion of the action is frequently seen through the eyes of the central figure. The result is a structure in which the audience and the principal command the greatest levels of awareness and other figures in varying degrees possess less knowledge of the total nature of the conflict and its ramifications; obviously the price for such a close emotional rapport is the loss of at least a degree of objectivity. In *Women Beware Women,* to the contrary, no single character stands predominantly at the center. Instead the spectators observe a series of independent actions in which individuals, both the manipulator and the victim, share their private perceptions with the spectators through soliloquies or asides. Consequently, the gap of awareness between the audience with its omniscient view and any one of the characters with his signally limited view is far more extensive than in other tragedies. No fewer than ten characters deliver an incredible seventy-three private passages (compared, for example, to five characters and eighteen passages in *Hamlet* or three characters and sixteen passages in *Othello*). While Leantio with one hundred seventy-three lines in fifteen passages holds a clear majority in total lines, Brancha has thirteen passages (sixty-four lines), Guardiano (twenty-eight lines) eleven passages, Hippolito (fifty-eight lines) and Livia (forty-seven lines) nine passages, the Duke (twenty-two lines) and Isabella (seventeen lines) five passages, the Mother (thirty-two lines) four passages, and the Cardinal (twelve lines) and Sordido (two lines) one each. The number of such lines, four hundred forty-five, comprises 14 percent of the total lines in the play (compared to 7 percent in *Hamlet* and 6 percent in *Othello*).

More importantly (through this private correspondence between the characters and the audience), at least eleven independent lines of action are initiated. A major strand, for example, traces Leantio's relationship with Brancha—the joy, the consternation, finally the condemnation. A second major strand involves Hippolito's affair with Isabella; his admission of incestuous passion, her willingness to participate after being told falsely that she is not his niece, her determination to keep this new knowledge secret, his ecstatic bliss stemming from the seduction—each of these points is registered first in soliloquy. The Duke's attraction to Brancha forms another separate strand which includes Guardiano's description of the scheme for Brancha's rape, her impassioned comments immediately following the act, and the mother's reaction to the daughter-in-law's increasing irritability over the period of the next few days; again these are concerns voiced privately to the spectators, not developed through dialogue among the characters on stage. The same is true for such unrelated matters as Livia's admission of love for Leantio, Guardiano's methods for securing Fabritio's support for joining his daughter and the Ward in marriage, and the genuine disdain for the Ward which Isabella masks behind coquetry in using the marriage as a cover for her own concupiscence. Consider finally the multiple strands of individual intrigue in the final scenes. Of the six deaths in V, ii, only two are planned in concert. Livia seeks Guardiano's counsel in devising the means of death for Hippolito and Isabella through a pageantic entertainment "at the Dukes hasty Nuptial's" (IV, ii, 175). Meanwhile Isabella indicates in an aside that she perceives the duplicity in Livia's feigned reconciliation (195–99) and during the mask she offers up poisoned incense to Livia with the private quip:

> And if it keep true touch, my good Aunt *Juno*,
> 'Twill try your immortality er't belong:
> I fear you'll never get so nigh Heaven again,
> When you're once down.
> $\qquad$ (V, ii, 106–109)

Similarly, at the very moment the Cardinal professes peace and reconciliation, Brancha informs the audience that this envious Brother, next heir to the Duke, will die this night:

> He that begins so early to reprove,
> Quickly rid him, or look for little love.
> . . . .
> In time of sports, Death may steal in securely;
> Then 'tis least thought on.
> $\qquad$ (21–22, 25–26)

Neither Isabella nor Brancha, one should note, discusses her projected action with those closest to her. Livia's murder presumably is totally unanticipated by Hippolito, just as Brancha's unsuccessful attempt on the Cardinal's life comes as a complete surprise to the Duke; indeed, if the Duke had possessed even the slightest inclination of the device, he surely would have been a bit more apprehensive about receiving the correct cup from Ganymed. For that matter, in Act IV Hippolito decides to challenge Leantio (in order, as he puts it, to "purge the air / Of [the] corruption" of this "apparent sinner" "To the perpetual honor of our house" [ii, 14–15, 9, 13]) without once consulting his heart's mate.

It is true that these private passages are not moments of decision in which the character makes an agonizing choice to commit himself to a particular line of action. Since, as we have already observed, the inhabitants of this stage world are peculiarly devoid of moral sensitivity and seem to base their decisions solely on personal

interest and pleasure, the soliloquies and asides are almost exclusively statements of intent which establish a pattern of anticipation for
the spectators. It is self-evident, then, that no character is led
through suffering to illumination either about himself or about
society at large; no principal possesses the degree of comprehension
of the total action vital to the experience of an effective anagnorisis.
Time and again, though, the characters turn to the spectators rather
than close companions during their most critical moments, and as a
consequence the spectators quite literally become a kind of silent
partner or confidante. They alone command anything approaching
a full view of the pattern of events; like Jonson in *Catiline* or
Webster in *The White Devil*, Middleton depends upon the spectators to exercise judgment predicated on their personal scale of
values. On the one hand, their omniscient perspective provides the
factual information necessary for each plot line to make causal
sense. On the other, it encourages them to consider the thematic
relationships of the strands of action which to anyone on stage remain unresolved and disparate. And certainly the multiple plot
lines converge on a single theme. Whether through elopement,
overpossessiveness, rape, adultery, a cuckolded husband ignorant
of the situation, a cuckolded husband whose compliance is purchased with gifts, panderism, incest, a male lover whose services
are bought, an arranged marriage in which love is less significant
than wealth—in all instances one individual is manipulated for the
sake of another in a society in which each person is a law unto
himself and the single viable goal is self-satisfaction. Of that portion of Florentine society which the spectators have confronted,
a majority—seven of the twelve named characters—have been
destroyed by the end of the play, and something akin to a vision
of doomsday hangs over the scene. The triple revenge plots have
destroyed all principals to be sure, but it is hardly a sense of purgation which emerges. The stage world is left only with two representatives of the older generation—Fabritio and the Widow,
Leantio's mother. Of the younger group only the foolish Ward
remains. None of these is capable of reviving this society riddled
and destroyed by lust and greed. Brancha's final words provide a
fitting testimonial to this social nightmare; like Leantio an act
earlier she dies without thought of repentance, bemoaning the
"deadly snares / That women set for women" (V, ii, 232–33).
Admitting that "Pride, Greatness, Honors, Beauty, Youth, / [and]
Ambition" must all die together, she takes a kind of perverse plea-

sure in snatching death from the "cup of love" which also claimed
the "Duke" (239, 242).

If the stage world of *Women Beware Women* has seemed lacking
in moral force and direction, the end results are almost rigidly conventional. The reward of sin is death, and, although no positive
force has been visibly active throughout the play, the guilty destroy
themselves with precise effectiveness. With the spectators in a
position to place all of the pieces together, they alone can receive
the full impact of the tragedy. And, as in the work of Jonson,
Tourneur, and Ford, for them alone is catharsis possible. Without
question they will face society beyond the theatrical doors with a
renewed conviction of teleological design. They will face their
Jacobean realities with the additional reminder that tragedy is rarely a matter of isolated private decision, that more frequently it will
be the consequence of human interaction. Hell has come to earth
and its name is humanity disposed to using others merely as means
of achieving its own satisfaction. While this stage world lacks
characters of full tragic stature, the greatest degree of sympathy—
albeit mixed with disdain and condemnation—is reserved for
Brancha, Isabella, and Leantio—figures whose descents into corruption and villainy are not entirely self-motivated and who most
clearly reflect the complex societal forces culminating in the
tragedy of the individual.

When one compares the work of Middleton, Ford, Tourneur, and
Jonson with Marlowe's and Shakespeare's powerfully internalized
tragedies, it becomes temptingly simplistic to speak of the increasingly decadent clientele to which the later playwrights catered or
of the absence of dominant protagonists in their work as a failure
of imagination and spiritual energy, an indication of an artistic
vision of a lower order than Shakespeare's. While any comparisons
with Shakespeare are perhaps odious, the truth surely lies elsewhere.
Clearly, it was Shakespeare himself who was among the first to
move away from intensely personal spiritual tragedy in order, it
would seem, to capture a broader view of the corrosive nature of
selfish human interactions. Consistently, the dramatists of the first
decades of the seventeenth century address the same theme; for
them, as for the tragedians of any age, drama becomes a vehicle
for measuring the experience of life against the spiritual and material values inherent to their own period. And the greatest artists
inevitably translate the tensions and conflicts of the particular age
into universal terms which engage each generation anew. For

Jacobean tragedy the result is a structural movement away from the heavily internalized protagonists of Elizabethan drama to a focus which, while retaining the central figure whose actions lend coherence to the plot, clearly reveals also the tragic dimensions of the surrounding social corruption and bestiality.

At first glance the dramatic worlds of *Women Beware Women* and *The Changeling* appear to be widely divergent. The one, set in a major Italian city, teems with over a dozen characters representing a broad social spectrum from the ducal family and the aristocracy to the mercantile class and its factors, all of them directly involved in the central intrigues of the play. With no single dominant figure and no character who develops through adversity to a point of significant insight, the perspective is demonstrably broad, focusing on a variety of relationships in order to stress the human chain which contributes to and is affected by the tragedy of an individual. *The Changeling,* on the other hand, employs only eight characters in its principal design. Set in a citadel in a Valencian seaport on the east coast of Spain, the action involves a single aristocratic household and focuses predominantly on Beatrice-Joanna, who through extensive soliloquies and asides, develops a compelling relationship with the spectators as they privately share the decisions on which her fall to lust is predicated and the agony of her moral regeneration moments prior to her death.

Such differences of focus, however, converge on the fundamentally important concept of tragedy. More specifically, Middleton forces the spectators to observe Beatrice-Joanna's experience in the context of a larger vision encompassing the tragedies of De Flores and Diaphanta, both of whom are destroyed by a combination of personal flaw and their manipulation by Beatrice, and she herself is impelled to her disastrous decision by a father's intractable will, just as later she is victimized by the servant De Flores she had previously employed for her own selfish designs.[14] Tragedy in both plays is the consequence of a vicious circle in which individuals abuse each other in the infantile and bestial pursuit of material and emotional satisfaction.

Different in kind from the consciously limited characterization of *Women Beware Women*, Beatrice-Joanna adds a powerful emotional dimension to this tragic design. Like Vittoria Corombona, she is a dynamic tragic figure who, following a series of ambiguous and progressively corrupting decisions, gains a degree of self-knowledge from her suffering and acknowledges the justice of her destruction moments before her death.[15] And quite literally she dominates the spectators' interest, appearing in eight of fourteen scenes and delivering 25 percent of the lines in the play (541 of 2,191). Moreover, Middleton carefully develops her characterization through four distinct phases. At the outset she is an individual who apparently has never had reason publicly to cross her father's will on serious issues, even his current choice of Alonzo de Piracquo as her mate. This ostensible submissiveness, however, belies a headstrong, opportunistic, and egotistical personality unhampered by moral reservation and unhesitating in the manipulation of others to selfish advantage. Ironically, her first words smack of restraint and caution, as she responds to Alsemero's declaration of love:

> Be better advis'd sir:
> Our eyes are sentinels unto our judgments[16]
> . . . .
> But they are rash sometimes, . . . which when our judgments find,
> They can then check the eyes, and call them blind.
> (I, i, 71–72, 74, 75–76)[17]

But within eighteen lines she snaps at her father's servant De Flores, a man whose very presence she loathes and whom she delights in insulting.[18] This strange flash of temper is the prelude to her private admission concerning Alsemero that she "find[s] / A giddy turning in [herself]" (155–56) and that she is not acquiescent to her father's will that she wed Alonzo post haste (220). If Beatrice gains the spectators' sympathy through the heavy-handed "command of parents" (II, ii, 20) that she marry by his arrangement (twice he openly calls Alonzo "son" [II, i, 113], and her delay he envisions as merely an attempt "to reprieve / A maidenhead" [114–15]), they can only be disturbed by her implicit assumption that, since public defiance of her father would endanger her inheritance (II, i, 20–21), her proper course of action is deception. To this end she uses Diaphanta as a messenger to arrange a secret tryst, goads Alsemero into an offer to challenge Piracquo (a plan which she rejects as too dangerous), and then privately manipulates De Flores as her henchman to perform the murder. The lust which motivates De Flores to cater anxiously to her every wish is admittedly deplorable, but it pales by comparison with her crass intention to employ this "ugliest creature / Creation fram'd for some use" (ii,

43–44) as a poison to expel another poison (47), and her subsequent coquetry in touching his face and complimenting him for his improved complexion reveals how flagrantly she can regard a human being as a mere instrument for self-gratification.

From the beginning, then, Beatrice acts individually to satisfy her own passions. Once she has committed De Flores in her behalf, however, she no longer enjoys the luxury of privacy, and in this second stage of development (III—IV) she hardens in duplicity as the concealing of one sin provokes the commission of others. Here, of course, she is guilty of murder and adultery, not coquetry and discourtesy. Her first expression of fear results from De Flores' demand of sexual favor as the reward for his services. To be sure, her shock is genuine when he refuses monetary compensation—the ring from Alonzo's finger worth three thousand ducats, three thousand golden florins, double the sum, whatever sum he would name: "I'm in a labyrinth; / What will content him? . . . I am now in worse plight than I was" (III, iv, 71–72, 75). Significantly, though, she recognizes her own responsibility ("He speaks home. . . . He's bold, and I am blam'd for't" [87, 97]), and, with the servant deaf to her tearful pleas to protect her honor, she acknowledges her guilt and its consequences:

> Oh misery of sin! Would I had been bound
> Perpetually unto my living hate
> In that Piracquo, than to hear these words.
> . . . Vengeance begins.
> Murder I see is followed by more sins.
> (127-29, 163-64)

This situation leads not to repentance, though, but to more extensive and progressively more serious moral compromise. Now her concern is to conceal the loss of her virginity from Alsemero on their wedding night, and to this end she crassly provokes a second loss of honor. Discovering among Alsemero's private possessions a liquid by which to ascertain virginity, she is able to feign the symptoms of honesty when her husband administers the potion. By a similar test she establishes Diaphanta's virginity and then with a thousand ducats ("a by-bet to wedge in that honour" [IV, i, 88]) tempts the maid to sacrifice it as her surrogate on the wedding night. Obviously Beatrice-Joanna at this point has manipulated both De Flores and Diaphanta into deeds which ultimately will destroy them, and obviously also, as her web of deceit grows, the involvement of these two individuals directly increases the probabilities of her own exposure.

The final stages of Beatrice's development occur in Act V. In the first scene she has become a totally adiaphorous creature committed only to self-preservation. She realizes, for example, that Diaphanta knows too much and that there is "No trusting of her life with such a secret" (6). Consequently, when De Flores devises a fire in the maid's room as a convenient means of murder, Beatrice leaps at the suggestion with no moral qualms whatever. Her attitude toward De Flores, moreover, signals her ultimate degradation. The creature whom she abhorred beyond words and abused at every opportunity she now is "forc'd to love" because he "provid'st so carefully for [her] honour" (47–48), which she at this stage envisions purely as a thing of appearance, a matter of public image:

> How rare is that man's speed!
> How heartily he serves me! His face loathes me,
> But look upon his care, who would not love him?
> The east is not more beauteous than his service.
>   (69–72)

This image of honor she inflexibly defends two scenes later in the face of Alsemero's charge that she is a whore and a murderess:

> 'Tis innocence that smiles, and no rough brow
> Can take away the dimple in her cheek.
> . . . .
>   oh, you have ruin'd
> What you can ne'er repair again.
>   (iii, 24–25, 34–35)

Her "spotless virtue," she proclaims, will "tread on" (42) any evidence he can produce.

This façade of courage collapses in her final moments, leading ultimately to an anagnorisis in which Beatrice-Joanna's "moral awareness," as Robert Ornstein (p. 185) prefers, forces her to acknowledge "the consequence of her sin." The initial admission of guilt is to her husband: for his love she has "kiss'd poison [and] strok'd a serpent" (66) and from him she desperately hopes to gain protection from full public exposure. He, however, repudiates "this dangerous bridge of blood" (81); to him the bed is a charnel and the sheets a shroud for murdered carcasses. After her fatal blow

from De Flores, her remorse is without qualification as she gives
full voice to the vileness of her actions. She warns her father to

> come not near me, sir, I shall defile you:
> I am that of your blood was taken from you
> For your better health; look no more upon't,
> But cast it to the ground regardlessly:
> Let the common sewer take it from distinction.
>
> (149–53)

She acknowledges that her honor fell with De Flores and assures
Alsemero she is a stranger to his bed; and with her final breath she
begs forgiveness from all: "'Tis time to die, when 'tis a shame to
live" (179).

Almost Shakespearean in its depth, the characterization of
Beatrice-Joanna provides the full tragic exposure of growth through
error and suffering to ultimate illumination and self-responsibility.
In itself it would provoke a strong emotional identification with the
spectators. At the same time, her pointed comment about defiling
others along with Vermandero's reference to hell's circumscribing
their present situation aims directly at the societal perspective of
this tragedy and the extent to which the destruction and misery
have resulted from the manipulation of others to selfish advantage.
Middleton, in other words, strives simultaneously for engagement
and detachment. The emotional and psychological experience with
Beatrice-Joanna is conditioned by a broad view exploring the interaction of numerous individuals who contribute to the tragedy.

Middleton achieves this detachment through three specific structural devices—numerous soliloquies and asides in characters other
than Beatrice-Joanna, sporadic irony which creates and sustains a
tone of satiric detachment, and a carefully modulated subplot
which treats comically the serious issues faced by the central figure.
The use of private lines is particularly significant. In *Women Beware Women* we have noted that Middleton makes more extensive
use of this device than any preceding playwright, scattering four
hundred forty-five lines, 14 percent of the total in the play, among
ten characters in seventy-three separate passages. The result is to
place the spectators alone in a position to perceive fully the various
strands of action as they share private perceptions with manipulator and victim alike. Since no single character's level of perception
approximates that of the spectators, they are compelled to exercise
judgment predicated on their personal scale of values and their

broad view of the societal forces which comprise the tragedy. Admittedly, no character in *Women Beware Women* is as fully developed as Beatrice-Joanna, and admittedly she herself delivers many private lines—thirty-four asides and seven soliloquies for a total of one hundred eighty-three lines (8 percent). The more significant point, however, is that fully 19 percent of the play is made up of private lines. Nine other characters combine with Beatrice-Joanna to deliver a total of ninety-three passages (De Flores—twenty-three asides and four soliloquies for one hundred twenty-one lines, Alsemero—six asides and six soliloquies for forty-one lines, Tomazo—three soliloquies for thirty-three lines, Jasperino—two asides for twelve lines, Isabella—one soliloquy for six lines, Lollio—two asides and one soliloquy for five lines, the Second Servant—two asides for four lines, Diaphanta—two asides for three lines, and Vermandero—one soliloquy for one line). In effect, Middleton does establish a powerful relationship between the spectators and Beatrice-Joanna, but he places the relationship in a context in which the spectators' perspective is far larger than hers, thereby forcing them to interrelate the various strands of plot to which they alone are privy and limiting the emotional engagement with any single figure. They alone, for example, perceive the anguish in De Flores' compulsive attraction for Beatrice: "I know she hates me, / Yet cannot choose but love her" (I, i, 234–35); he can "as well be hang'd as refrain seeing her" though she "baits [him] still / Every time worse than other" (II, i, 28, 32–33); like the bull at the Beargarden, he breathes but "to be lugg'd again" (81). They alone share his ecstatic joy when she finally deigns civilly to recognize his presence, when she calls him by name and touches his face with her amber-scented hands (II, ii, 70 ff.); thus only they realize how easily he can be manipulated to her devilish purpose. And they alone share with him the momentary fear pursuant to the deed—the grimly disturbing remembrance of murder in the presence of Alonzo's brother (IV, ii, 40–41, 43–44, 56) and his paralytic inability to answer Tomazo's direct challenge: "I cannot strike; I see his brother's wounds / Fresh bleeding in his eye, as in a crystal" (V, ii, 32–33); indeed Beatrice-Joanna sees only the De Flores who defies danger and welcomes death with the boast that he drank the full sweetness of life. This additional dimension of De Flores' sensitivity inevitably colors the spectators' attitude toward the woman who manipulates him without regard to human consequences. The same is true for Tomazo, who privately reveals the effects of grief for his

murdered brother, his loss of the "relish" of life (V, ii, 2) and
renunciation of "All league with mankind" (43). Or compare
Alsemero's initial exaltation in his love for Beatrice (his "joy on
earth" [I, 1]) and his firm assumption of her innocence ("modesty's
shrine is set in yonder forehead" [IV, ii, 125]) with the pathos of
the "sad story" (V, iii, 88) with which their marriage ends.[19] As in
Women Beware Women, then, the spectators share the private experience of tragedy with several characters; while Beatrice-Joanna
commands their major interest, their view transcends her individual
experience and focuses upon the general tragedy of human abuse in
which she is villain as well as protagonist.

A sporadic level of irony through the major plot is a second
means by which Middleton assures the distance vital to this societal
perspective. In I, i, for instance, Alsemero's spiritualized conception of love for Beatrice-Joanna is flanked by two blatantly earthly
concerns—the Second Servant's quips that the delay provides a
measure of physical security ("We must not to sea to-day; this smoke
will bring forth fire. . . . Let him e'en take his leisure too, we are
safer on land" [50, 56]) and Jasperino's determination to seek similar satisfaction—but of a decidedly sexual nature—from the maid
Diaphanta:.

> Methinks I should do something too;
> I meant to be a venturer in this voyage.
> Yonder's another vessel, I'll board her,
> If she be lawful prize, down goes her top-sail.
>   (89–92)

His blunt overtures of affection stand in marked constrast with
those of Alsemero, as he offers the "mad" state of his body to be
cured by Diaphanta. He would "show [her] such a thing with an
ingredient that [they] would compound together" (143–44); Poppy
("a pop i' th' lips") is one simple; cuckoo another. Similarly,
Tomazo's perceptive observations concerning Beatrice's actual feelings for his brother deflate Alonzo's rhapsodic flights. Tomazo sees
"small welcome in her eye" and marks the "dulness of her parting"
(II, i, 106, 124); he would have his brother "Unsettle [his] affection with all speed" since it is likely that Beatrice's "heart is leap'd
into another's bosom" (129, 132). In IV, i, Beatrice's deadly earnest
stratagem of placing the virgin Diaphanta in Alsemero's bed on their
wedding night is virtually mocked by the maid's prurient anticipation of bodily pleasure. Envying Beatrice's reasons for looking upon

Alsemero on this day and "the first night's pleasure," she readily
agrees to carry her mistress' load on this occasion because she
"love[s] the burthen," and she promises to "be cool" by midnight
so that Beatrice may exchange places with her (57, 86, 122, 125).
One final example, in the fifth act De Flores speaks of the devil's
itch in Diaphanta when she fails to come from the bed on schedule.
Finally roused, she apologizes for being "so well" that she forgot
herself; "I never made / So sweet a bargain" (i, 78, 80–81). And
surely during the fire there is grotesque humor for the spectators
in Vermandero's reference to Diaphanta as a sleepy slut and in De
Flores' lamentation over the "poor virginity" that perished in the
blaze (103, 104). So also scene iii provides another touch of the
ironically macabre in Vermandero's confronting Alsemero with the
smug assurance that in Franciscus and Antonio he has apprehended
Alonzo's murderers, in Tomazo's obvious lust for blood revenge
against them, and in Alsemero's efforts to explain his solution to
the crime; this action takes place, of course, directly in front of
the closet in which Beatrice-Joanna and De Flores are enclosed (as
Dorothy Kehler would have it, engaged in their final sexual act)[20]
and from which Beatrice's scream finally jolts them into a stunned
silence. Quite consciously, then, throughout the play Middleton
has forced comedy to serve the purposes of tragedy, using it to
prevent the myopic vision which close emotional identification
would produce.

Certainly the most significant utilization of comedy to reinforce
the broad perspective of societal tragedy is the extensive double
plot. A *cause célèbre* among the critics of the tragedy, the subplot
—once rejected as silly and nauseating—is now generally considered
an artistic fusion "invit[ing] the audience to be sensitive to *double-
entendre*" (Williams, p. xv). Both views are extensively documented
by Holzknecht (p. 264) and, more recently, by Richard Levin, who
describes the subplot as "a negative analogy built on direct moral
contrast."[21] Like the Ward-Isabella plot in *Women Beware Women*
this material—comprising fully one-third of the text—in realistic
fashion provides an overtly comic parallel to the major action. The
persistently rutty language, for example, graphically sets forth the
theme of lurid sexual attraction and characters run mad with passion which the tragic plot treats with high seriousness. Alibius fears
that, if he is careless of his ring (his wife), "one or other will be
thrusting into't" (I, ii, 30–31); she is kept in the "pinfold" of the
madhouse because she "might be pounded in another place" (III,

iii, 10). Franciscus in song begs leave to lie with his love while "love creeps in at a mousehold" (90, 94). Similarly, Antonio brings to Isabella "shafts to strike you with" (130); and Lollio, who would lay his hand on what pleases men (237), asserts that Antonio will "put her down" (211). If Antonio can eliminate his rival, Lollio promises that the "fool shall ride her" (IV, iii, 151).

Admittedly, one can push precise parallels too far—the madhouse and the society of Alicant, Alibius' control and Vermandero's governorship, the old man's confinement of his young wife and Vermandero's heavy-handed parental influence in the choice of Beatrice's mate, the rival wooers Antonio and Franciscus and the rival wooers Alonzo and Alsemero, Lollio's observing Isabella's presumed tryst and assuming he can also enjoy her intimacy once she has transgressed and De Flores' similar assumption while observing Beatrice-Joanna's private meeting with Alsemero, Antonio's belief that he can enjoy Isabella's favor if he will get rid of the rival Franciscus and De Flores' similar belief concerning Beatrice-Joanna if he will eliminate Alonzo. Nevertheless, if overprecision may distort, the general similarity is unmistakable; and it is inconceivable—whatever the exact nature of the collaborative authorship —that these three scenes were not intended to form a comically phantasmagoric reflection of the major action. Isabella, though the victim of a January-May marriage, withstands temptation, of course, and for the secondary plot a comic ending is possible. Beatrice-Joanna, on the other hand, destroys two men and taints an entire society in her willful pursuit of self-satisfaction. The two plots run separately throughout the play, but the projected point of connection is grimly and symbolically appropriate—a dance of madmen at nuptial festivities in which the groom has been replaced with inordinate haste and the original has mysteriously disappeared amid strong suspicions of murder. One must indeed question where true sanity lies.

Middleton, in a word, has structured his play in such a manner as to prevent the preoccupation with a single figure which close emotional identification would provoke; at the same time he has delineated a full and compelling tragic experience in Beatrice-Joanna. In effect, he has placed an Elizabethan tragic figure who assumes that life accommodates the determinations of the dominant will which sets its own standards of conduct in a Jacobean tragic world which emphasizes the inseparability of the principal from his society and the manner in which various surrounding figures both contribute

to and suffer from the consequences of the individual's decisions
and actions. We have noted earlier that man's philosophic views in
the early seventeenth century wavered between faith in a metaphysical absolute which placed a premium on individual accountability
to a spiritual code of conduct and a secular humanism which—by
suggesting some lesser standard—conceptualized man, with all his
contrarieties, as his own measure. While Marlowe, Chapman, and
the early Shakespeare emphasize the titanic protagonist who defies
a higher law but ultimately grows to reconciliation with a cosmic
principle of order, the most powerful Jacobean playwrights in
various ways register a fundamental ambiguity in the tragic cata-
strophe itself.

Middleton's particular method is to create, through the extensively scattered soliloquies and asides described earlier, such a large gap
between the spectators' view and that of any single figure that the
moral basis for resolution in one instance does not accommodate
the dilemma of another. As a consequence the spectators themselves must define the ethical parameters which govern the stage
world and which determine the consequences of their action.[22] In
Women Beware Women, to repeat, the pattern is relatively simple.
No character directly involved in the action is brought through
suffering and adversity to any kind of tragic illumination or
anagnorisis; Leantio, Brancha, Isabella, the Duke, Livia, the Ward—
each pursues his personal pleasures with an amazing disregard for
genuine standards of conduct. The Cardinal in the final act emerges
as a spokesman for conventional morality, but his perception and
judgment are limited to the Duke's lechery and thus cannot effectively establish a moral basis for the full resolution of the action.
At the same time, the spectators, sharing private lines of action
with each of the affected characters, are forced to perceive an inexorable force at work which methodically destroys these characters
through their own vices. The net result is that a rigid moral standard
does indeed operate in the world of *Women Beware Women;* but,
since it is fully visible only to the spectators and since it seems so
markedly absent as a motivational force among the characters who
comprise the fictional world, the spectators can only be genuinely
disturbed by the extent of the corruption and decadence which have
transformed society into a bestial jungle largely oblivious of the
moral ramification of its actions.

The pattern of *The Changeling* is more complex. In the first
place there is, as we have discussed, a genuine anagnorisis in the

principal figure; and, with Beatrice-Joanna's acknowledgment of a power of retributive justice, the moral standard would appear to be self-evident. Certainly, this assumption is supported by the specifically Christian imagery of the play (in the first scene alone, for instance, "temple," "holy," "first creation," "blest," "church," "God's," "prayers," "orisons," "devotion," "saint," "Saint Jacques," "soul," and "serpent") and by the use of Alonzo's ghost which, though the device is never fully developed, briefly confronts both De Flores (Dumb Show, Act IV) and Beatrice-Joanna (V, i, 61) as a visual reminder of their sinful deeds.

Again, however, the spectators have shared private perceptions with other individuals for whom the moral standard is inapplicable or inappropriate. Isabella, for example, is dismissed to a continuing marriage with an older man who, insanely jealous, virtually prohibits her access to normal society; Alibius, presumably totally unaware of the designs upon his wife until the final moments, bumbles badly in an unconvincing assertion that he "will change now / Into a better husband" (V, iii, 213–14); Franciscus and Antonio apparently suffer little more than embarrassment for their adulterous designs; nowhere does the tragedy require Tomazo to consider the moral implications of his determination to gain blood revenge or Vermandero to consider the dangerously restrictive policy concerning his daughter's marital choice. In a word, those who "stare at the dead criminals" simply cannot be dismissed as "shallow innocents . . . incapable of deep emotion" (Ornstein, p. 189). Nor is it a matter of loose ends of the plot which are never completely tied together; in fact, as elements of plot, they probably would never give the spectators a second thought. What is disturbing is that several of these characters engage the spectators emotionally through soliloquies and asides; they are involved in the tragedy—in some instances they are contributing factors to it—and their failure to come to grips morally with their particular issues undermines confidence in the universal validity of the teleological design which Beatrice-Joanna espouses. In the final analysis the problem is essentially the same as that involving the Cardinal as spokesman for the moral structure of *Women Beware Women*. Middleton has provided the spectators a larger and more comprehensive view of the tragedy than that of the principal; and, while her tragic situation is resolved on moral grounds, the fact that significant figures are required neither to answer morally to their decisions and actions nor directly pay the consequences impresses once more upon the spectators a deep sense of the corruption of human society and of the ethical ambiguities intrinsic to human interactions.

In one particular aspect the conclusion of *The Changeling* anticipates a structural device which John Ford is to utilize with signal effectiveness to register this profound ambivalence—the double anagnorisis. In both Annabella and Giovanni in *'Tis Pity She's a Whore* and Ithocles and Orgilus in *The Broken Heart* diametrically opposing philosophies emerge from the tragic experience, one based on the recognition and acceptance of traditional moral values, the other based on a private code which repudiates all external values as corrupt and hypocritical. Certainly, it would be an overstatement to speak of an anagnorisis in De Flores, just as it would be a mistake to suggest that the action of his final moments is of a dramatic interest and power equal to that of Beatrice-Joanna; nor for that matter does he specifically condemn conventional values or draw a comparison with his own private values. The pattern, nevertheless, is there. On two previous occasions he has evinced at least a degree of moral sensitivity. But here, at the exact moment that Beatrice-Joanna experiences a moral rejuvenation, he in the face of death asserts the defiance of a life which has realized the full measure of sensual ecstasy. Indeed, his final words are addressed only to her, and his only moral reference is in the metaphor of a game as he boasts of coupling with her in "hell" (the center position) at barley-brake.[23] With calm assurance he asserts that he earned Beatrice's love through Alonzo's murder and that he loved her "in spite of her heart"; her "honour's prize / Was [his] reward" (V, iii, 165, 167-68). And he most explicitly offers no regrets and no fear of judgment to come:

> I thank life for nothing
> But that pleasure: it was so sweet to me
> That I have drunk up all, left none behind
> For any man to pledge me.
>
> (168-71)

His only final concern is that Beatrice-Joanna, whom he has fatally stabbed, should hasten to meet him in death: "Make haste, Joanna, by that token to thee; . . . / I would not go to leave thee far behind" (175, 177). De Flores' Hobbesian philosophy is not fully developed —that is, it does not come as the anticipated action of a consistently presented characterization. Clearly, however, instead of reinforcing

Beatrice-Joanna's final moments, it stands in direct contradiction and contributes directly to the complex design. Middleton's structure thus provides a firm teleological basis for the tragic experience of the principal and yet also reflects the amorality and hedonism of a world in which, like the madmen, each individual follows his own bent and makes his own rules—and society, with no center of values acknowledged and accepted by all, lacks the cohesion and self-responsibility which constitute a form of sanity. Perhaps most importantly, by dramatically increasing the number of individuals who communicate privately with the spectators, Middleton has captured amidst his broad scene of societal corruption and tragedy the sheer loneliness and isolation of its victims. In a world in which human depravity sets its own rules of conduct, the individual is ultimately a stranger and genuine love and friendship are virtual impossibilities.

VII. Ford

—'TIS PITY SHE'S A WHORE, THE BROKEN HEART

John Ford, who had a hand in some eighteen plays between 1621 and 1638, was probably well into his forties before he composed any of his eight unaided plays. He was only twenty-one or twenty-two when Shakespeare wrote his final tragedies; and, indeed it is unlikely that Ford ever met Shakespeare, Tourneur, or Webster. An equally wide gap appears in the tastes of the theatrical clientele, by 1633 predominantly aristocratic and catering to private or court performance. By Harbage's count tragicomedies begin to outnumber tragedies considerably during the two decades between *The Duchess of Malfi* and Ford's major pieces. In a sense the increasingly isolated audience became addicted to sensationalism, easy reconciliation, and the exploitation of intellectual and moral fashion which in effect functioned as self-gratification. Ford himself has not infrequently been identified with such dramatic narcissism. By artistic inclination, however, in his three extant tragedies—presumably all composed within a four-year period (1629–32), he is firmly in the tradition of the Elizabethan and Jacobean playwrights whose tragedies were vehicles for genuine explorations of the relationship between human suffering and the actions which provoke it and whose vision came increasingly to focus on the social malaise not only as a reflection of the crisis of values peculiar to the age but also universally as a principal contributing factor to the tragedy of the individual.

Love's Sacrifice requires only brief notice. A rather confused and muddled play, it deals with the conflicting demands of passion and honor, and like *'Tis Pity She's a Whore* and *The Broken Heart* it raises fundamental questions concerning the assignment of guilt in a complex affair of the heart. Bianca, wedded unhappily to an old and somewhat effeminate aristocrat, finds true love in a gallant courtier Fernando. While the relationship between the two young lovers is chaste, the Duke suspects his wife, surprises them together, and kills her without permitting an explanation. Fernando subsequently hides within her vault and poisons himself when threatened by the Duke, who in turn kills himself in a fit of remorse for the destruction of two innocent lives. While the Duke experiences the spiritual anguish concomitant with the recognition and acknowledgment of a transcendent moral presence, Fernando, who like Giovanni sacrifices himself to the honor of love—albeit unconsummated—clearly postulates a private code as man's highest value, and it is he who provokes the greater degree of sympathy from the spectators. The action admittedly is fantastic and ultimately unconvincing, and a grotesque subplot in which Ferentes seduces three ladies and in turn is killed by them in a court entertainment only compounds the objections. *Love's Sacrifice,* however, does establish both a theme and a structure which is effectively explored in Ford's more powerful tragedies.

One such piece is *'Tis Pity She's a Whore,* and it is a grim commentary on the society of this stage world that the most flagrant criminal escapes with his life and the relatively mild decree of banishment from what is not even his native land while eight characters reflecting various lesser degrees of involvement and guilt lie dead. This is but the final irony, however, in the pervasive moral ambivalence which Ford has so meticulously built into his plot. Clearly, the protagonists' incestuous love is sinful and fundamentally repellent; yet this relationship is set in the context of a decadent society in which each individual is a law unto himself, pursuing his own interests at whatever cost to those around him.

'Tis Pity She's a Whore, like several of the plays we have examined, is a tragedy of a whole society as much as it is the tragedy of an individual. The causes of the disaster exist not in the isolation of an individual flaw but as a combination of destructive forces from within and from without. The emotional focus is indeed upon Giovanni and Annabella; but their affection, if unrighteous, is also intensely sincere, and the spectators are constantly required to weigh that sincere immorality against the lust, avarice, treachery, vindictiveness, and hypocrisy of the society whose morality the lovers have rejected. The carefully contrived world of the play, as R. J. Kaufmann has remarked, "is made to act (in its negation of beauty) as a foil to the desperate choices of Giovanni and his sister."[1] The moral norms, then, exist outside this stage world—in the minds of the spectators who can never fully embrace the lovers but certainly find no point of emotional reference in the society which has produced them. The result is a

sustained ambivalence forcing the spectators simultaneously to sympathize vicariously with the lovers and to sit in judgment on their actions. The present purpose is to examine the peculiar subtleties of this perspective and the major structural features by which Ford controls the audience's response, both emotionally and intellectually.

Such double vision is in itself nothing new to Elizabethan drama, and, as we approach the culmination of the dramaturgical movement in Jacobean-Caroline tragedy, it may well be beneficial to review briefly the essential thrust of this development. The Elizabethan protagonists Hieronimo and Edward II, for example, are characters who provoke pity and disdain from the spectators, even though the tension is not sustained. Similarly, Tamburlaine emerges as a character who possesses in combination the cruelty and the rapaciousness of a barbarian and the regality and magnetism of a prince; Faustus, through the soliloquies reflecting the protagonist's inner tension, is a brilliant illustration of fallible mortality torn by immortal ambitions. And, as A. P. Rossiter and Norman Rabkin, among others, have described, one of Shakespeare's central concerns in tragedy is to provoke the spectators to a sympathetic collaboration of mind with the protagonist while at the same time creating a more expansive vision through which they observe the character, moving against the larger backdrop of the effects of his decisions and actions upon the surrounding characters, and his inevitable conflict with and destruction by the powers which control the stage universe. The spectators attain a "privileged" vision[2] which Edmond Cherbonnier has termed the "ultimate perspective of the detached observer" set against the "finite perspective of the man in action."[3]

Narrative and philosophic coherence is achieved in such tragedies through the experience of the protagonist and, most importantly, the manner in which he accommodates himself—or fails to accommodate himself—to the ambivalent value structure within which his decisions must be made. Hamlet's accommodation to God's will, while it does not remove either the ghost's ambiguities or his responsibility for earlier crimes, does produce a clarity of direction and a sense of purpose which give meaning to his life. Similarly, while Lear's final moments do not minimize the daughters' cruelty or his own petty egotism, they do reflect one man's ability to rediscover the value of human affection in a society whose very axis is compounded of hatred and violence. In Webster's *The White*

Devil, Vittoria's courage and recognition of guilt—though irre-
deemably stained by her own passion and egocentricity—provide a
plausible conception of the animalistic barbarity in which she herself has participated and to which she ultimately falls victim. The
tragedies are subject, of course, to shades of interpretation, but the
significant point is that the anagnorisis furnishes the teleology. The
insights achieved by the protagonist or the conclusions that he
draws upon his existence in such a stage world provide a meaningful frame of reference for what has happened to him by imposing
a human logic upon the sequence of events which have comprised
his tragedy. It is as if for one brief moment, in the most powerful
dramas, the central figure achieves a vision comparable to that of
the spectators; obviously, he is not privy to all the events through
which the playwright has constructed the spectators' double vision,
but his judgments are supported by their more expansive perspective. And for a brief space he, like them, can simultaneously condemn and lament his actions.

Ford's most crucial structural modification occurs in this
anagnorisis. Both in *'Tis Pity She's a Whore* and *The Broken Heart*
he refuses to provide a culminating experience through which to
lend single moral and emotional perspective to the tragic events.
The anagnorisis as well as the protagonist is doubled in each
instance, and the insights achieved by the two characters are flatly
contradictory. Thus ambivalence emerges as the central thrust of
'Tis Pity as both Annabella, with her Christian repentance, and
Giovanni, with his stoic insistence on the sanctity of his private
values, provide apparent resolutions to the tragic dilemma. The
spectator is left to choose for himself between the wisdom of passive endurance and the attraction of egocentric defiance of external values.[4] The metaphysics of the stage world neither exclusively
repudiates the one nor supports the other.

Annabella's anagnorisis builds in three increasingly powerful
waves. Actually, in III, vi, she speaks only thirty-one words to
Bonaventura's three hundred sixty-nine, but the scene establishes
the framework for repentance. The friar approvingly notes her
tears as he graphically describes the horrors and tortures of hell
which await the guilty. In this "black and hollow vault," where
"dwell many thousand thousand sundry sorts / Of never-dying
deaths," shines only the "flaming horror of consuming fires" (i,
14–15, 11).[5] Each individual is punished according to his particular sin, the glutton fed with toads and adders, the drunkard's

throat scalded with burning oil, the murderer stabbed repeatedly;
the wanton lies "on racks of burning steel, whiles in his soul / He
feels the torment of his raging lust" (22–23). Annabella, terrified,
pleads for counsel by which she might "redeem [her] miseries" (33)
and vows henceforth to spurn "the baits of sin" (39). Her remaining appearances in effect confirm both her contrition and her
pledge. When Soranzo, discovering her pregnancy, brands her
"strumpet," "whore," and "quean" (IV, iii, 1, 25), she does not
deny the charges (although she defies his fury by refusing to name
her lover).[6] More pertinent, to Soranzo's feigned anguish that the
treasure of his heart has been mocked by her "lewd womb" (114),
she responds that such words "wound deeper than [his] sword
could do" (130) and would "on [her] knees" (142) beg his forgiveness. Her full repentance is articulated in soliloquy in the final act.
She repudiates the "false joys" for which "conscience now stands
up against [her] lust / With depositions character'd in guilt" (i, 1, 2,
9–10). She would now accept total guilt for the "black offense"
(21), if by doing so Giovanni might escape "the torment of an uncontrolled flame" (23). In such a spirit she sends a message to her
brother acknowledging her transformation and admonishing him
to repent. Herself resolved to death, she also cautions him not to
believe Soranzo's friendship. Similarly, in her last moments she
urges him not to waste "precious hours in vain and useless speech"
(V, v, 19), but prepare himself for death by acknowledging
heaven's laws. And her greatest expression of love is with her final
breath to forgive Giovanni for her murder and to beg heaven's
mercy. Admittedly, Annabella's position is undercut to some
degree by the fact that the friar's counsel has involved concealing
her pregnancy through a marriage of convenience and by the generally disreputable nature of the Cardinal's actions in the name of
the Church. Nevertheless, her renunciation of the incestuous relationship casts a more opprobrious light upon Soranzo's brutality
and his intended vengeance, and, in general, her experience suggests a resolution to the tragic dilemma through Christian repentance and submission to God's will.

Giovanni, by comparison, blatantly rejects such a notion. Following Annabella's marriage to Soranzo, he comments privately that
he "would dare confusion, / And stand the horror of ten thousand
deaths" (IV, i, 17–18) before he would again permit such a ceremony. His clear defiance of Christian morality is voiced in soliloquy
in V, iii. The "glory / Of two united hearts like hers and mine" (11–

12) makes a mockery of those who dream of happiness in some
other world. Moments later he asserts to Bonaventura that hell is
"naught else / But slavish and fond superstitious fear" (19–20); the
friar's moral strictures are "religion-masked sorceries" (29), an
"old prescription" (75) which would bar him both from the ecstasy
of love's consummation and the glory of courageous death in defense of his passion.[7] Convinced that the intensity of their love
belies the obloquy of a corrupt society, he describes Annabella as
one "white in . . . soul" who is fit "to fill a throne / Of innocence
and sanctity" (V, v, 64–65). Just as the necessity of living a lie
compromises Annabella's Christian posture, so Giovanni's subsequent grisly acts of passion subvert his proclamation of the
inviolability of private values. His conception of her honor is more
significant than her life; hence, stabbing her to death, he proclaims
he has saved her fame:

> Revenge is mine; honor doth love command. . . .
> How over-glorious art thou in thy wounds,
> Triumphing over infamy and hate!
> (86, 103–104)

It remains now only for him defiantly to face Soranzo, with Annabella's heart upon his dagger,[8] to affirm publicly his undying love
for his sister, and to claim "brave revenge" as he fatally stabs
Soranzo before falling—unrepentant—at the hands of the banditti.
During the last scenes Giovanni falls prey to hubris, to be sure, in
his assumption that man is the final measure of things and in his
crass disregard for human life. But to brand him a "maniacal villain,"[9] a "grotesque and almost ludicrous figure"[10] incapable of
eliciting sympathy is to disregard completely the context in which
his actions occur. The assumption that at his death he is the only
"wonderful and terrible" figure on stage, surmounting his ruin by
despising it,[11] may also be extreme. But a comment by Juliet
McMaster bears remembering: "Central figures in any work of the
imagination, if their motivation is fully and adequately worked,
will always capture our sympathy, whether or not they have our
moral approval."[12]

In truth the spectators at the conclusion of the tragedy have no
viable point of emotional reference. Certainly, their fundamental
association has been with the protagonists, and just as certainly
both Annabella's Christian repentance and Giovanni's egocentric

code are possible reflections of human wisdom gained through
agony and pain. The spectator may well feel that, in comparison
with Giovanni's passion and defiance, Annabella's repentance
seems valid and warranted; but, given the context of Giovanni's
love, his actions are not without appeal. In a word, the flat contradiction of their responses prevents the spectators from fully accepting the position of either as exclusive philosophic justification
for the spectacle of suffering. This condition, clearly, is the result
not of the accident of Ford's moral chaos but of sheer design. Indeed, the value structure of Ford's stage world is not unformed
and unorganized; it is instead ambivalent from beginning to end
as a result of two clearly defined theories of human conduct, both
of which in part impose logical coherence upon existence in such
a society.

   This ambivalence is central to the drama from the opening
scenes. On the one hand the conventional moral attitude toward
incest is voiced sharply by Friar Bonaventura, who flatly condemns
such a relationship as an abomination to God and man. On the
other, in both soliloquy and dialogue, the lovers speak with a passion not without appeal in its intensity and its ostensible sincerity.
The result is an immediate blurring of the ethical polarities of the
stage world and consequently a division of sympathy within the
spectators.

   Certainly, Ford minces no words in establishing the central love
affair as sinful. Giovanni confidentially has described his agony to
Bonaventura, daring even to defend the morality of his secret
passion. The Friar peremptorily informs him that "Heaven admits
no jest" (I, i, 4) on this issue. Such a "lust" (59) is "the nearest
way to hell" (7), demanding:

> Repentance, son, and sorrow. . . .
> For thou hast mov'd a Majesty above,
> With thy unranged-almost blasphemy.
>   (43–45)

He should "fall down / On both [his] knees, and grovel on the
ground"; his words must be washed in tears as he begs Heaven "to
cleanse the leprosy of lust / That rots [his] soul" (70–71, 74–75).
Bonaventura appears in six additional scenes, in every act reiterating his condemnation of this sinful love. Indeed, with no active
role in the plot except that of a messenger in the final act, he exists
primarily to give voice to what the spectators would certainly per-

ceive as a reflection and reinforcement of traditional social and religious values. In II, v, more specifically, learning that the physical union has been consummated, he avers that "Heaven is angry" (9). Giovanni's action "threatens eternal slaughter to the soul" (2); he is "too far sold to hell, / It lies not in the compass of [Bonaventura's] prayers / To call [him] back" (37–39). If the passionate lovers do not through shriving admit that the "throne of mercy is above [their] trespass" (64), a "pair of souls" are doomed to "a second death" (69, 61). Called to Annabella's bed in III, iv, for "ghostly comfort" (29), he is delighted to find her receptive to his counsel as he describes at length the grotesque abode which awaits those engaged in "lawless sheets" and "secret incests" (25–26). When Hippolita appears at the wedding of Annabella and Soranzo with her vicious curses, Bonaventura seizes the opportunity to warn Giovanni in aside to "take heed" (IV, i, 109) lest these events portend a disastrous marriage. Finally in V, iii, he again denounces the "conscience . . . seared" (30) Giovanni blind to both spiritual and physical danger. Reminiscent of the Old Man departing from Faustus,[13] he withdraws from the lover who again repudiates his spiritual counsel: "since no prayer / Can make thee safe, I leave thee to despair" (70).

From first to last, then, this love affair is branded as abominably sinful and spiritually destructive by one who, despite the occasional equivocation of his position,[14] basically strikes the pose of normality and objectivity. At the same time Ford is careful not to provoke the spectators' total condemnation. Certainly, for one thing, it speaks well for Giovanni that, like Romeo, he has turned to his spiritual counselor for advice before acting. For another, he readily accepts Bonaventura's suggestion that he acknowledge his need of God and for seven days pray earnestly that the temptation be removed: "All this I'll do, to free me from the rod / Of vengeance" (I, i, 83–84). Moreover, Giovanni and Annabella are humanized through the devices of internalization. Nine characters at one point or another speak in soliloquy or aside, but the lines for the most part serve expositional or rhetorical ends. Hippolita, Grimaldi, and Richardetto, for example, delight in privately informing the audience of the nature of their intended revenge on Soranzo (III, v, 1–7; II, ii, 121, 159–60; II, iii, 62–63). Similarly, a well-placed aside by Poggio emphasizes the buffoonish qualities of Bergetto (I, ii, 115–16) just as Vasques' remark underscores Soranzo's brutal disdain for Hippolita once he has had his will with her (II, ii, 100).

Only the two principals, by contrast, are dynamic or developing
characters. Delivering more than 62 percent of the soliloquies and
asides (Giovanni 109 lines, 45.4 percent; Annabella 30 lines, 17.3
percent), they provoke the spectators to share the spiritual turmoil
attendant upon decisions in which emotions and logic fail to
cohere. Giovanni, for instance, in I, iii, voices his agony concerning
his love for his sister. He all too clearly realizes that such passion
presages his ruin, but he can find no adequate "judgment or endeavors [to] . . . apply / To [his] incurable and restless wounds" (I, ii,
142–43). The greater he strives, the more he loves and the less he
hopes. He has "wearied Heaven with prayers, dried up / The spring
of [his] continual tears, even starv'd / [His] veins with daily fasts"
(147–49). In short, his efforts to purge his soul are painfully
deliberate, and he asserts that the persistence of his affection affirms
love rather than lust; thus, he mournfully concludes, his fate—not
his act of free will—has "doom'd [his] death" (139). Albeit logi-
cally specious, the argument is emotionally appealing as a forthright
expression of human agony free from the guilt-ridden public posture
of either defensiveness or secrecy.[15] Similarly, in V, iii, he laments
that his love for Annabella has not waned, as he had hoped, with
her contract to Soranzo: "I find no change. . . . She is still one to
me, and every kiss / As sweet and as delicious as the first" (6, 8–9).

All told, the principals deliver thirteen soliloquies and asides, and
their divided response to their passion is central to these moments
of private introspection. They must readily admit, as Giovanni
remarks to Annabella in V, v, that the "laws of conscience and of
civil use / May justly blame us" (70–71); at the same time they
would desperately assert that, were it but possible for others to
"know / Our loves, that love [would] wipe away that rigor / Which
. . . in other incests [is] abhorr'd" (71–73). It is interesting in this
respect that, despite Friar Bonaventura's counsel and specific
condemnation, Giovanni rarely describes his love in Christian context. He defends the virtues of their love, for instance, on the
Platonic principle that outward appearance reflects the spiritual
essence:

> So where the body's furniture is beauty,
> The mind's must needs be virtue; which allowed,
> Virtue itself is reason but refin'd,
> And love the quintessence of that. This proves
> My sister's beauty being rarely fair
> Is rarely virtuous; chiefly in her love,

> And chiefly in that love, her love to me.
> If hers to me, then so is mine to her;
> Since in like causes are effects alike.
>   (II, v, 18–26)

His love is so beautiful that the "gods" themselves would "kneel" to her as he does to "them" (I, i, 21, 23). Annabella's fair forehead exceeds that of Juno (I, ii, 187); her eyes shine "like Promethean fire" (191). As they kneel ritualistically and pledge their mutual love, Giovanni "would not change this moment for Elysium" (260; see also V, iii, 16). He sucks "divine ambrosia from her lips" as did Jove from Leda (II, i, 17).

The mythological imagery provides Giovanni a means of drawing Annabella's beauty and their mutual passion larger than life. Equally important, the celestial comparisons evoke responses in the spectators free from the moral attitudes associated with Christianity. Juxtaposed to the Friar's consistent view of incest in relation to God, sin, lust, destruction, the pagan imagery mirrors in little the clashing values central to this tragedy. A second significant strand which lends a degree of sympathy by reflecting the intensity of their affection is the cosmological imagery. Giovanni's unrequited love for his sister in Act I has "untun'd / All harmony both of [his] rest and life" (I, ii, 213–14); conversely, when she later has returned his affection, her voice resembles the music of the spheres (II, vi, 55–56). Her love empowers him to "command the course / Of time's eternal motion" (V, v, 12–13); lest they can embrace, time itself will "be struck quite out of number" (II, v, 66). Annabella is "a world of variety" (50), and in her love Giovanni "env[ies] not the mightiest men alive / But hold[s himself] in being king of [her] / More great than were [he] king of all the world" (II, i, 18–20).

By thus establishing a framework which Clifford Leech has described as a battleground for "ever-resurgent skepticism" and "an inherited scheme of values,"[16] Ford forces the spectators simultaneously to condemnation of and sympathy with the incestuous lovers. And there are yet additional structural devices which preclude a simplistic distinction in values. Giovanni's love is set in a context of rival wooers, each of whom in his own way is more despicable than Giovanni. Thus the viewers are barred from an easy transfer of sympathy away from Giovanni, and their condemnation of the aberrational passion is mitigated further. More specifically, inserted between Giovanni's declaration to Friar

Bonaventura in scene i of his love for Annabella and the siblings' ritualistic betrothal late in scene ii, Grimaldi, Soranzo, and Bergetto assert their interest in "Senor Florio's daughter." Grimaldi, first seen bested in a petty quarrel and sword fight with Vasques (I, ii, 19), is a vindictive and cowardly creature. From the tactics of spiteful tale-telling against his rival in love, Soranzo, he turns to a physician's potion to "move [her] affection" for him (II, iii, 41), then gleefully settles for a deadly poison with which to anoint his rapier's point and dispatch Soranzo. Admitting that the act is "unnoble" and not "becom[ing] / A soldier's valor" (III, v, 3–4), he brazenly asserts that "in terms of love, / Where merit cannot sway, policy must" (4–5). His "policy" is to lie in wait in a dark lane, to strike from the darkness the wrong man, and then to run to his friend, the Cardinal, and beg "his Holiness' protection" (III, ix, 54). Bergetto, Grimaldi's unintentional victim, is too stupid to develop into much more than a buffoon. Described as a cipher "to fill up the number," an "idiot" (I, ii, 101, 117), and a "dunce" (I, iii, 24), he proclaims fatuously that he "shall have the wench. . . . I will but wash my face, and shift socks, and then have at her, i'faith" (I, ii, 112–14). His best efforts in wooing involve his swearing that he loves her almost as much as he loves Parmesan (I, iii, 58) and assuring her that he will inherit a goodly fortune (70). In writing he commends his "best parts" to her and observes that he "will marry [her], in spite of [her] teeth" (II, iv, 26, 25). "Stuff indeed to shame us all," as his uncle observes, he is little more than "apish running to motions and fopperies" (29, 40–41). To his credit, the fop at least is incapable of hypocrisy, and the spectators are hardly surprised that, shortly before his death, he turns his affection to Philotis, who befriended him when a "swaggering fellow . . . maul[ed him] with the hilts of his rapier" (II, vi, 69–70, 73–74).

Soranzo is quite a different matter. Both his virtues and his vices are revealed more slowly as he becomes Giovanni's primary dramatic foil. At the outset he is quite obviously the favored suitor. Florio assures him that he need not be concerned with Grimaldi: "Why [should you] storm, having my word engag'd; / Owing her heart, what need you doubt her ear?" (I, ii, 54–55). "Wise," "rich," "kind," "a nobleman," "bountiful," "handsome," "wholesome," "liberal," and "loving," this "gallant of three and twenty" is one, according to Putana, whom Annabella should "wish and pray for" (86 *passim*). Only a fleeting reference to an

affair "with Hippolita, the lusty widow, in her husband's lifetime"
(93-94) mars our introduction to this masculine paragon. Four
scenes later he is in training for love, reciting Sannazzaro's sonnets
and chiding the poet for complaining of love's discomfort; "Had
Annabella liv'd when Sannazar," he would have written only of
her and her divine cheeks (II, ii, 12-13). The first insight into his
true nature comes with Hippolita's bursting in upon this reverie.
The accusations that he has wooed her into sin with pleas and
oaths, vowing to marry her when her husband died, are the more
shocking through juxtaposition with the posture of innocence and
purity in his poetic meditations. And his response is hardly convincing as he avers that he "cannot mask [his] penitence" (87):

> The vows I made, if you remember well,
> Were wicked and unlawful; 'Twere more sin
> To keep them than to break them. . . .
> Learn to repent and die, for by my honor
> I hate thee and thy lust: you have been too foul.
>
> (84-86, 98-99)

Even his servant Vasques acknowledges in aside that Soranzo has
played a scurvy role (100).

Not privy to this information, Florio on three subsequent occasions reaffirms his choice of Soranzo (II, vi, 123; III, ii, 4; III, iv,
15). The gallant, meanwhile, concerns himself no further with his
earlier assignation, glibly vowing that he has loved Annabella long
and truly (III, ii, 31) and thanking "the hand of goodness" for
enriching his "life / With this most precious jewel" (IV, i, 7, 9-10).
With the words scarcely out of his mouth, Hippolita appears again—
among a group of maskers—to denounce the nuptials. Again
Soranzo refuses to acknowledge his earlier affair, and he displays
crass unconcern as she dies of poison before his eyes. His cruelest
moment, to be sure, is his subsequent mistreatment of Annabella
when he discovers her pregnancy. Branding her "strumpet,"
"whore," "harlot," and "quean" (IV, iii, 1, 4, 25), he drags her by
the hair and shakes her mercilessly while threatening to hew her
flesh to shreds and rip out her heart (53, 58). That the discovery
of his wife's infidelity provokes him to rage is not in itself surprising; the spectators, however, can hardly miss the grim irony in the
parallels with his own earlier relationship and his assumptions that
he bears no responsibility and no guilt for his previous sexual actions. Certainly, despite the general physical revulsion against an

incestuous relationship, the spectators are hard pressed to feel any preference for this hypocritical and brutal legitimate husband.

The choice is all the more difficult because the plot strand of the rival wooers unfolds the squalid and vicious qualities which permeate human society. No fewer than three occasions, for instance, find blood revenge sworn as the lines of lust and avarice cross to create the web of intrigue. In each instance Soranzo is marked the victim. Grimaldi in I, ii, swears vengeance for the beating administered by Vasques. "Holding a man so base no match for [him]" (40), Soranzo has "will'd [his] servant to correct [Grimaldi's] tongue" for verbally abusing him. The oath receives renewed impetus in II, iii, when Richardetto—disguised as a physician—informs Grimaldi that his love for Annabella will never prosper until his chief rival is eliminated and supplies him with a poison for his rapier's point so deadly that Soranzo would die had he "as many heads as Hydra had" (60). There is method in Richardetto's madness, of course. Cuckolded by Soranzo, he has perceived in Grimaldi the opportunity for his own vengeance, noting in aside with grim satisfaction that the fates have thus decreed that Soranzo shall fall by him whom he ruined (62–63). Hippolita, too, designs her attack upon Soranzo. Having played the mistress only to be peremptorily spurned in favor of the fair Annabella, she enlists Vasques' aid in "bring[ing] to pass a plot" (II, ii, 147) for which she would give both herself and her estate: "On this delicious bane my thoughts shall banquet: / Revenge shall sweeten what my griefs have tasted" (159–60).

All three attempts misfire in the bloody carnage of the last half of the play in which the innocent is slain, the guilty is protected from justice, and the schemer is betrayed. More specifically, Hippolita's efforts conclude only in bizarre futility. Betrayed by Vasques, whom she assumes to be her confidant in treachery, she unwittingly quaffs the poisoned wine intended for Soranzo and dies the object of her erstwhile lover's contempt and scorn. From the moment Hippolita's scheme is unmasked, Soranzo speaks only two words to her—"Villain!" "Monster!"—before turning to his new bride to usher her home from "this mirth" (IV, i, 106). Grimaldi's results are no less grotesque and sordid. He chooses to fight, not by openly challenging Soranzo, but by villainously striking him down with a poisoned sword in the dark of night. To make matters worse, he stabs Bergetto by mistake, then is too cowardly to face the judgment of his error. Racing to the Cardinal's home,

he begs and receives the Nuncio's privileged protection. Nor does
the Cardinal hesitate to pervert the law to his own pleasure, an-
nouncing with haughty superiority:

> For this offense I here receive Grimaldi
> Into his holiness' protection. . . .
> If more you seek for, you must go to Rome,
> For he shall thither; learn more wit, for shame.
> Bury your dead.—Away, Grimaldi—leave 'em!
> (III, ix, 53-54, 58-60)

The Cardinal's flagrant disregard for the law and for human
dignity seriously undermines Friar Bonaventura's impact upon the
spectators.[17] Spokesman for the Church as a residuum of righteousness and salvation, the friar in the name of the Church has pro-
nounced the severest damnation upon the incestuous love of
Giovanni and Annabella, and the viewers have for the most part
accepted his judgment at face value in Act I. Heaven, hell, devilish
atheism, pray, soul, deity, shrine, penance—such words in I, i; II, v;
and III, vi—align the Friar and the Church against everything for
which Giovanni's incestuous love stands. While the Cardinal's actions obviously neither negate the essential value of Bonaventura's
counsel nor compromise his integrity, they do tend to provoke the
spectators' disdain for the institution in which the Nuncio occupies
a high position of authority. With the Church stained in this manner and at least by association guilty of crime and impropriety, the
spectators understandably might be less inclined to accept the
Friar's pronouncements at face value. And well might they feel a
momentary sympathy with Giovanni's assertion that the Church
with its "religion-masked sorceries" conjures up a "petty devil"
(V, iii, 29, 28) when they observe the Nuncio's further actions in
the final act. Crying first for protection from the general violence
(V, vi, 110), the Cardinal—even when fully apprised of Vasques'
role—would but banish the Spaniard who is guilty at the least of
murder, yet would condemn a serving lady to be burned to ashes
for her mere knowledge of the incest. And all too quickly he would
leap to seize "to the Pope's proper use" (151) the gold and jewels
from Soranzo's and Florio's estates, almost flippantly belying the
complexity of the tragic situation with his final judgmental quip,
"'tis pity she's a whore."

Both Putana and Vasques merit further attention as self-serving
representatives of the decadent society which comprises the back-

ground to the protagonists' destructive passion. Putana, like the Nell Quickly of *Merry Wives,* sells her support for Annabella's various wooers. Though, for example, she never utters a word on Bergetto's behalf, she assures Donado—for proper compensation—that she commends the nephew to Annabella "every night before her first sleep, because I would have her dream of him, and she hearkens to that most religiously" (II, vi, 15–17). It is the similar assurance of "everlasting love and preferment" (203) which prompts her to reveal in IV, iii, that Annabella is pregnant by Giovanni. Moreover, like that of Juliet's nurse, her language is peppered with prurient puns. She suspects Grimaldi of "some privy maim" which "mars [his] standing upright" (I, ii, 80–81); Soranzo, on the other hand, is "a plain-sufficient, naked man; such a one is for your bed" (95–96); Bergetto is a fool whose "bauble" might be "a lady's playfellow" were Annabella not wealthy enough to spurn "the dearth of flesh" (123, 125). When Putana first learns of the incestuous relationship, her thoughts seize immediately upon the sensual delights as she jests about the "paradise of joy" Annabella has "pass'd under. . . . Your brother's a man, I hope, and I say still, if a young wench feel the fit upon her, let her take anybody, father or brother, all is one" (II, i, 45, 47–49).

Vasques is the most vicious character in this macabre society, his barbarity masked behind a fanatic loyalty to Soranzo. Indeed, his first moments on stage find him inviting Grimaldi to a duel because the Roman soldier has verbally disparaged his master. Only the intervention of Florio and others prevents bloodshed, as Vasques himself arrogantly boasts: "had not your sudden coming prevented us, I had let my gentleman blood under the gills; I should have worm'd [him] for running mad" (I, ii, 43–45). In his second ap-pearance (II, ii) he feigns compliance with Hippolita in order to learn the details of her intended vengeance against Soranzo. In this way he is able flamboyantly to foil her scheme as the poisoned cup is passed to Soranzo in IV, i. Denouncing Hippolita as a "She-Devil," a "foolish woman," and a "thing of malice" (68, 72, 77), he pro-vokes from all present exclamations of "wonderful justice!" and righteous heaven. In such dramatic excitement it is all too easy to miss the blood lust which Vasques has satisfied through Hippolita's unnecessary death. More specifically, he is careful not to expose the former mistress's treacherous design until she has drunk the lethal potion, and his feeble assertion that he would have let her live but for her vindictiveness is hardly justification for murder. His most grisly actions occur late in the drama. After coaxing Putana to reveal the identity of Annabella's lover, he orders her to be gagged, her eyes put out, and (if she yells) her nose slit; like Hippolita's murder, these atrocities, having nothing to do with public justice or punishment, are acts of wanton cruelty initiated by Vasques, who organizes his private banditti and now vows to "tutor [his master] better in his points of vengeance" (IV, iii, 237). At Vasques' bidding, Soranzo agrees to hold a birthday feast, thus setting the stage for Giovanni's murder by the banditti. In the final analysis Vasques is despicably arrogant, justifying his actions in the name of loyalty to his master and "rejoic[ing] that a / Spaniard outwent an Italian in revenge" (V, vi, 146–47).

In brief, the complexity of *'Tis Pity She's a Whore,* painfully evident to a theatrical audience, defies those readers and critics who inveterately leap to distinguish villain from hero, vice from virtue, and the ethics of sensationalistic theatrical illusion from the responses of the spectators whose values in effective tragedy have been attuned by the playwright's artistry to the richest aesthetic experience. As Seymour Reiter has noted in his study of the structure and meaning of drama, in the perception of a play "no being is worlds away, no value is incredible; there is no separateness, we are all one in our mental nature."[18]

The structure of *The Broken Heart* is equally complex. Not only is the protagonist again doubled; the conventional lines between protagonists and antagonists are totally blurred. Orgilus, to be sure, considers Ithocles his deadly enemy for aborting his nuptials with Penthea, but the spectators view the Spartan soldier as a man torn between private desire and public commitment. The play, in effect, has no antagonist.[19] The two central figures are developed essentially as protagonists, and with both the spectators achieve the ambivalent double vision involving sympathy and judgment. While each is deeply flawed and in part is responsible for his own downfall, each also plays a major role in destroying the other. This societal aspect of tragedy gains further emphasis through the delineation of Penthea and Calantha; depicted as virtuous and blameless characters, both are destroyed in spirit and in body by the actions of others who use them for self-advantage.[20]

Orgilus is established as the single apparent protagonist in the opening scene of the tragedy. Describing his love for Penthea which grew out of the engagement arranged by Crotolon and Thrasus, he reminds his father of Penthea's forced marriage to Bassanes involving

Ithocles' violation of a bond viewed by Ford's audience as "something conforming very closely to a public and approved civil contract of marriage."[21] Ostensibly, Orgilus desires to travel to Athens where through contemplation he may escape the agony of his public life; even more pointedly, he would "undertake a voluntary exile" (I, i, 77)[22] to relieve Penthea from the "hell on earth" (80) resulting from Bassanes' obsessive jealousy. Concerned for his sister's honor, he bids her an affectionate farewell and secures her pledge never to wed without his consent. Immediate signals, however, suggest the inner turmoil of this distraught lover. In an aside he observes that his grief is not so lightly worn that it can be discarded for a change of air. Moreover, in scene iii we observe that he has no intention of traveling to Athens, but rather will disguise himself as a student in Sparta. Again, he may swear to Tecnicus that he desires to study in order to assuage his "silent griefs" (9) and "unsettled mind" (28), but the spectators see beyond his pledge that he acts without malice to the soliloquy in which he delights in the opportunity—thus "metamorphos'd"—to "harken after / Penthea's usage and Euphranea's faith" (34–35). Revealing also is his assertion that the lover's wound is beyond the cure of physic and his sudden concern that his sister would dare befriend Ithocles' companion. Overhearing the conversation between Euphranea and Prophilus and incensed at her apparent love for his enemy's friend, he exclaims, "There is no faith in woman. / Passion, O, be contain'd! My very heartstrings / Are on the tenters" (90–92). And, after he (as Aplotes) has agreed to serve as their messenger for further correspondence, his second soliloquy contains unmistakably ominous implications as he invokes Mercury to inspire him "with swift deceits" (177) to quench Hymen's torch.

Orgilus, then, at the end of the first act is a man sinned against and apparently anxious to sin in return. While the determination to move against Prophilus seems at best peripheral to the main issue, his two soliloquies and eleven asides (totaling forty-two lines) reveal a brooding malcontent whose implicit desires to gain vengeance the spectators can quite understand, if not fully condone. Apparently, before involving himself in an intricate and macabre scheme against Ithocles, Orgilus does attempt unsuccessfully to renew his relationship with Penthea. In II, iii, for instance, proclaiming that he can no longer tolerate the misery of a "heart divided / From intercourse of troth-contracted loves" (38–39), he throws off his scholar-disguise and, kneeling hand in hand, claims

Penthea still as his own. Twice he reiterates their union: "I would possess my wife" (71); "Penthea is the wife to Orgilus, / And ever shall be" (96–97). When, in the name of honor, she firmly repudiates him, he swears to tear off his "veil of politic French" (124) and henceforth to be known by action rather than by words. If the spectators can infer an internal conflict in which Orgilus earnestly attempts to avoid a confrontation with Ithocles, they can certainly infer a developing scheme of vengeance in Act III.[23] Denying Tecnicus' warning that "giddy rashness" may be "chok[ing] the breath of reason" (i, 2), he insists on leaving his program of study immediately. Moreover, his stated reasons are, in part at least, suspect; "the present state" (14) may command him because the Prince of Argos comes to woo the King's daughter and because his sister Euphranea is disposed to Prophilus, but the King has hardly sent letters to Athens to order him home. Later, Crotolon's assertion that his son has "come unsent for" (III, iv, 37) with politic plots and with the "wolf of hatred snarling in [his] breast" (33) provokes the direct lie in response that care of his health "cut short [his] journey / For there [in Athens] a general infection / Threatens a desolation" (40–42). Orgilus no longer can hide his discontent, complaining first of the King's will and absolute power which confound justice, then of Prophilus as Ithocles' creature, and finally of Ithocles' "arrogance and spleen which wrought the rape / On griev'd Penthea's purity" (26–27). Admittedly, when Crotolon observes that his son has brought back an infection of the mind far worse than any of body which he fled, Orgilus swears he is free of malicious intent. But his assertion is unconvincing, and his subsequent obsequiousness in addressing Ithocles as "most honored" and "ever famous" (57) while terming himself a "too unworthy worm" (93) even the casual observer perceives as a ploy. Even more suspicious is his offer to entertain Ithocles and his friends with "a poor invention" of his own making.

Orgilus, in other words, to this point has developed consistently and steadily as a tragic figure caught between the mandates of conscience and revenge. Admittedly, however, Ford has provided in Acts II and III not a single glimpse of the protagonist's inner conflicts, with the consequence that the spectators—forced to gauge his development exclusively by his actions and the observations of surrounding characters—do not achieve a compelling emotional association with him. Any such relationship is further blocked in the initial scenes of Act IV by what momentarily at least appears to

be an inconsistency in his characterization. By the conclusion of
Act III he has presumably committed himself to private vengeance;
yet for three consecutive and lengthy scenes (by actual count, 22
percent of the play), Orgilus appears to have forgotten the matter
of personal revenge, and there is not a single moment of internalization which permits the spectators to perceive any such intent behind his actions. In IV, ii, he taunts the erstwhile irascible Bassanes
for cruelty to Penthea; he would "damn all [Bassanes'] comforts
to a lasting fast / From every joy of life" (55-56); Bassanes should
"dig out / The jealousies that hatch'd this thralldom first / With
[his] own poniard" (101-103). And pointedly in scenes i and iii
Orgilus feeds Ithocles' ego, urging him first to opposition to the
royal Nearchus and then firing his anticipation of the throne. In i
he defends Ithocles as "matchless" (89), "the clear mirror / Of
absolute perfection": (82-83); and, when Armostes warns the Spartan soldier that his fronting Nearchus with unruly passions will
provoke a madness, Orgilus counters with the assertion that "in
point of honor / Discretion knows no bounds. . . . Griefs will have
their vent" (105-106, 116). In iii he addresses Ithocles as a "brave
man" (89), the "minion of the time" (90), "most good, . . . most
great" (102), "princely," even "royal" (103); he will be "a just
monarch" before whom "Greece must . . . tremble" (125-26);
with the "glory / Of numerous children" and the "potency of
nobles," he will revel in "bent knees" and "hearts pav'd to tread
on" (128-30).

Convinced that Ithocles is wound in pride and ripe for plucking,
Orgilus springs the mechanical chair on his enemy in IV, iv. But he
springs it on the spectators as well. Despite the reference in soliloquy that Tecnicus' warning against revenge is but the "dotage of a
withered brain" (IV, i, 154), the spectators have little reason to
assume that Orgilus is contriving his device in silence, and their
shock admittedly diverts the primary focus from the protagonist
by casting attention upon the event itself rather than upon his
involvement and reaction. In truth, the focus upon Orgilus has
steadily decreased since Act I, from a point in which the spectators
shared fully his conflicting emotions to a point at which they are
frankly uncertain either of his immediate or ultimate intentions.

The pattern, however, is by design. Ford here faces the task of
establishing two protagonists; whereas in 'Tis Pity She's a Whore
the two central figures were lovers whose personalities and relationships with the audience could be developed simultaneously,

here the spectators must achieve a perspective which encompasses both a sympathetic concern for each individual and also a comprehension of their mutual distrust or antipathy. Such development can hardly be simultaneous without diffusion of effect. More specifically, the spectators cannot become vitally concerned with Ithocles' struggle against the temptation of ambition or with his remorse for forcing his sister to wed against her will if each of these moments is countered by scenes in which they share Orgilus' torments concerning the proper course of action against him. Ford's method is to intersect the development of the two. The focus is exclusively upon Orgilus in Act I; but, when Ford blocks this preoccupation in Act II, the spectators become more profoundly involved with Ithocles through the devices of internalization. By the fourth act interest is independently established, and the spectators find themselves effectively involved with two dominant figures whose culminating stages of tragedy are separate though their destinies are inseparably linked.

Ithocles is seen in Act I only in external terms. Orgilus, of course, describes him as a despicably proud individual who, both for vengeance against the house of Crotolon and for material profit, forced his sister to wed out of heartlock. Quite contrary is the public view of the returning Spartan soldier. The king lauds him as a "death-braving" (ii, 11) warrior who, bringing "triumphs and peace upon his conquering sword" (12), deserves a temple in his honor. And Prophilus reports him as a man of great moderation and calmness, constant as "a star fix'd, not mov'd with any thunder / Of popular applause, or sudden lightning / Of self-opinion" (44–46). When Ithocles himself enters, his first words are humble and self-effacing. Insisting that he has done nothing more than any man would do for his country, he berates those who, victorious, would give ear to the madding applause and style themselves demigods. To his companions he is expressly gracious in his refusal to accept the individual credit for victory over the Messenians: "All there did strive their best, and 'twas our duty" (98).

The human side of Ithocles surfaces in Act II. Neither the arrogant monster Orgilus has pictured nor the "miracle of man" military victory has reflected, he is a man torn by remorse for his peremptory action antecedent to the play—primarily because he now experiences in himself the misery to which he earlier had subjected Orgilus. Publicly acclaimed a hero, he keenly senses in soliloquy the bitter irony of his private torment. Ambition he now can readily

denounce as self-destructive, "of vipers' breed" (ii, 1); mounting
higher "to perch on clouds" (4), it inevitably will tumble "head-
long down with heavier ruin" (5). So, too, he can admit the necessity of morality, which "keeps the soul in tune, / At whose sweet
music all our actions dance" (9–10). Neither insight, however,
assuages "the sickness of a mind / Broken with griefs" (12–13). In
this frame of mind he faces twenty-five lines later Crotolon's specific charge that he has buried a sister in a "bridebed" and destroyed Orgilus' hopes for a life fulfilled through true love. Significantly, there is not the least flash of haughty disdain. Instead,
Ithocles freely acknowledges his fault and lays it to his immaturity
("the heat / Of an unsteady youth, a giddy brain, / Green indiscretion, flattery of greatness, / Rawness of judgment, willfulness in
folly, / Thoughts vagrant . . . and . . . uncertain" [44–48]). Admitting that he now knows the "secrets of commanding love" (51),
he pledges to redeem these errors "with any service / Your satisfaction can require for current" (54–55). Twice more Ithocles
reiterates in Act III his change of heart, once when he publicly
welcomes Orgilus back to Sparta, expressing joy at the meeting and
"covet[ing] to deserve the title / Of [his] respected friend" (iii,
47–48). The scene is reminiscent of Romeo's meeting with Tybalt;
just as new love for Juliet has buried the hatred of her cousin, so
Ithocles' unrequited love for Calantha has forced upon him a
sympathy for Orgilus' misery—but Orgilus, like Tybalt, inevitably
misinterprets the intention. Most extensively Ithocles opens his
heart to the sister whom he has wronged, lamenting that his "rash
spleen / Hath with a violent hand pluck'd from [her] bosom / A
lover-bless'd heart" (ii, 43–45). For this trespass his own heart is
now breaking as he is consumed "in languishing affections" (53).

    Ithocles' real tragedy, however, arises from his regression in Act
IV. When Calantha suggests a romantic interest by tossing a ring
before his feet, his autocratic pride suddenly bursts forth anew. To
Amelus, Nearchus' attendant who offers to take up the ring for
the Prince, Ithocles snaps, "Learn manners" (i, 31). And, similarly,
seven lines later as Nearchus exits, he haughtily orders the "spaniel"
(35) to follow; "I'll force 'ee to a fawning else" (36). Nor does his
incredible disdain stop with the attendant. When the Prince himself observes that such "pride turns heretic in loyalty" (97), Ithocles
mutters for him to come back so that his presence "may bait a
muzzled lion" (104), and in the second scene Nearchus enters on
an insult which the director might well have Ithocles voice just

loud enough for the Prince to hear: "th' augury thing returns
again; / Shall's welcome him with thunder? We are haunted, / And
must use exorcism to conjure down / This spirit of malevolence"
(177–80). Two seemingly insignificant moments early in the act,
by juxtaposing his penitence with his resurgent pride, underscore
the awesome rapidity of this transformation and the agitation and
turmoil of his mind. First, his words in IV, i, 8–14, suggest that a
lifetime of remorse will not expiate his injury to Penthea and
Orgilus: his "folly . . . stand[s] tallied / Without all possibilities of
payment"; yet within forty lines, flushed with Calantha's favor, he
banishes such thoughts, calling for a "real, visible, material happiness" (50), a "felicity / Of which [his] senses waking are partakers"
(48–49). Second, prideful irritation at Prince Nearchus—whom he
would defy even if the royal breath could toss "servile slaves . . .
into a vapour" (62, 63)—breaks quite literally into the middle of a
sentence in which he contemplates Penthea's innocent and sacrificial love. Calantha's attention, in short, instead of provoking a
humble and long-suffering devotion, rekindles the malevolently
competitive pride which had characterized his earlier relations with
Orgilus and his sister. Nowhere is this clearer than in the choric
comments of Armostes. The Counsellor of State cautions Ithocles
against his forwardness, his uncontrolled tongue, and his vain unruly passions. He decries the individual "who is not privy counsellor to himself" (78) and quite pointedly identifies the pride which
forms the basis of such demeanor:

> Contain yourself, my lord. Ixion, aiming
> To embrace Juno, bosom'd but a cloud,
> And begat centaurs. 'Tis an useful moral:
> Ambition, hatch'd in clouds of mere opinion,
> Proves but in birth a prodigy.
>
> (69–73)

Savoring suggestions of royalty and monarchy and realizing that his
wedding contract with the Princess is firm, he offers Orgilus easy
friendship and fortune. As a consequence of his pride and apparent
good fortune, he is blind to the animosity behind his adversary's
fair words.

For each of the principals, then, the sympathy provoked by the
dilemma and anguish reflected in soliloquies and asides is tempered
by the judgment of the spectators who perceive the passion in its
true colors and the egregious manipulation of others to its satisfac-

tion. Ford utilizes a variety of minor plot strands to maintain and to sharpen this pervasive ambiguity. Certainly, Orgilus' animosity toward Ithocles, for example, gains sympathetic support through the delineation of Bassanes.[24] His maniacal jealousy makes a mockery of the marriage into which the brother has consciously forced Penthea as a device for enhancing the family's material fortunes. The window facing the street must be "damn'd up" (II, i, 1) because it gives "too full a prospect to temptation" (2); he fears her eye will invite adultery through its sweat, travail, plot, and contrivance. All women indeed he views as creatures of lust: the city housewives, "cunning in the traffic / Of chamber merchandise" (23-24); dames at court, running the bias of pleasure; the country mistress, "more wary" (37) but false—"No woman but can fall, and doth, or would" (40). Convinced that it would "puzzle all the gods" (II, ii, 90) to create a constant woman, he even suspects incest when Ithocles requests a private audience with his sister: "Brothers and sisters are but flesh and blood, / And this same whoreson court-ease is temptation / To a rebellion of the veins" (117-19). And in his most audacious moment, convinced that the matted floor conceals the sounds but not the feelings of chamber combats, he crashes in upon the siblings and proclaims that he will not be party to "bed sports" smacking of "bestial incest" (III, ii, 135, 150). Since throughout these scenes Penthea's purity and chastity are carefully established for the spectators, and since Ithocles forced the marriage in despite of true heartlock, Orgilus' hatred gains emotional credence as the spectators react to Bassanes with derisive mockery.

At the same time, Orgilus' antipathy for Prophilus gives the spectators pause. It is understandable that Euphranea's romantic interest in Prophilus should agitate her brother. After all, Orgilus parts from his sister on her pledge never to "pass" to any man without his consent and on his vow that his "first care" will be to see her "match'd / As may become [their mutual] choice" (I, i, 108-109); yet, a mere two scenes later he observes her strolling arm and arm with Prophilus—a man, to make it worse, who is Ithocles' bosom companion. Even so, his feelings run dangerously deeper than agitation, and in his disguise as Aplotes his asides form a sinister obbligato to the lovers' conversation. And, indeed, his soliloquy at the end of the first act explicitly reflects the extent of his depraved fury as he envisions a "darkness of eternal night" for Prophilus (I, iii, 176). Fate has "leapt into [his] arms" (178), and he sees himself as Her agent: "Mortality / Creeps on the dung of earth and cannot reach / The riddles which are purpos'd by the gods" (179–81).

Ford, then, utilizes the secondary characters to establish an ambiguous view of Orgilus. If Bassanes' mistreatment of Penthea evokes a strong sympathy for his hatred of Ithocles, his attitude toward Prophilus reveals both a deep-seated passion which would reach beyond hatred to vengeful murder of an innocent associate and also (in his threatening to bar the genuine romance between Prophilus and his sister) a willingness to play the same role for which he condemns his adversary. Similarly, Ford through the subplot carefully modulates the spectators' attitude toward Ithocles. In the first act, for instance, the view that "nothing is lost and much is gained by excising" the comic material[25] is surely shortsighted. Not only do Hemophil and Groneas provide humorous relief; more importantly, they serve as comic foils to enhance the spectators' early impressions of Ithocles. The Spartan soldier, who has trodden Messene underfoot, humbly acknowledges that his motivation for fighting has been a "debt of service" (ii, 77) to his country in "gratitude for life" (76). By contrast, the companion soldiers, arrogant and boastful, demand sexual pleasures as a reward for military services. Blunt, they move directly for the lip; their "valour / Is of a mounting nature" (108–109). In actuality, they have dealt no fatal blows, and they can produce no spoils—despite Hemophil's offer of one of his conquered cities to his mistress. Aptly, Christalla berates the absence of valor and wit in these "corn-cutters" (137) whose self-serving cowardice underscores Ithocles' heroism. Similarly, when pride and ambition turn Ithocles' head in Act IV, the dramatist maintains a sympathetic view through the pomposity and arrogance of Nearchus. The Prince describes Ithocles as "saucy" for taking up the ring Calantha tosses at his feet, asserting that he lacks both "civility" and "good manners" and thrasonically proclaiming: "You might have understood who I am. . . . Sirrah, low mushrooms never rival cedars" (i, 90, 98).

Significantly, the subplot characters are utilized in IV, ii, to underscore the least desirable moments of the protagonists as well. The initially strong rapport with the spectators already badly eroded, Orgilus faces a Bassanes genuinely remorseful for his jealous antics and intent now upon studying reformation and pouring humility before the deities. When Orgilus berates him as a patron of horrors, Bassanes welcomes the taunts as an "addition to

[his] penance" (45). Certainly, as Orgilus curses him to everlasting misery and challenges him to the one worthy act of suicide—and as Bassanes continuously returns patience for irascibility—the dislocation between spectators and protagonist becomes extensive. A similar situation develops with the second central figure. Confronting Ithocles' mounting pride, Nearchus in a sudden reversal of attitude both graciously excuses the soldier's peremptory manner and also withdraws from the romantic struggle over Calantha rather than be party to a marriage of convenience; and, in the face of such magnanimity of spirit, Ithocles' arrogance appears all the more petty and vain.

Ford, then, carefully employs the subplot characters to manipulate the spectators' attitude toward the dual protagonists. The initially intense rapport with Orgilus, while supported through Bassanes, is tempered by Prophilus, thus prompting the viewers to a more sympathetic interest in Ithocles, an interest then reinforced through Hemophil and Groneas and through Nearchus. In turn, Bassanes and Nearchus later provoke the audience's sternest judgment upon the central figures moments before their crises and deaths.

As in 'Tis Pity She's a Whore, the major ambiguity of the tragedy arises from these critical moments. For again the anagnorisis, which normally provides in the experience of the protagonist the philosophic coherence and thus the thematic impact of the drama, is doubled; and again the insights gained by the two figures are blatantly contradictory.[26] Ithocles, more specifically, dies reconciled with his enemy, providing the traditional figure of Elizabethan tragedy who has gained wisdom through suffering and who dies more nobly than he lived. Not only does he submit silently to Orgilus' taunts concerning tyranny, royalty, and pride ("You dreamt of kingdoms, did 'ee? How to bosom / The delicacies of a youngling princess, / How with this nod to grace that noble courtier, / How with that frown to make this noble tremble" [IV, iv, 30–33]); he freely admits his sins of overreaching, voicing specific remorse for dreams of the ambition and "delicious banquet" (67) which dictated the actions of his public life. He asserts his courage, to be sure; armed with a stately resolution, he will neither whine nor beg compassion. But, clearly, his attitude stems from contrition rather than arrogance. As his life's blood ebbs from the wound which Orgilus has inflicted, he freely forgives his adversary and counsels him to seek "safety; with success" (64). More specifically, he voices the hope that his death will provide recompense for the misdeeds of his life:

"Penthea, by thy side thy brother bleeds, / The earnest of his wrong to thy forc'd faith" (65-66); and he dies in expectation of a "heaven" (70) and "a long-look'd-for peace" (70). The dramatic setting is pre-Christian, of course, but Ithocles' final moments reflect the moral and psychological insights common to the protagonists of the most profound tragedy of the Tudor-Stuart age. No longer the egotistic center of his universe, he acknowledges the self-centered aims which have motivated his crass manipulation of those around him; and, his final comments, which fleetingly mirror both the titanic glory of human assertion and the recognition of the passion which lethally taints such noble aspiration, reflect the acceptance of the teleology inherited from the medieval age and adapted by the Renaissance humanists, a hierarchically ordered universe controlled by a power which for the sake of the whole society places constraints upon the actions of the individual member.

Orgilus, to the contrary, never wavers in his commitment to self during the final act; never once does he question the right to judge and to condemn another by his personal scale of values. To Calantha at the court dance he whispers the news that Ithocles is "murdered cruelly" (V, ii, 16), and a few moments later with undeniable pride he announces Ithocles' butchery, admits his guilt, and brandishes the weapon which was "instrument to [his] revenge" (45). Twice within one hundred sixteen lines he flatly proclaims himself above the law: his "reasons / Are just and known" (45-46); the "goodness of [his] cause" (143) he would not trust to Fortune. Requesting that no "common hand" (86) separate him from life, he will be his own executioner since he is "well skill'd in letting blood" (101), and he sternly rejects pity or scorn—either of which would presume moral judgment. His last moments display the firm assurance that in death he will join a "pair-royal" (136) as liege man to his sovereign and devoted servant to his mistress. Yet, unlike Ithocles, he envisions no heaven or continuation of existence; instead, unflinchingly he faces the "everlasting shadow" (153) which closes around him, the "ice that sitt'st about my heart [which] / No heat can ever thaw" (154-55). And the comments of those present are appropriately ambiguous as they observe his "desperate courage" and his "honorable infamy" (123).

Thus, the tragic insights gained by Ithocles and Orgilus tend to cancel each other. Like Annabella, Ithocles submits to the judgment of his peers, admitting his fault of pride and tacitly acknowledging a social order which places the law above the will of the individual. Orgilus, though, like Giovanni, rejects even in his dying agony the right of anyone else to condemn his actions. Convinced of the moral validity of his private judgments, he has defied his father, who warned him of the infection of mind which threatened his entire family, and his King, who openly had accepted Ithocles as suitor for his daughter's hand. In effect, he has even repudiated the gods. When the philosopher Tecnicus first cautioned Orgilus not to permit passion to choke the breath of reason and later, while delivering Apollo's oracle, proclaimed that revenge would prove "its own executioner" (IV, i, 152), Orgilus scoffed that he was no Oedipus to interpret such "dark sentences" (139). He dies, in short, as he has lived—at least since his private meeting with Penthea in Act II—resolutely convinced that man is his own final measure.

The ambivalence arising from this double anagnorisis is certainly in part responsible for the pervasive pessimism of Ford's society. The constant emphasis "not on fruition or fertility but on barrenness and obstruction"[27] ultimately mirrors the human condition in which, as Maynard Mack has described it, men are "stripped to their naked humanity and mortality, and torn loose from accustomed moorings."[28] Spectators are never permitted the luxury of a particular philosophic view which the artistic pattern upholds through the experiences of the central figure. Instead, they must hold in simultaneous suspension the humanist's view that man is a creature whose good life is to be found in proper subordination to the deity and his social and personal laws and the seventeenth-century view of the New Man that the body is a garden to which the will is unrestricted gardener. By refusing to resolve this tension, Ford tragically captures the uncertainties involving protean Nature which are central to the philosophic trauma of the age.

Perhaps most directly responsible for the darkened tone of this stage world are the two women from whom the tragedy draws its title—two individuals who seem created to be scapegoats to the cruelty of those around them. Indeed, the action of the play turns on their innocent suffering and death. Penthea, though appearing in only six scenes, is the catalyst both for Ithocles' intense pride and for Orgilus' commitment to vengeance. She herself is clearly above the passions which possess those closest to her; each of her appearances underscores the temptations to which she is subject and the strength of character which enables her to repudiate them.[29]

Bassanes, for instance, although privately possessed of an insane
fear of cuckoldry, insists in II, i, that Penthea should appear at
court "in such a ravishing lustre / Of jewels above value" (78–79)
that all other dames shall hide themselves for shame; she shall be
"a queen" (84) of whatever recreations delight her and "do all
things / Youth can command" (86–87). Her response is that, desir-
ing no "braveries" (93) or "gaudy outsides" (98) and coveting not
the admiration of the curious, her "attires / Shall suit the inward
fashion of [her] mind" (98–99). The sincerity of her simplicity
and honesty is dramatically established two scenes later when
Orgilus, suddenly removing his disguise as Aplotes, confronts her
and claims in private the affection which her brother's tyranny has
denied them in public. Even though he is her true love and she
laments the "divorce betwixt" (57) body and heart which has
committed a "rape . . . on [her] truth" (79), she firmly rejects his
rash advances which lay "a blemish on [her] honor. . . . Honor, /
How much we fight with weakness to preserve thee!" (52, 130–
31). In III, ii, even in the face of her assertions that Ithocles is an
unnatural brother whose bloody guilt is directly responsible for
her whoredom within a loveless marriage, she listens compassion-
ately to his declaration of love for Calantha. Agreeing to act as his
intercessor with the Princess and, true to her word, speaking
eloquently and effectively in his behalf in III, v, she ironically
provides access to a heart's mate for the same brother who has
earlier blocked her own. Torn irrevocably between her commitment to the moral law which demands fidelity in marriage and the
personal conviction which proclaims the integrity of her love for
Orgilus, she quite literally destroys herself through starvation, her
final words noting pathetically how she might have been a mother
"to many pretty prattling babes . . . 'Tis not my fault" (IV, ii, 88,
94).

Thus manipulated by a brother into a marriage for profit and
pressed by a lover for an affection she can no longer reciprocate,
she is crushed by converging external forces, and her death in turn
prompts Orgilus to move decisively against Ithocles. Similarly, the
action of the final act centers upon the Princess Calantha. To be
sure, she has appeared in every act, but in six previous scenes she
has spoken an incredibly brief ninety-seven lines. Her actions, moreover, have been totally stylized. Whether graciously welcoming
Ithocles as the conquering hero (I, ii), mingling at court as
Prophilus' betrothal to Euphranea is discussed (II, ii), receiving

Prince Nearchus as a suitor for her hand and the kingdom (III, iii), listening with a calm detachment which conceals any genuine emotional response to Penthea's description of Ithocles' languishing love for her (III, v), coyly tossing a ring before Ithocles as a signal both to Ithocles and Nearchus of her shifting affection (IV, i), or even requesting publicly her father's blessings on Ithocles as her wooer (IV, iii)—she functions as a court dignitary who, without emotional life, does not vitally command the spectators' attention. Her full development occurs in the final act, in which she speaks in two scenes a greater number of lines (one hundred twelve) than in the first four acts combined, and in which her fate becomes a painful iteration of Penthea's grief and death. Leading the dance in honor of Prophilus' and Euphranea's nuptials, she receives reports within a matter of seconds of her father's death, Penthea's starvation, and her fiancé's murder. With apparently remarkable composure she accepts Orgilus' confession of vengeance against Ithocles, sentencing him to present death and calling to mind the irrefutable logic of consolation that, had her loved ones "not now died, of necessity / They must have paid the debt they ow'd to nature, / One time or other" (ii, 90–92). Her true sensitivity is perceived only in the final scene, in which she reveals that her "antic gesture" (iii, 68) was but a cover for the sorrows which "struck home" (71) and "cut the heartstrings" (75). Concerned in the face of death for the security of her kingdom, she recognizes Nearchus as ruler, Crotolon as viceroy of Messene, Bassanes as Marshall of Sparta, Groneas and Hemophil as lords of the chamber, and Prophilus as heir of Ithocles' titles and preferments.[30] Turning then to her husband, from whom death "shall not separate" (67) her, she places her mother's wedding-ring on his finger, kisses his cold lips, and dies smiling even as her heart breaks.

Like Penthea, then, Calantha dies an innocent victim to the evil which surrounds her, and here the consequences of such senseless destruction funnel out from the private grief for Penthea to touch the lives of all in the kingdom. Charles Lamb's[31] and Swinburne's (II, 379) effusions over the final scene may be extreme, but Saintsbury's view that Calantha is "wholly artificial" (p. 408) and Burbridge's that she is indifferent to her fate (p. 406) disregard the manner in which her death—paralleling that of Penthea—reinforces the societal nature of tragedy by expanding the consequences while simultaneously reiterating the personal agony of unrequited love.[32] In successive stages, the price which society must pay for such tragedy becomes increasingly painful and obvious. In *'Tis Pity She's a Whore* the principal victims themselves share at least a portion of the blame for creating the situation which destroys them. Annabella, Giovanni, and Soranzo are all flawed individuals, guilty of actions which corrode their own lives and the lives of those with whom they have intimate contact. Though Annabella's repentance and submission to Christian values juxtaposed with Giovanni's defiant insistence on the sanctity of private values create a similar moral ambiguity, the deaths which occur reflect a kind of poetic justice embodying the fundamental—if primitive—law of cause and effect. Penthea and Calantha, on the other hand, are totally innocent creatures whose only fault is a love so intense that, thwarted and unrequited, the heart is broken. Like Ophelia, Desdemona, or Cordelia, they die a stark testimony to the sheer waste of tragedy, their destruction all the more painful since it is a consequence of their own genuine affection. Stavig may well argue (p. 161) that the "purgation of the evil that has been corrupting the state" provides "the basis for a new and more stable society," but Joan Sargeaunt (p. 81) perceptively observes that we can have little confidence in the stability of a society whose leadership has been so totally annihilated that Bassanes must fill a post of honor.[33] Coupled with the double anagnorisis, the contrasting teleologies, and the senseless deaths of Penthea and Calantha, this restoration of order in *The Broken Heart* produces the most oppressively pessimistic atmosphere in Jacobean-Caroline drama.

VIII. Epilogue

In a very real sense John Ford's drama represents the culmination of the basic dramaturgical trend toward the societal perspective of tragedy. As we have seen, this tragedy, in the full Jacobean sense, is an indictment of the individual and of his society, emphasizing both the flaw of the protagonist and of those in society who have manipulated him for selfish interests. Each of the major Jacobean playwrights develops this broader societal perspective in slightly differing fashion. Shakespeare, for example, places no additional direct emphasis upon the antagonist. Instead, by virtually eliminating the soliloquy as an instrument of the divided mind, he sharply limits the development of philosophic depth in the protagonist and thereby directs the spectator's attention in larger measure to the surrounding characters who abuse him. He also is instrumental in developing a variation in the anagnorisis and the concomitant restitution of reason in the individual and the society at large. Through secondary figures such as Alcibiades, Aufidius, and above all Cleopatra, whose experiences parallel those of the central figures, Shakespeare projects a catharsis arising from the ordeal of the protagonist, at the same time avoiding the kind of emotional engagement that would be the consequence of the spectators' directly confronting this occurrence within the principal figure. Jonson, like Shakespeare in his final tragedies, places his central characters in a pagan setting in which metaphysical assumptions tend only to reflect the manner in which unprincipled individuals manipulate religion to serve their personal ends. Viciously corrupt figures, both Sejanus and Catiline are ultimately destroyed by equally adept Machiavellian opportunists. Jonson's structure involves a confrontation, not of characters postulated on any sort of moral or ethical scale, but of bestial antagonists bent on survival and the achievement of power by any method. Tourneur distances the spectators by total elimination of philosophic depth in the protagonist and, simultaneously, by accretive intensification of the evil in the characters who surround him; the consequence, however, is virtual alienation of the spectators, who—with no characters through whom to relate to the action and hence no meaningful perspective— remain outside the action. Vindice's mounting cruelty in his private dispensation of justice—coupled with the multiplicity of antagonists who form a crescendo of deceit and decadence—sharply emphasizes both the pervasive corruption of the stage world and the interrelationship of the hero's flaw with the actions of those who misuse him for selfish gratification. In D'Amville, Tourneur, like Jonson, even more strikingly moves the villain to center stage. A creature of increasing fascination, he is clearly the dominant force, and the spectators view the action through his eyes as he engages in satanic machinations to secure his brother's estate for himself and for his progeny. If such a character is ultimately too stylized to provoke genuine emotional concern, there is no denying the brilliance and the impact of his vision of a society festering with corruption. Such a vision Webster in turn establishes by doubling the antagonist and methodically emphasizing the greed and lust of other significant characters surrounding Vittoria and the pitiful impotence of the few with moral integrity; at the same time, he achieves emotional coherence through the internal focus upon the protagonist and her private struggle, and through transferring the anagnorisis in part to her brother Flamineo. The design is repeated more effectively in his second piece in which the corrupt and designing force of both Church and State is ranged against the innocent—if naïve—Duchess, whose cathartic experience is again registered most effectively in the transformation of the Machiavellian Bosola. In *Women Beware Women* no single character stands predominantly at the center. Instead Middleton through expansive use of the soliloquy forces the spectator to observe the activities of a sordid and decadent society from diverse perspectives; no fewer than ten characters— manipulator as well as victim—share their private perceptions, and the spectator alone possesses a full view of the pattern of events and consequently must exercise judgment predicated on his own scale of values. While *The Changeling* focuses primarily on the character of Beatrice-Joanna, her experience, set within a broad context encompassing the tragedies of others and again utilizing the soliloquy to prompt the spectator to become an active participant in the moral judgments, stresses the human chain which contributes to and is affected by the tragedy of the individual.

To a considerable extent, Ford's technique seems to build upon

Webster's and Middleton's. Through the rival wooers, the multiple
revenge plots, the Cardinal, and the servant characters, he sketches
in *'Tis Pity* a society teeming with corruption; at the same time,
through the devices of internalization, he creates in Annabella a
character—somewhat reminiscent of Vittoria—who commands the
spectators' genuine interest. Whereas Webster reinforces the spectators' sympathetic concern through a character such as Flamineo,
who is profoundly influenced by the protagonist's experience,
Ford—like Middleton with De Flores—blocks the association
through the counter philosophy of a second protagonist. And since
conflicting philosophies limit the intensity of the audience's identification with either of these principals, he is able to create a dramatic situation in which the spectator, though not without an emotional attachment to the protagonists, is—from the first scene to the
last—sufficiently distanced from them to perceive corruption at
every turn, in them as well as in the characters surrounding them.
Moreover, Ford's refusal to provide a single convincing teleology
for the stage world projects a fundamentally pessimistic view of life
in which man's challenge is not the heroic deed or the new horizon
but the ambiguity of moral values constantly frustrating his search
for a meaningful life.

Similarly, by blurring the distinction between protagonist and
antagonist in *The Broken Heart,* the playwright gives sharp emphasis
both to Ithocles' arrogance and to the abiding hatred which it provokes in Orgilus; coupled with the insane jealousies of Bassanes, the
prurience of Grausis, the lust of the braggadocios Groneas and
Hemophil, and the pomposity of Nearchus, Ford sketches a society
in which, in the name of decorum and respectability, normal affection and genuine integrity are sacrificed to prideful ambition and
lustful gratification. At the same time, through the devices of internalization he depicts in Orgilus and Ithocles characters who again
provide the emotional center for the play and who again experience
contradictory tragic illuminations. The resulting pessimism is compounded by the delineation of Penthea and Calantha as totally innocent and fully sympathetic figures whose destruction poignantly
focuses upon the sheer waste and irrevocable loss. The insights
gained by those who at the end must attempt to reorder the shattered society is small recompense indeed for the woefully painful
price.

The best of the Jacobean and Caroline stage worlds, then—both
the tragedies examined in some detail in this study and those of

Shakespeare, Marston, Massinger, Chapman, and Fletcher addressed at best only cursorily—effectively capture the spiritual uncertainties of an increasingly analytical age which no longer accepted without question either a universe informed by transcendent and inscrutable reason or human conduct predicated fundamentally on traditional religio-social values. In such a period of growing skepticism, soon to be conceptualized by Hobbes and Descartes, society is envisioned on occasion not as a microcosmic unit of God's larger order but as a cluster of degree-vizarding individuals bent on material and emotional gratification. While tragedy may well focus on the central figure, suffering and destruction clearly result both from individual error and from the interaction of others who selfishly and cruelly pursue their own interests at his expense. The path from Faustus to Orgilus is winding and multiform, but in its general direction it is the journey of Jacobean and Caroline tragedy.

Abbreviations USED IN THE NOTES

CLAJ	*College Language Association Journal*
CQ	*Critical Quarterly*
ECS	*Eighteenth-Century Studies*
EJ	*English Journal*
ELH	*English Literary History*
ELN	*English Language Notes*
ES	*English Studies*
HLQ	*Huntington Library Quarterly*
JEGP	*Journal of English and Germanic Philology*
MLN	*Modern Language Notes*
MLQ	*Modern Language Quarterly*
MLR	*Modern Language Review*
MP	*Modern Philology*
N&Q	*Notes and Queries*
PLL	*Papers on Language and Literature*
PMLA	*Publications of the Modern Language Association*
PQ	*Philological Quarterly*
RES	*Review of English Studies*
SAB	*Shakespeare Association Bulletin*
SEL	*Studies in English Literature*
SP	*Studies in Philology*
SQ	*Shakespeare Quarterly*
TSLL	*Texas Studies in Literature and Language*
YES	*Yearbook of English Studies*

Notes

CHAPTER I

1. "The Rise of the Gentry, 1558–1640," *Economic History Review*, 11 (1941), 8 ff.

2. "The Gentry, 1540–1640," *Economic History Review*, Supplement 1 (1953).

3. *The Causes of the English Revolution 1529–1642* (New York: Harper, 1972), p. 30.

4. Paul Oskar Kristeller and John Herman Randall, Jr., *The Renaissance Philosophy of Man*, ed. Ernst Cassirer (Chicago: Univ. of Chicago Press, 1948), p. 11.

5. Christopher H. Dawson, *Christianity and the New Age* (London: Sheed and Ward, 1931), p. 66.

6. E. A. Burtt, *The Metaphysical Foundations of Modern Science* (London: Routledge and Kegan Paul, 1932), pp. 236–37.

7. Jacob Burckhardt, *The Civilization of the Renaissance in Italy* (1878; rpt. New York: Random House, 1960), p. 39.

8. L. C. Knights, *Drama and Society in the Age of Jonson* (New York: Stewart, 1936), p. 5.

9. *Shakespeare and the Nature of Man* (New York: Macmillan, 1942), p. ix.

10. *The Counter-Renaissance* (New York: Scribner's, 1950), p. 4.

11. *The Shakespearean Moment and Its Place in the Poetry of the Seventeenth Century* (New York: Random House, 1960), p. 39.

12. See, for example, Arthur Lovejoy, *The Great Chain of Being* (Cambridge, Mass.: Harvard Univ. Press, 1936); Marjorie Hope Nicholson, *The Breaking of the Circle: Studies in the Effect of the "New Science" upon Seventeenth Century Poetry* (New York: Columbia Univ. Press, 1960); Victor Harris, *All Coherence Gone: A Study of the Seventeenth Century Controversy over Disorder and Decay in the Universe* (London: Cass, 1966); Richard Foster Jones, *Ancients and Moderns: A Study of the Rise of the Scientific Movement in Seventeenth Century England* (St. Louis: Washington Univ. Press, 1961); Steven E. Ozmont, *Mysticism and Dissent: Religious Ideology and Social Protest in the Sixteenth Century* (New Haven: Yale Univ. Press, 1976).

13. Alvin B. Kernan, *The Cankered Muse: Satire of the English Renaissance* (New Haven: Yale Univ. Press, 1959), pp. 86–87. For the best discussions of

this new form, see further Hallet Smith, *Elizabethan Poetry* (Cambridge, Mass.: Harvard Univ. Press, 1952); John Peter, *Complaint and Satire in Early English Literature* (Oxford: Oxford Univ. Press, 1956); O. J. Campbell, *Comicall Satyre and Shakespeare's Troilus and Cressida* (San Marino: Huntington Library, 1938); John Wilcox, "Informal Publication of Late Sixteenth-Century Verse Satire," *HLQ,* 13 (1949–50), 191–200; and William Frost, "English Persius: The Golden Age," *ECS,* 2 (1968), 77–101.

14. See *Virgidemiae, Pigmalion's Image and Certaine Satyres, The Scourge of Villanie, Skialetheia, Microcynicon or Sixe Snarling Satyres, Seven Satyres, Satyres, The Scourge of Folly,* and *Abuses Stript and Whipt.*

15. Hardin Craig describes the conflict between Aristotelian and Stoic ethics ("Ethics in the Jacobean Drama: The Case of Chapman," in *Parrott Presentation Volume,* ed. Hardin Craig, Princeton: Princeton Univ. Press, 1935, p. 281); in a later article ("The Shackling of Accidents: A Study of Elizabethan Tragedy," *PQ,* 19, 1940, 1–19) he expands the conflict to include Aristotelian, Stoic, and Christian ethics. Mark Stavig argues that "thinkers in the eclectic Renaissance" fused these views into a consistent philosophy (*John Ford and the Traditional Moral Order,* Madison: Univ. of Wisconsin Press, 1968, p. 61), while Irving Ribner sees the tragic dramatists engaged in "philosophic exploration" (*Jacobean Tragedy,* New York: Barnes and Noble, 1962, p. 21).

16. *Shakespeare and the Rival Traditions* (New York: Macmillan, 1952), p. 71.

17. *Elizabethan and Jacobean* (Oxford: Clarendon Press, 1945), p. 20.

18. Robert Ornstein, *The Moral Vision of Jacobean Tragedy* (Madison: Univ. of Wisconsin Press, 1960), p. 4.

19. Cyrus Hoy, "Jacobean Tragedy and the Mannerist Style," *Shakespeare Survey,* 26 (1973), 50.

20. W. R. Elton, "Shakespeare and the Thought of His Age," in *A New Companion to Shakespeare Studies,* ed. Kenneth Muir and Samuel Schoenbaum (Cambridge: Cambridge Univ. Press, 1971), p. 197.

21. *Shakespeare's Dramatic Heritage* (New York: Barnes and Noble, 1969), p. 42.

22. A. C. Bradley, *Shakespearean Tragedy* (London: Macmillan, 1904), p. 33. S. F. Johnson considers *King John* and *Gorboduc,* with their emphasis on tragedy's resulting from an individual flaw and its consequences rather than "the power of Fortune and of Providential retribution," to be "outstanding forerunners" of Elizabethan heroic tragedy ("The Tragic Hero in Early Elizabethan Drama," in *Studies in the English Renaissance Drama,* ed. J. W. Bennett, O. Coghill, and V. Hall, Jr., New York: New York Univ. Press, 1959, p. 159).

23. See Walter Clyde Curry, *Shakespeare's Philosophical Patterns* (Baton Rouge: Louisiana State Univ. Press, 1937), p. 155; and Marco Mincoff, "Shakespeare, Fletcher, and Baroque Tragedy," *Shakespeare Survey,* 20 (1967), 1–15.

24. *Angel with Horns,* ed. Graham Storey (New York: Theatre Arts Books, 1961), p. 51.

25. *Shakespeare and the Common Understanding* (New York: Free Press, 1967), p. 144.

26. Clifford Leech, *Shakespeare's Tragedies* (New York: Oxford Univ. Press, 1950), p. 15.

27. This type of tragic perspective Northrop Frye presumed in his assertion that "a tragic figure is *fully* tragic only to its spectators; heroes do not suffer except when they become objective to themselves" (*Fools of Time,* Toronto: Univ. of Toronto Press, 1967, p. 61); similarly the critic must hold himself in suspension between the hero and the advocate of Eternal Law (Helen Gardner, "Milton's 'Satan' and the Theme of Damnation in Elizabethan Tragedy," *Essays and Studies,* 1, 1948, 63).

28. For discussion of the growing influence of the private stage and of the court, see Allardyce Nicoll, *English Drama: A Modern Viewpoint* (London: Harrap, 1968), p. 58; G. E. Bentley, "Shakespeare and the Blackfriars Theatre," *Shakespeare Survey,* 1 (1948), 38–50; Harbage, pp. 29–57; and John F. Danby, *Poets on Fortune's Hill* (London: Faber and Faber, 1942), p. 156. J. A. Bastiaenen rather fervently exclaims against the "putrid cravings" of the audience (*The Moral Tone of Jacobean and Caroline Drama,* New York: Haskell House, 1966, p. 195). For an interesting discussion of Shakespeare's artistic use of the reactions and prejudices of this new audience, see J. L. Simmons, "*Antony and Cleopatra* and *Coriolanus,* Shakespeare's Heroic Tragedies: A Jacobean Adjustment," *Shakespeare Survey,* 26 (1973), 95–101.

29. Paul Siegel focuses upon the social, political, and economic tensions of the late Elizabethan era (*Shakespearean Tragedy and the Elizabethan Compromise,* New York: New York Univ. Press, 1957, chaps. 1–5); see also Knights, p. 174; and G. K. Hunter, "English Folly and Italian Vice: The Moral Landscape of John Marston," *Jacobean Theatre,* ed. J. R. Brown and B. Harris (London: Arnold, 1960), pp. 93–94.

30. G. Wilson Knight, *The Golden Labyrinth* (London: Phoenix House, 1962), p. 105.

31. L. G. Salingar ("*The Revenger's Tragedy* and the Morality Tradition," *Scrutiny,* 6, 1938,) 417) describes Jacobean England as a "happy hunting ground for adventurers and profiteers," for "the Machieavellian and the sychophant"; see also Hunter's description of the "whole group of Jacobean statements" reflecting the world of Hobbesian individualism and power politics (pp. 87–94).

32. Eugene Waith, *The Herculean Hero* (New York: Columbia Univ. Press, 1962), p. 144.

33. *Jacobean Dramatic Perspectives* (Charlottesville: Univ. Press of Virginia, 1972), p. 128.

34. See Alfred Harbage, *Annals of English Drama,* 2d ed., rev. S. Schoenbaum (1940; Philadelphia: Univ. of Pennsylvania Press, 1964).

CHAPTER II

1. *Shakespeare's Tragic Perspective: The Development of His Dramatic Technique* (Athens: Univ. of Georgia Press, 1976).

2. All line references to Shakespeare's plays throughout this study are to the Pelican Shakespeare, *William Shakespeare: The Complete Works,* general editor Alfred Harbage (Baltimore: Penguin Books, 1969).

3. Virgil K. Whitaker asserts that, except for Marlowe, Shakespeare was "the only dramatist who worked seriously at solving the structural problem presented by the dramatic treatment of English history" (*The Mirror Up To Nature,* San Marino: Huntington Library, 1965, p. 16). The "cyclical structure" (A. P. Rossiter, "The Structure of *Richard III,*" *Durham University Journal,* 1938–39, 46) suggests "a rhetorical symphony of five movements, with first and second subjects and some Wagnerian *Leitmotifs*" (*Angel With Horns,* ed. Graham Storey, London: Longmans, 1961, p. 7).

4. Both this scene (Kristian Smidt, *Iniurious Imposters and Richard III,* New York: Humanities Press, 1964, p. 168) and the earlier scene of Margaret's curse (E. K. Chambers, *William Shakespeare,* Oxford: Clarendon Press, 1930, II, 301) may well be afterthoughts, but the effect in each instance is to heighten the architectonic structure of the piece.

5. Aerol Arnold, "The Recapitulation Dream in *Richard III* and *Macbeth,*" *SQ,* 6 (1955), 53.

6. Richard becomes "Mankind, . . . resisting oppression and being destroyed" ("Reflecting Gems and Dead Bones: Tragedy Versus History in *Richard III,*" *CQ,* 7, 1955, 134); Daniel E. Hughes, "The 'Worm of Conscience' in *Richard III* and *Macbeth,*" *EJ,* 55 (1966), 851. For a recent analysis of Richard's terrifying dream, see Bettie Anne Doebler, " 'Despair and Dye': The Ultimate Temptation of *Richard III,*" *Shakespeare Studies,* 7 (1974), 75–85.

7. "Each of Shakespeare's histories serves a special purpose in elucidating a political problem of Elizabeth's day" (Lily Bess Campbell, *Shakespeare's Histories: Mirrors of Elizabethan Policy,* San Marino: Huntington Library, 1947, p. 125); Richard II is "shot full of warnings and advice and prophecies and pictures of England" (Donald Stauffer, *Shakespeare's World of Images,* New York: Norton, 1949, p. 90).

8. "A large part of the play's imaginative framework" (R. A. Foakes, "An Approach to *Julius Caesar,*" *SQ,* 5, 1954, 263), the outer conflict "serve[s] to order the human action by relating it to some hinted outerness" (R. H. West, *Shakespeare and the Outer Mystery,* Lexington: Univ. of Kentucky Press, 1968, p. 97).

9. *Shakespeare's Use of Learning* (San Marino: Huntington Library, 1953), p. 246.

10. J. A. Bryant sees Richard as "microchristus" and "microcosmos," as the "Lord's anointed" and as "Everyman" ("The Linked Analogies of *Richard II,*" *Sewanee Review,* 65, 1957, 425). Both Travis Bogard in the king's

suffering ("Shakespeare's Second Richard," *PMLA,* 70, 1955, 208) and P. G. Phialas in the nature of the tragic process (*"Richard II* and Shakepeare's Tragic Mode," *TSLL,* 5, 1963, 344) view Richard as a significant step in Shakespeare's development of tragic character. For a similar view, see Harold F. Folland, "King Richard's Pallid Victory," *SQ,* 24 (1973), 390, 398.

    11. Richard becomes "man and martyr" (Karl F. Thompson, "Richard II: Matyr," *SQ,* 8, 1957, 160) as the scenes "are played against each other for effect" (W. B. C. Watkins, *Shakespeare and Spenser,* Princeton: Princeton Univ. Press, 1950, p. 80). See also Paul A. Jorgensen, "A Formative Shake-spearean Legacy: Elizabethan Views of God, Fortune, and War," *PMLA,* 90 (1975), 232.

    12. Richard's final words have been branded as "the merest of lip-service" (Willard Farnham, *The Medieval Heritage of Elizabethan Drama,* Oxford: Blackwell, 1956, p. 417). To the contrary, Michael Quinn avers that Richard "dies as Somebody, a lion overpowered, a king deposed" ("'The King is Not Himself': The Personal Tragedy of Richard II," *SP,* 56, 1959, 184) who has learned "to distinguish in himself shadow from substance" (D. H. Rieman, "Appearance, Reality, and Moral Order in *Richard II,"MLQ,* 25, 1964, 40).

    13. Harry Levin describes the love of Romeo and Juliet as "the one organic relation amid an overplus of stylized expressions and attitudes" ("Form and Formality in *Romeo and Juliet,"SQ,* 11, 1960, 9). The lovers alone "are pos-sessed of a light incomprehensible to the rest of Verona's citizens" (Ruth Nevo, *Tragic Form in Shakespeare,* Princeton: Princeton Univ. Press, 1972, p. 40.

    14. F. M. Dickey (*Not Wisely But Too Well,* San Marino: Huntington Library, 1957, p. 106) and T. P. Harrison ("Hang Up Philosophy," *SAB,* 22, 1947, 208) consider the Friar a key figure in the play. On the other hand, G. I. Duthie (ed., with J. D. Wilson, *Romeo and Juliet,* Cambridge: Cambridge Univ. Press, 1955, p. xix) and Theodore Spencer (*Shakespeare and the Nature of Man,* New York: Macmillan, 1942, p. 92) argue that for all his comment the Friar does not "increase an understanding of the protagonists."

    15. The lovers "idolize each other, and in doing so make a religion of their passion" (*Shakespearean Tragedy,* Bloomington: Indiana Univ. Press, 1969, p. 103); suffering an "'ulcerate' condition of soul" (H. Edward Cain, *"Romeo and Juliet:* A Reinterpretation," *SAB,* 22, 1947, 186), Romeo *"loses* himself in love" (M. A. Goldberg, "The Multiple Masks of Romeo," *Antioch Review,* 28, 1968, 425).

    16. G. A. Bonnard, *"Romeo and Juliet:* A Possible Significance," *RES,* 2 (1951), 325; G. M. Matthews observes that the feud is "an 'expanded meta-phor' for the conflict in Elizabethan sex-relations," reflecting the antagonisms toward arranged marriage ("Sex and the Sonnet," *Essays in Criticism,* 2, 1951, 134).

    17. A cultural elitist (Marvin L. Vawter, "'Division 'Tween Our Souls': Shakespeare's Stoic Brutus," *Shakespeare Studies,* 7, 1974, 192), Brutus, on

the one hand, is "pompous, opinionated, and self-righteous" (T. S. Dorsch, ed., *Julius Caesar,* London: Methuen, 1955, p. xxxix), an "intellectually limited do-gooder" (W. R. Bowden, "The Mind of Brutus," *SQ,* 17, 1966, 67). On the other hand, he is a "liberal intellectual in a world of *Realpolitik*" (David Daiches, *Literary Essays,* London: Oliver and Boyd, 1956, p. 3).

18. Several critics see the effect as deliberate: Rene Fortin, "*Julius Caesar:* An Experiment in Point of View," *SQ,* 19 (1968), 342; Adrien Bonjour, *The Structure of Julius Caesar* (Liverpool: Liverpool Univ. Press, 1958), p. 3; Ernest Schanzer, "The Problem of Julius Caesar," *PMLA,* 81 (1966), 58. Brutus' vision is necessarily limited by the Christian concept of Roman history (J. L. Simmons, *Shakespeare's Pagan World,* Charlottesville: Univ. Press of Virginia, 1973, p. 14).

19. In this soliloquy his "virtue and his intellect worked together to produce only rationalization" (G. R. Smith, "Brutus, Virtue, and Will," *SQ,* 10, 1959, 373). We watch "Brutus' attempt to defend his decision before the court of his conscience" (Ernest Schanzer, *The Problem Plays of Shakespeare,* New York: Schocken, 1963, pp. 54-55); see also D. J. Palmer, "Tragic Error in *Julius Caesar,*" *SQ,* 21 (1970), 404.

20. Such critics as Irving Ribner (*Patterns in Shakespearian Tragedy,* London: Methuen, 1960, p. 53) and Anne Paolucci ("The Tragic Hero in *Julius Caesar,*" *SQ,* 11, 1960, 333) insist that Brutus has gained significant insight. As M. N. Proser observes, however, Brutus simply never articulates such insight; nor does he ever seem to realize that Pompey and Caesar in their turn probably also conceived of themselves as "saviors of Rome" (*The Heroic Image in Five Shakespearean Tragedies,* Princeton: Princeton Univ. Press, 1965, p. 14).

21. The play concerns the "process by which a new Caesar emerges from the wreckage of the conspiracy" (J.W. Velz, " 'If I were Brutus now . . .': Role-Playing in *Julius Caesar,*" *Shakespeare Studies,* 4, 1968, 152), a "tyranny of the triumvirate . . . far more terrible than those of which the conspirators could accuse Caesar" (J. E. Phillips, *The State in Shakespeare's Greek and Roman Plays,* New York: Columbia Univ. Press, 1940, p. 186).

22. As R. A. Foakes has recently observed, "While Hamlet is concerned with the nature of revenge and the horror of the act of cruelty, we see in Vindice a growing detachment from the nature of what he is doing" ("The Art of Cruelty: Hamlet and Vindice," *Shakespeare Survey,* 26, 1973, 28).

23. Both Madeleine Doran ("The Language of *Hamlet,*" *HLQ,* 27, 1963-64, 259-78) and Maurice Charney (*Style in Hamlet,* Princeton: Princeton Univ. Press, 1969) refer to Hamlet's various styles which reflect the complexity of his personality, the "first attribute [of which] . . . is mysteriousness" (Maynard Mack, "The World of *Hamlet,*" *Yale Review,* 41, 1952, 504).

24. On the one hand, given the conventions of revenge tragedy, we cannot assume—as do Roy Walker (*The Time Is Out of Joint,* London: Dakers, 1948) and Paul N. Siegel (*Shakespearean Tragedy and Elizabethan Compromise,*

New York: New York Univ. Press, 1957,—that the average Elizabethan would have condemned blood revenge in dramatic context any more than we would morally judge James Bond for an act of political assassination. On the other, we have no reason to assume that Hamlet, like Hieronimo, attempts to distinguish between the morality of public and private revenge (see Fredson Bowers, "Hamlet as Minister and Scourge," *PMLA,* 70, 1955, 740–49; "Dramatic Structure and Criticism: Plot in *Hamlet,*" *SQ,* 15, 1964, 217). All we can say with assurance is that he, in Act V, stands ready to act in either capacity "as the instrument of justice rather than the dispenser of it" (H. S. Wilson, *On the Design of Shakespearian Tragedy,* Toronto: Univ. of Toronto Press, 1957, p. 39).

25. Theodore Spencer, "Hamlet and the Nature of Reality," *ELH,* 5 (1938), 258; David Bevington, ed., *Twentieth-Century Interpretations of Hamlet* (Englewood Cliffs, N.J.: Prentice Hall, 1968), p. 12.

26. Thomas MacAlindon, "Indecorum in Hamlet," *Shakespeare Studies,* 5 (1969), 78; see also *Shakespeare and Decorum* (New York: Barnes and Noble, 1973). Hamlet's personality takes shape in terms of its confrontations with the other inhabitants of the *Hamlet*-world (Bernard McElroy, *Shakespeare's Mature Tragedies,* Princeton: Princeton Univ. Press, 1973, p. 67).

27. Neville Coghill (*Shakespeare's Professional Skills,* Cambridge: Cambridge Univ. Press, 1964, pp. 6–19) and Eleanor Prosser (*Hamlet and Revenge,* Stanford: Stanford Univ. Press, 1967, pp. 140–41) find in the action proof of the evil nature of the ghost. According to J. Dover Wilson (*What Happens in Hamlet,* Cambridge: Cambridge Univ. Press, 1935, p. 48) the ambiguity of the nature of the ghost is built into the action.

28. Thomas McFarland, *Tragic Meanings in Shakespeare* (New York: Random House, 1966), p. 17.

29. Spencer, *Nature of Man,* p. 125.

30. Alvin Kernan, ed., *Othello* (New York: New American Library, 1963), p. xxix.

31. Iago is "the champion of the absolute autonomy of the will" (Daniel Stempel, "The Silence of Iago," *PMLA,* 84, 1969, 258). Ralph Berry calls the Iago-Emilia relationship a key to understanding the major struggle of the play ("Pattern in *Othello,*" *SQ,* 23, 1972, 17).

32. Recently Othello has been described as a composite character: "normal," "romantic," "psychotic" (Robert Rogers, "Endopsychic Drama in *Othello,*" *SQ,* 20, 1969, 213); he is "magnanimous" but "egotistic" (F. R. Leavis, "Diabolic Intellect and the Noble Hero," *Scrutiny,* 5, 1937, 265), "too much of a romantic idealist" (Leo Kirschbaum, "The Modern Othello," *ELH,* 2, 1944, 287). Like the Pelegians, he understands justice but not mercy (Ruth Levitsky, "All in All Sufficiency in *Othello,*" *Shakespeare Studies,* 6, 1970, 219).

33. Albert Gerard, "'Egregiously An Ass': The Dark Side of the Moor," *Shakespeare Survey,* 10 (1957), 195. On the complex connotations of color

in the play, see Doris Adler, "The Rhetoric of *Black* and *White* in *Othello*," *SQ*, 25 (1974), 248–57. Whatever moral judgments one may draw (at his own risk), the spectators are made to feel that Othello in his final moments achieves a kind of purgation, a "swearing of the truth" (Madeleine Doran, "Good Name in *Othello*," *SEL*, 7, 1967, 216).

34. Mark Van Doren, *Shakespeare* (New York: Holt, 1939), p. 215. Each at the outset is blinded by a kind of hubris (Lawrence Rosinger, "Gloucester and Lear: Men Who Act Like Gods," *ELH*, 35, 1968, 491–504; Russell A. Fraser, *Shakespeare's Poetics*, London: Routledge and Kegan Paul, 1972, p. 119).

35. The Gloucester plot "helps us to understand, and feel, the enduring agony of Lear" (G. Wilson Knight, *The Wheel of Fire*, Oxford: Oxford Univ. Press, 1930, p. 169). Maynard Mack has described this structure as homiletic (*King Lear in Our Time*, Berkeley: Univ. of California Press, 1965, p. 71); see also John Ellis, "The Gulling of Gloucester: Credibility in the Subplot of *King Lear*," *SEL*, 12 (1972), 289.

36. As Harold Skulsky observes, "The finest intelligence that Lear learns . . . is to resolve his abortive attempts at formulating a causal problem of evil" (*"King Lear* and the Meaning of Chaos," *SQ*, 17, 1966, 14). Initially guilty of what J. Leeds Barroll calls "ontological self-sufficiency" (*Artificial Persons: The Formation of Character in the Tragedies of Shakespeare*, Columbia: Univ. of South Carolina Press, 1974, p. 194), Lear in his final words, while ambivalent (Phyllis Rackin, "Delusion as Resolution in *King Lear*," *SQ*, 21, 1970, 30), does establish a sense of humility and integrity (Emily W. Leider, "Plainness of Style in *King Lear*," *SQ*, 21, 1970, 45).

37. E. W. Talbert, "Lear, the King," in *Medieval and Renaissance Studies* (Chapel Hill: Univ. of North Carolina Press, 1966), p. 98. The play is a "successive stripping away of the layers of appearance" (Ivor Morris, *Shakespeare's God: The Role of Religion in the Tragedies*, New York: St. Martin's, 1972, p. 184).

38. Judah Stampfer, "The Catharsis of *King Lear*," *Shakespeare Survey*, 13 (1960), 153.

39. Robert J. Brauer, "Despite of Mine Own Nature: Edmund and the Orders, Cosmic and Moral," *TSLL*, 10 (1968), 359. See also R. C. Bald, "'Thou, Nature, Art My Goddess': Edmund and Renaissance Free Thought," in *J. Q. Adams Memorial Studies* (Washington, D.C.: Folger Library, 1948), pp. 337–49; Harry Rusche, "Edmund's Conception and Nativity in *King Lear*," *SQ*, 20 (1969), 161–64; and G. T. Buckley, "Was Edmund Guilty of Capital Treason?" *SQ*, 23 (1972), 94.

40. Nature, which both "preserves" and "impedes" (L. C. Knights, "On the Background of Shakespeare's Use of Nature in *Macbeth*," *Sewanee Review*, 64, 1956, 214), is "seen as the mirror of psychic and metaphysical convulsions" (Speaight, p. 53). Ultimately, as Paul Jorgensen has observed, the most striking quality of the play is the "dark and painful power resulting from unparalleled sensational artistry" (*Our Naked Frailties*, Berkeley: Univ. of California Press, 1971, p. 4).

41. Knights, *Some Shakespearean Themes* (Stanford: Stanford Univ. Press, 1959), p. 122.

42. Whether one perceives them as Destinies or Norns (G. L. Kittredge, ed., *The Complete Works of Shakespeare*, Boston: Ginn, 1936, p. 1114), or demons credible to the Jacobean audience (W. C. Curry, *Shakespeare's Philosophical Patterns*, Baton Rouge: Louisiana State Univ. Press, 1937, p. 60; Arthur R. McGee, "*Macbeth* and the Furies," *Shakespeare Survey*, 19, 1966, 65), Shakespeare forces each reader to "make his own rationale of the supernatural in *Macbeth*, . . . just as he might for similar phenomena in the real world" (West, p. 78).

43. G. B. Harrison, for example, maintains that Macbeth can be a "tragic victim" only to those who believe in predestination (*Shakespeare's Tragedies*, New York: Oxford Univ. Press, 1966, pp. 193–94).

44. E. E. Stoll, *From Shakespeare to Joyce* (Garden City, N.Y.: Doubleday, 1944), p. 305.

45. J. I. M. Stewart, *Character and Motive in Shakespeare* (London: Longmans, Green, 1949), p. 96.

46. Hardin Craig, *The Enchanted Glass* (New York: Oxford Univ. Press, 1936), p. 232. We never forget his potentiality for goodness (Wayne Booth, "Macbeth as Tragic Hero," *JGE*, 6, 1951–52, 20).

47. "Shakespeare's encompassing framework is not heaven and hell, but the life of man within the kingdom of Scotland" (R. M. Frye, "Theological and Non-Theological Structures in Tragedy," *Shakespeare Studies*, 4, 1968, 135).

48. "The utmost he attains," as J. C. Maxwell writes, "is to *see through* particular shams and injustices" (ed., *Timon of Athens*, Cambridge: Cambridge Univ. Press, 1957, p. xxxvii). Dehumanized by grief (Harry Levin, "Shakespeare's Misanthrope," *Shakespeare Survey*, 26, 1973, 94), he represents Everyman in Shakespeare's inverted morality play (Anne Lancashire, "*Timon of Athens:* Shakespeare's *Dr. Faustus*," *SQ*, 21, 1970, 41).

49. Una Ellis-Fermor, "*Timon of Athens:* An Unfinished Play," *RES*, 18 (1942), 271; A. C. Bradley, *Shakespearean Tragedy* (London: Macmillan, 1904), p. 14.

50. Margaret Webster, *Shakespeare Without Tears* (New York: MacGraw Hill, 1947), p. 184.

51. O. J. Campbell, *Shakespeare's Satire* (New York: Oxford Univ. Press, 1943), p. 168. Whitaker, *The Mirror*, p. 87; Knights, "Timon of Athens," in *The Morality of Art*, ed. D. W. Jefferson (London: Routledge and Kegan Paul, 1969), pp. 4–5; A. S. Collins, "*Timon of Athens:* A Reconsideration," *RES*, 22 (1946), 96–108; David M. Bergeron, "*Timon of Athens* and Morality Drama," *CLAJ*, 10 (1967); Maurice Charney, ed., *Timon of Athens* (New York: New American Library, 1965), p. xxxiii. The concept of the play as pageant, discussed by E. A. J. Honigmann ("*Timon of Athens, SQ*, 12, 1961, 14–16), has been most fully developed by M. C. Bradbrook in *The Tragic Pageant of 'Timon of Athens'* (Cambridge: Cambridge Univ. Press, 1966).

52. The principle of connection, according to H. J. Oliver, is not a "plot-link" but "counterpoint" (ed., *Timon of Athens,* London: Methuen, 1959, pp. xlviii–xlix).

53. In this sense the heroes of the late tragedies are by no means "more deeply flawed" than the earlier (Willard Farnham, *Shakespeare's Tragic Frontier,* Berkeley: Univ. of California Press, 1950, p. 11). On the other hand, neither do they represent a form of goodness which cannot "make the necessary kinds of adjustment to hard reality" (Oliver, "Coriolanus As Tragic Hero," *SQ,* 10, 1959, 60). See further Simmons, *Shakespeare's Pagan World,* p. 49.

54. He blindly adheres to the ancient hero's creed, the concept of *virtus* (D. J. Gordon, "Name and Fame: Shakespeare's *Coriolanus,*" *Papers Mainly Shakespearean,* ed. G. I. Duthie, Edinburgh: Oliver and Boyd, 1964, 40–57). Shakespeare is reflecting, according to Clifford C. Huffman, the potential tyranny of both royal absolutism and of strictly limited monarchy (*Coriolanus in Context,* Lewisburg: Bucknell Univ. Press, 1971, 169, 222).

55. It is suggested, for instance, that Shakespeare "has become tedious" (E. K. Chambers, *Shakespeare: A Survey,* London: Sidgwick and Jackson, 1925, p. 258); the play is "a success altogether of a lower order than that of *Macbeth*" (D. J. Enright, "*Coriolanus:* Tragedy or Debate?" *Essays in Criticism,* 4, 1954, 19).

56. It is a "newly discovered human feeling that [leads] him to make peace" (E. A. M. Colman, "The End of Coriolanus," *ELH,* 34, 1967, 18). See also: S. K. Sen, "What Happens in *Coriolanus,*" *SQ,* 9 (1958), 332; Ivor Browning, "Coriolanus: Boy of Tears," *Essays in Criticism,* 5 (1955), 18–31. On the significance of Aufidius' last lines to the theme of reconciliation, see Jay L. Halio, "*Coriolanus:* Shakespeare's Drama of Reconciliation," *Shakespeare Studies,* 6 (1970), 302, 303.

57. "The audience is carefully placed," as Michael McCanles has recently noted, "outside the play as well as outside Coriolanus and is left to contemplate without involvement" ("The Dialectic of Transcendence in *Coriolanus,*" *PMLA,* 82, 1967, 53). The audience views the first half as a political tragedy, the last half as an individual tragedy (D. C. Hale, "The Death of a Political Metaphor," *SQ,* 22, 1971, 202).

58. Clifford Davidson, "Coriolanus: A Study in Political Dislocation," *Shakespeare Studies,* 4 (1968), 263–72.

59. Setting forth "two richly endowed but very imperfect people" in a "poetic frame which creates an aura of uniqueness and greatness" (Madeleine Doran, "'High Events as These': The Language of Hyperbole in *Antony and Cleopatra,*" *Queens Quarterly,* 72, 1965, 33), *Antony and Cleopatra* achieves "swinging ambivalence" (John F. Danby, *Poets on Fortune's Hill,* London: Faber and Faber, 1952, p. 135). The protagonists' language sets them apart as "bigger than lifesize" (Rosalie Colie, *Shakespeare's Living Art,* Princeton: Princeton Univ. Press, 1974, p. 298).

60. Depicting dissension on three levels—the individual, the family, and the state (L. E. Bowling, "Antony's Internal Disunity," *SEL,* 4, 1964, 239), the play brings "aristocratic and heroic appeals into tension with a popular and unheroic world" (J. L. Simmons, *"Antony and Cleopatra* and *Coriolanus,* Shakespeare's Heroic Tragedies: A Jacobean Adjustment," *Shakespeare Survey,* 26, 1973, 97).

61. Those who judge the play on this moral issue alone condemn Antony as a victim of a sinful "passionate lust [which] dominate[s] his life and obliterate[s] his sense of duty" (Louis B. Wright, ed., *Antony and Cleopatra,* New York: Washington Square, 1961, p. xi). To the contrary, according to Julian Markels, "Step by step through this play Shakespeare has made us amoral" (*The Pillar of the World,* Columbus: Ohio State Univ. Press, 1968, p. 7).

62. "The politics from which Antony secedes are . . . the treacheries and back-stabbing of a drunken party on a pirate's barge" (W. K. Wimsatt, *The Verbal Icon,* Lexington: Univ. of Kentucky Press, 1954, p. 96).

63. Antony asserts "not the integrity of a Roman general" but his "individual integrity" (Eugene M. Waith, *The Herculean Hero in Marlowe, Chapman, Shakespeare, and Dryden,* New York: Columbia Univ. Press, 1962, p. 118). He symbolizes several significant alternative postures concerning the passing of time (Arthur H. Bell, "Time and Convention in *Antony and Cleopatra," SQ,* 24, 1973, 264).

64. As R. A. Foakes has observed, the late plays "show us men and women as they are rather than as they might be" (Shakespeare's Later Tragedies," in *Shakespeare: 1564-1964,* ed. E. A. Bloom, Providence: Brown Univ. Press, 1964, p. 109). Shakespeare forces us to judge at the same time he reveals to us the folly of judging (Janet Adelman, *The Common Liar,* New Haven: Yale Univ. Press, 1973, p. 39).

CHAPTER III

1. C. H. Herford and Percy Simpson describe *Sejanus* as "the tragedy of a satirist" (*Ben Jonson,* Oxford: Clarendon, 1925, II, 27) while C. G. Thayer sees a "unique rendering, in tragic-historical terms, of the themes of Old Comedy" (*Ben Jonson: Studies in the Plays,* Norman: Univ. of Oklahoma Press, 1963, p. 117); to J. A. Bryant it is tragedy which instructs "through the medium of an authentic reconstruction of the past" ("The Significance of Ben Jonson's First Requirement for Tragedy: 'Truth of Argument,'" *SP,* 49, 1952, 204). L. C. Knights maintains that it is a "triumph," a "unique vision" of men and affairs with "a contemporary relevance" both in theme and in technique ("Tradition and Ben Jonson," *Scrutiny,* 4, 1935-36, 145, 157); for less enthusiastic appraisals, see T. S. Eliot (*Essays on Elizabethan Literature,* New York: Harcourt, 1932, 67); G. G. Smith (*Ben Jonson,* London: Macmillan, 1926, p. 197); and J. B. Bamborough (*Ben Jonson,* London: Longmans, Green, 1959, 28).

2. The resultant "scientific method" of presenting "moral and psychological truths" (Una Ellis-Fermor, *The Jacobean Drama*, London: Methuen, 1936, p. 99) reveals that "what most men regard as the cause of the fall—irrational Fortune—is actually the work of a clever Machiavellian tyrant" (Gary D. Hamilton, "Irony and Fortune in *Sejanus*," *SEL*, 11, 1971, 268).

3. Line references to Jonson's plays are to the edition of C. H. Herford and Percy Simpson, IV (1932).

4. Barbara N. Lindsay, "The Structure of Tragedy in *Sejanus*," *English Studies,* 50, Anglo-American Supplement (1969), xlvi. It is beside the point to argue either Jonson's "republican" posture (A. C. Swinburne, *A Study of Ben Jonson,* 1889, rpt. New York: Haskell House, 1968, p. 26) or his defense of "a strong and consecrated monarchy" (K. W. Evans, "*Sejanus* and the Ideal Prince Tradition," *SEL*, 11, 1971, 250). J. A. Bryant sees only a single scene in the play (III, i) as a clear confrontation of good and evil ("The Nature of the Conflict in Jonson's *Sejanus*," *Vanderbilt Studies in the Humanities,* ed. R. C. Beatty *et al.*, Nashville: Vanderbilt Univ. Press, 1951, p. 215).

5. A variation of the choric device (W. A. Armstrong, "Ben Jonson and Jacobean Stage Craft," in *Jacobean Theatre,* ed. J. R. Brown and B. Harris, London: Edward Arnold, 1960, p. 55), this group is led by Arruntius, the "spokesman of legitimacy" (Daniel C. Boughner, "Sejanus and Machiavelli," *SEL,* 1, 1961, 84), whose "tone of moral aversion to the life of the empire is Juvenalian" (Boughner, "Juvenal, Horace, and Sejanus," *MLN,* 75, 1960, 546).

6. His concern, according to K. M. Burton, is with "the tragic flaw *within the social order,* not within the individual" ("The Political Tragedies of Chapman and Ben Jonson," *Essays in Criticism,* 2, 1952, 397). A Roman play with "massive intrusion of Machiavellian elements" (Boughner, *The Devil's Disciple: Ben Jonson's Debt to Machiavelli,* New York: Philosophical Library, 1968, p. 89), this tragedy inveighs against "society-at-large rather than against the solitary villain" (Geoffrey Hill, "'The World's Proportion,' Jonson's Dramatic Poetry in *Sejanus* and *Catiline*," in *Jacobean Theatre,* p. 120).

7. M. C. Bradbrook, *Themes and Conventions of Elizabethan Tragedy* (Cambridge: Cambridge Univ. Press, 1957), p. 131. Sejanus has been compared profitably with Marlowe's overreachers (Robert Ornstein, *The Moral Vision of Jacobean Tragedy,* Madison: Univ. of Wisconsin Press, 1960, p. 86), with the public Vice in the late morality (Alan C. Dessen, *Jonson's Moral Comedy,* Evanston: Northwestern Univ. Press, 1971, p. 74), with Richard III (Eugene Waith, *The Herculean Hero in Marlowe, Chapman, Shakespeare and Dryden,* London: Chatto and Windus, 1962, p. 145), and with Coriolanus (Edwin Honig, "*Sejanus* and *Coriolanus:* A Study in Alienation," *PMLA,* 12, 1951, 407).

8. Jonas A. Barish, ed., *Ben Jonson: Sejanus* (New Haven: Yale Univ. Press, 1965), p. 9.

9. This is the culminating action, C. R. Ricks notes, in a pattern of imagery

reflecting the dismemberment of Sejanus, Tiberius, and Rome itself (*"Sejanus and Dismemberment," MLN,* 76, 1961, 301–308).

10. If the assertion that *Sejanus* "teaches the virtue of humility before the will of God" (Robert E. Knoll, *Ben Jonson's Plays,* Lincoln: Univ. of Nebraska Press, 1964, p. 78) is overly simplistic, we must agree that what ultimately prevails is Jonson's "deep-rooted and energetic belief in modesty, moderation, a categorical 'norm' in matters social and religious" (D. J. Enright, "Crime and Punishment in Ben Jonson," *Scrutiny,* 9, 1940–41, 235).

11. In Jonson's case the structure goes beyond what Harry Levin has called the "almost medieval stress upon tragic reversal of fortune" (ed., *Ben Jonson: Selected Works,* New York: Random House, 1938, p. 15) to achieve, "on three different levels simultaneously"—the personal, the historical, and the ontological (Lindsay, p. xliv)—a "unity of theme, a seeking out of all things within a limited subject, as a means of achieving 'dilation' or fulness" (L. A. Beaurline, "Ben Jonson and the Illusion of Completeness," *PMLA,* 84, 1969, 55).

12. Critics in general have not been kind. Leonard Digges in 1640 called the tragedy "irksome" (quoted in Smith, p. 188) and Samuel Pepys thought it "the worst upon the stage" (*Diary,* ed. H. B. Wheatley, London: Bell, 1924, VIII, 172). Eliot calls it a "dreary Pyrrhic victory of tragedy" (p. 129); more recently Jacob I. DeVilliers has described the "turgid weariness" ("Ben Jonson's Tragedies," *ES,* 45, 1964, 440) of what is to Dessen Jonson's "greatest debacle" (p. 138).

13. In a general sense W. D. Briggs was no doubt correct in his view that every one of Jonson's undertakings has an immediate bearing on his own day ("Studies in Ben Jonson," *Anglia,* 37, 1913, 488), but Irving Ribner is surely shortsighted in his assertion that Jonson "is concerned not with mankind but with the corruption in the court of King James" (*Jacobean Tragedy: The Quest for Moral Order,* New York: Barnes and Noble, 1962, p. 14). Even more restrictively, Barbara N. De Luna has argued that the play is a "classical parallelograph on the Gun powder Plot of 1605" (*Jonson's Romish Plot,* Oxford: Clarendon, 1967, p. 360).

14. See W. F. Bolton and Jane F. Gardner, eds., *Catiline* (Lincoln: Univ. of Nebraska Press, 1973), p. xv.

15. Geoffrey Hill (p. 121) perceptively notes the irony of juxtaposing Catiline's Petrarchan posturings with his "cynical confession of wife-removal."

16. *Jonson and the Comic Truth* (Madison: Univ. of Wisconsin Press, 1957), p. 177. Herford and Simpson speak of "the sublimity of a desperate and prodigal heroism" in Catiline's last stand and death (II, 125).

17. Bryant views the situation in which Cicero is pitted against Catiline while the real conspirator Caesar bides his time "for another attempt to assassinate the body politic" as "an extension rather than a restriction of the scope of tragedy" ("*Catiline* and the Nature of Jonson's Tragic Fable," *PMLA,* 69, 1954, 270, 277); to another it is "an extension of the scope of history"

(Angela G. Dorenkamp, "Jonson's *Catiline:* History as a Trying Faculty," *SP*, 67, 1970, 220).

18. *Essay of Dramatic Poesy,* in *Essays of John Dryden,* ed. W. P. Ker (Oxford: Clarendon, 1900), pp. 60, 61.

19. Eliot, p. 131.

20. Bolton and Gardner, p. xxii; Burton, p. 403; G. B. Jackson, *Vision and Judgment in Ben Jonson's Drama* (New Haven: Yale Univ. Press, 1968), p. 129.

21. For those who view Cicero as simplistically a thoroughly "good man" (Dessen, p. 138), who symbolizes the "self-transcendence" of "true ambition" (Jackson, p. 152) and whom Jonson all too obviously admired (Barish, *Ben Jonson and the Language of Prose Comedy,* Cambridge, Mass.: Harvard Univ. Press, 1960, p. 48), it is easy to write off the tragedy as "the decline and fall of an obviously bad man and . . . the rise of an all-too-obviously good one" (DeVilliers, p. 441). Actually, Jonson "lay[s] Cicero's claims to virtue . . . open to qualification on several counts" (Miachael J. C. Echuero, "The Conscience of Politics and Jonson's *Catiline,"SEL*, 1966, 348).

22. Bolton and Gardner, p. xiv. Jonson "clung tenaciously to the unorthodox humanistic credo that, finally, what is important in life is the work of art itself and our moral attitude toward it" (John T. French, "Ben Jonson: His Aesthetic of Relief," *TSLL,* 10, 1968–69, 174).

23. A Senecan anachronism to Herford and Simpson (II, 116), Sylla serves to create an atmosphere of the "world turned upside down" (Thayer, p. 124); a "historical link between preceding events and the play to follow" (Dorenkamp, p. 211), it substitutes a statement of conspiratorial politics for one of blood revenge (Weldon M. Williams, "The Influence of Ben Jonson's *Catiline* upon John Oldham's *Satyrs Upon the Jesuits," ELH,* 11, 1944, 40).

24. Armstrong, p. 52; L. H. Harris, "Lucan's *Pharsalia* and Jonson's *Catiline," MLN,* 34 (1919), 399.

25. *Shakespeare and the Nature of Man* (New York: Macmillan, 1942), p. 49.

CHAPTER IV

1. Lacy Lockert, "The Greatest of Elizabethan Melodramas," *Essays in Dramatic Literature: The Parrott Presentation Volume,* ed. Hardin Craig (Princeton: Princeton Univ. Press, 1935), 103; James L. Rosenberg, ed., *The Revenger's Tragedy* (San Francisco: Chandler, 1962), p. vii.

2. Richard Hindry Barker, *Thomas Middleton* (New York: Columbia Univ. Press, 1958), p. 73.

3. Samuel Schoenbaum, *"The Revenger's Tragedy:* Jacobean Dance of Death," *MLQ,* 15 (1954), 203; Alvin Kernan, *The Cankered Muse* (New Haven: Yale Univ. Press, 1959), p. 231.

4. Inga-Stina Ekeblad, "An Approach to Tourneur's Imagery," *MLR,* 54

(1959), 489; "On the Authorship of *The Revenger's Tragedy*," *English Studies*, 41 (1960), 227; Lawrence J. Ross, ed., *The Revenger's Tragedy* (Lincoln: Nebraska Univ. Press, 1966), p. xxiii.

5. *The Tragic Satire of John Webster* (Berkeley: Univ. of California Press, 1955); for a similar view but a contrary conclusion, see George F. Sensabaugh, "Tragic Effect in Webster's *The White Devil*," *SEL*, 5 (1965), 346.

6. L. G. Salingar, "*The Revenger's Tragedy:* Some Possible Sources," *MLR*, 60 (1965), 12.

7. *A Study of Elizabethan and Jacobean Tragedy* (Cambridge: Melbourne Univ. Press, 1964), pp. 126-27.

8. *The Revenger's Tragedy* (1607) appeared without indication of authorship. By critical consensus Tourneur (first associated with the play by Archer in 1656) is the author, though a heated argument has been made for Middleton. All line references in this essay to *The Revenger's Tragedy* are to the edition of R. A. Foakes (Cambridge, Mass.: Harvard Univ. Press, 1966).

9. M. C. Bradbrook describes the play as "an enlarged series of peripeteia" (*Themes and Conventions of Elizabethan Tragedy*, Cambridge: Cambridge Univ. Press, 1957, p. 165).

10. Irving Ribner, *Jacobean Tragedy* (New York: Barnes and Noble, 1962), pp. 72, 73.

11. Robert Ornstein, *The Moral Vision of Jacobean Tragedy* (Madison: Univ. of Wisconsin Press, 1960), p. 117. Tourneur's "implications are obviously positive, and orthodox" (John Peter, "*The Revenger's Tragedy* Reconsidered," *Essays in Criticism*, 6, 1956, 140), ultimately upholding the Christian view that vengeance belongs only to God (Henry Hitch Adams, "Cyril Tourneur on Revenge," *JEGP*, 48, 1949, 79). Whereas both Peter Lisca ("*The Revenger's Tragedy:* A Study in Irony," *PQ*, 38, 1959, 242) and Michael H. Higgins ("The Influence of Calvinistic Thought in Tourneur's *The Atheist's Tragedy*," *RES*, 19, 1943, 255) stress the Calvinistic influence, Peter B. Murray (*A Study of Cyril Tourneur*, Philadelphia: Univ. of Pennsylvania Press, 1964, p. 246) and Inga-Stina Ekeblad ("Approach," p. 497; "Authorship," p. 229) stress the significance of imagery and symbolism to the moral structure.

12. The intent is apparently not clear, however; Adams (p. 77) notes Heaven's disapproval of murder through the thunder, whereas Thomas B. Stroup describes the sound as "the applause of the gods" (*Microcosmus: The Shape of the Elizabethan Play*, Lexington: Univ. of Kentucky Press, 1965, p. 72).

13. The morality "puzzles our response to [the] protagonist" (Madeleine Doran, *Endeavors of Art*, Madison: Univ. of Wisconsin Press, 1954, p. 357) and fails to compensate for Vindice's fall (L. G. Salingar, "*The Revenger's Tragedy* and The Morality Tradition," *Scrutiny*, 6, 1938, 417).

14. Vindice's role has been described in various ways—the "Jacobean 'reality instructor'" (George C. Herndl, *The High Design: English Renaissance Tragedy and the Natural Law*, Lexington: Univ. Press of Kentucky, 1970, p.

219), malcontent, revenger, and tool-villain all in one (E. E. Stoll, *John Webster,* New York: Mudge, 1905, p. 110), the moralist with the mask of the satirist (Murray, p. 250).

15. Interpretations of Antonio's final authority are flatly contradictory. On the one hand, he is a moral touchstone (Fredson Bowers, *Elizabethan Revenge Tragedy,* Princeton: Princeton Univ. Press, 1940, p. 134), "God's deputy" (Adams, p. 77) who wants only justice at the end (John Peter, *Complaint and Satire in Early English Literature,* Oxford: Oxford Univ. Press, 1956, pp. 255–87) and whose judgment on Vindice "restores our moral perspective" (Lockert, p. 125). On the other hand, his execution of Vindice is purely political (Doran, p. 358), a move to eliminate those who stand between him and power (Murray, p. 227); he is but one final example in the play of "retribution ironically accomplished through injustice" (Ross, p. xxv).

16. This *"drame a these"* (Bradbrook, p. 184) has provoked two complementary critical views: (1) that it was written to refute "all the philosophies that were undermining religious orthodoxy in Jacobean England" (Murray, pp. 142–43; Ribner, *Jacobean Tragedy,* New York: Barnes and Noble, 1962, p. 72), and (2) that it sets forth "a religious hero and a higher moral to compete with the traditional amoral revenge play with its anomalous revenger" (Bowers, p. 143; see further note 13). R. J. Kaufmann has described the play as an explicit dramatization of Psalm 127 on "the extent and nature of God's providence" ("Theodicy, Tragedy, and the Psalmist: Tourneur's *Atheist's Tragedy,*" *Comparative Drama,* 3, 1969–70, 250).

17. The tragedy depicts a bestial view of man which to J. A. Bastiaenen is repulsive (*The Moral Tone of Jacobean and Caroline Drama,* Amsterdam: H. J. Paris, 1930, p. 177) and to Michael H. Higgins (p. 256) reflects the Calvinistic doctrine of the utter depravity of man. T. B. Tomlinson affirms the powerful social decadence of the stage world but argues that too rigid an insistence on the dubious parallels between the tragedy and the society of its time does an injustice to Tourneur's creative vision ("The Morality of Revenge: Tourneur's Critics," *Essays in Criticism,* 10, 1960, 146–47).

18. All line references in this essay to *The Atheist's Tragedy* are to the edition of Irving Ribner (Cambridge, Mass.: Harvard Univ. Press, 1964).

19. As Robert Ornstein has argued, D'Amville is a "compound of atheist, materialist, sensualist, nature worshiper, and politician" (*"The Atheist's Tragedy* and Renaissance Naturalism," *SP,* 51, 1954, 195).

20. Ed., p. lvii. "For all the show of reason," notes Harold Jenkins, "the ultimate appeal must still be to passion" ("Cyril Tourneur," *RES,* 17, 1941, 35).

21. *Elizabethan and Jacobean Playwrights* (New York: Columbia Univ. Press, 1939), p. 35.

22. J. M. S. Tompkins has observed that the stars, "which are symbols and instruments of the divine government of the world, are hidden" during the first three acts; the reverse is true when Heaven assumes control in IV-V ("Tourneur and the Stars," *RES,* 22, 1946, 318).

23. The imagery of building is one of the dominant patterns in the play, as Miss Ellis-Fermor has noted ("The Imagery of *The Revenger's Tragedy* and *The Atheist's Tragedy," MLR,* 30, 1935, 289); D'Amville's rise and fall can be traced in "the image of the founding, erecting and subsequent ruining of the building" (Ekeblad, "Approach," p. 492).

24. A. P. Rossiter, *English Drama from the Early Times to the Elizabethans* (London: Hutchinson, 1950), p. 155.

25. Kaufmann, p. 257. The most extensive discussion of the relationships is by Richard Levin ("The Subplot of *The Atheist's Tragedy," HLQ,* 29, 1965, 17-33).

26. If branding him a "prig" (Adams, p. 87) and a "cad" (Ellis-Fermor, *Jacobean Drama,* p. 166) is extreme, so is defending him as the Senecal man (Michael H. Higgins, "The Development of the 'Senecal Man': Chapman's Bussy D'Ambois and Some Precursors," *RES,* 23, 1947, 32) who is a sympathetic and dynamic character growing into right reason (Murray, pp. 59, 100). Inexplicably inactive, Charlemont was created perhaps as a Christian response to Bussy and Clermont D'Ambois as stoic heroes (Clifford Leech, "*The Atheist's Tragedy* as a Dramatic Comment on Chapman's *Bussy* Plays," *JEGP,* 48, 1949, 525-30).

27. Doran, p. 307. Of no "real dramatic value" (Charles Whitmore, *The Supernatural in Tragedy,* Cambridge, Mass.: Harvard Univ. Press, 1915, p. 245), this "least Senecan, most Christian, ghost in Elizabethan tragedy" (Lily Bess Campbell, "Theories of Revenge in Elizabethan England," *MP,* 28, 1930-31, 296) is clearly either Montferrers himself or his good angel (R. H. West, *The Invisible World,* Athens: Univ. of Georgia Press, 1939, p. 186).

28. *The Moral Vision of Jacobean Tragedy* (Madison: Univ. of Wisconsin Press, 1960), p. 119.

29. Ribner, ed., p. lxiii.

CHAPTER V

1. G. B. Shaw, *Our Theatres in the Nineties* (London: Constable, 1932), II, 130.

2. William Archer, "Webster, Lamb, and Swinburne," *New Review,* 8 (1893), rpt. in *John Webster,* ed. G. K. Hunter and S. K. Hunter (Baltimore: Penguin, 1969), p. 82.

3. Samuel Sheppard, *Epigrams Theological, Philosophical and Romantic* (London, 1851), in Hunter and Hunter, eds., p. 36.

4. Charles Lamb, *Specimens of the English Dramatic Poets Who Lived about the Time of Shakespeare* (New York: Putnam, 1848), p. 203.

5. "John Webster," *Nineteenth Century,* 19 (1886), 869.

6. Ed., *The White Devil* (Cambridge, Mass.: Harvard Univ. Press, 1960), p. xliii.

7. "The Case of John Webster," *Scrutiny,* 16 (1949), 38.

8. "Inverted Rituals in Webster's *The White Devil," JEGP,* 61 (1962), 45.

9. *John Webster* (Boston: Mudge, 1905), p. 128.

10. *Jacobean Tragedy: The Quest for Moral Order* (London: Baylis, 1962), p. 97. The "strongly moral theme" (Ian Scott-Kilvert, *John Webster*, London: Longmans, Green, 1964, p. 20) results from "opposing two negative values in such a way that neither dominates nor obscures the other" (James Smith, "The Tragedy of Blood," *Scrutiny*, 8, 1939, 270).

11. Lucy Lockert, "Marston, Webster, and the Decline of the Elizabethan Tragedy," *Sewanee Review*, 27 (1919), 65.

12. W. A. Edwards, "John Webster" in *Determinations*, ed. F. R. Leavis (London: Chatto and Windus, 1934), p. 176.

13. Harold Jenkins, "The Tragedy of Revenge in Shakespeare and Webster," *Shakespeare Survey*, 14 (1961), 52. T. S. Eliot describes Webster as "a very great literary and dramatic genius directed toward chaos" (*Selected Essays*, New York: Harcourt, 1932, p. 117).

14. Inga-Stina Ekeblad, "The Impure Art of John Webster," *RES*, NS 9 (1958), 267.

15. Travis Bogard, *The Tragic Satire of John Webster* (Berkeley: Univ. of California Press, 1955), p. 5; George F. Sensabaugh, to the contrary, blames the play's structural imbalance on precisely this blend of satire and tragedy ("Tragic Effect in Webster's *The White Devil*," *SEL*, 5, 1965, 346).

16. Fredson T. Bowers, *Elizabethan Revenge Tragedy* (Princeton: Princeton Univ. Press, 1940), p. 180.

17. Flamineo, described by Rupert Brooke as "cold, itchy, filthily knowing" (*John Webster and the Elizabethan Drama*, New York: Lane, 1916, p. 140) is considered by Bogard to be the center—both as commentator and as chief gull—of a satiric story (ed., *The White Devil*, San Francisco: Chandler, 1961, p. x).

18. All line references to *The White Devil* and *The Duchess of Malfi* are to the edition of F. L. Lucas, *The Complete Works of John Webster* (London: Chatto and Windus, 1927), Vols. 1-2.

19. As Roma Gill notes, it sets "our moral nature at variance with our instinctive sympathies" ("'Quaintly Done': A Reading of *The White Devil*," *Essays and Studies*, 1966, p. 57). To the audience Brachiano, Francisco, and Monticelso are on trial as well, and Vittoria emerges as the emotional victor as a result of her plainer, more earnest, and less artificial style (H. Bruce Franklin, "The Trial Scene of Webster's *The White Devil* Examined in Terms of Renaissance Rhetoric," *SEL*, 1, No. 2, 1961, 45).

20. This point is the critical linchpin for the diverse interpretations of the play. J. R. Mulryne (*"The White Devil* and *The Duchess of Malfi,"* in *Jacobean Theatre*, ed. J. R. Brown and B. Harris, London: Arnold, 1960, p. 212), Peter B. Murray (*A Study of John Webster*, The Hague: Mouton, 1969, p. 89), Sensabaugh (p. 360), Robert Ornstein (*The Moral Vision of Jacobean Tragedy*, Madison: Univ. of Wisconsin Press, 1960, p. 138), and R. W. Dent ("The White Devil, or Vittoria Corombona?" *Renaissance Drama*, 9, 1966,

197) deny Vittoria's anagnorisis altogether. With varying qualifications her growth in self-awareness is defended by Una Ellis-Fermor (*The Jacobean Drama*, London: Methuen, 1936, p. 176, 184), Lucas (p. 96), Ekeblad ("Webster's Constructional Rhythm," *ELH*, 24, 1957, 175), J. A. Symonds (ed., *Webster and Tourneur*, London: Vizetelly, 1888, p. xxi), Gamaliel Bradford ("The Women of Middleton and Webster," *Sewanee Review*, 29, 1921, 23), Bogard (*Tragic Satire*, p. 55), Stoll (p. 130), Clifford Leech (*John Webster*, London: Hogarth, 1951, p. 51), Ribner (97), and B. J. Layman ("The Equilibrium of Opposites in *The White Devil*," *PMLA*, 74, 1959, 347).

21. *Elements of Tragedy* (New Haven: Yale Univ. Press, 1969), pp. 44–45.

22. "Flamineo and the 'Comfortable Words,'" *Renaissance Papers* (1964), p. 15.

23. *The Vision of Tragedy* (New Haven: Yale Univ. Press, 1959), pp. 5, 36, 41, 79.

24. Page 117. See also, Mulryne, p. 214; Bogard, ed., p. xi; Brown, ed., p. lviii.

25. Alvin Kernan, *The Cankered Muse* (New Haven: Yale Univ. Press, 1959), p. 233. Elizabeth Brennan asserts that Webster, through the "conventional" marriage with Castruchio which leads to Julia's immorality, lends a kind of validity to the Duchess' secret betrothal ("The Relationship Between Brother and Sister in the Plays of John Webster," *MLR*, 58, 1963, 491).

26. "*The Duchess of Malfi:* Styles of Ceremony," *Essays in Criticism*, 12 (1962), 134.

27. Herbert J. Muller, *The Spirit of Tragedy* (New York: Knopf, 1956), p. 199.

28. Critical opinion on the Duchess' culpability varies widely. On the one hand, she is "vain, willful" (Ornstein, p. 147), a creature of folly (Stoll, p. 192) caught in the "context of sin and its atonement" (E. M. W. Tillyard, *The Elizabethan World Picture*, London: Chatto and Windus, 1948, p. 20). On the other hand, she "never violates . . . moral goodness" (Seymour L. Cross, "A Note on Webster's Tragic Attitude," *N&Q*, 4, 1957, 375); yearning only for domestic happiness, a husband to love and children to rear (Bradford, p. 24), she would not "automatically" be condemned either for remarrying (Frank W. Wadsworth, "Webster's *Duchess of Malfi* in the Light of Some Contemporary Ideas on Marriage and Remarriage," *PQ*, 35, 1956, 398) or for "irreligion"—all such phrases "are simply protestant" (William Empson, "Mine Eyes Dazzle," *Essays in Criticism*, 14, 1964, 83).

29. *The Duchess of Malfi: Sources, Themes, Characters* (Cambridge, Mass.: Harvard Univ. Press, 1962), p. 91. Webster maintains a careful ambiguity between "Fate and Chance" (M. C. Bradbrook, "Two Notes Upon Webster," *MLR*, 42, 1947, 289).

30. Calderwood, p. 136.

31. Surely Webster intends Antonio to be neither "the ideal husband" (Wadsworth, p. 403) nor totally "irresponsible" (Leech, p. 63). Don D. Moore

is essentially correct, I think, in branding him "pallid" and dramatically un-interesting (*John Webster and His Critics: 1617-1964*, Baton Rouge: Louisi-ana State Univ. Press, 1966, p. 165).

32. As Louis D. Gianetti has observed, Bosola's soliloquies are "crucial" because the spectators "see the two poles of characters through his eyes" ("A Contemporary View of *The Duchess of Malfi*," *Comparative Drama,* 3, 1969-70, 301). Bosola "so dominates any presentation of the play that the loves and crimes of the house of Aragon seem but a background to his tragedy" (Bradbrook, p. 289).

33. "The Ambiguity of Bosola," *SP,* 54 (1957), 170. Both Stoll (p. 126) and Bogard (*The Tragic Satire,* p. 55) deny that Bosola develops and achieves a kind of tragic insight. But critical consensus is against them. Through "a growth of pity and admiration for the Duchess" (John Russell Brown, ed., *The Duchess of Malfi,* Cambridge, Mass.: Harvard Univ. Press, 1964, p. li), Bosola makes "a nightmarish progress through himself and the twisting paths of his motives" (Murray, p. 182).

34. Explanations for the scene range from a claim that it is a "comic inter-lude" (Louis B. Wright, "Madmen as Vaudeville Performers on the Elizabethan Stage," *JEGP,* 30, 1931, 51), to a "grotesque horror" (Cecil W. Davies, "The Structure of *The Duchess of Malfi:* An Approach," *English,* 12, 1958, 92) totally devoid of humor (S. I. Hayakawa, "A Note on the Madman's Scene in Webster's *The Duchess of Malfi*," *PMLA,* 47, 1932, 904-909), to "a symboli-sation of the madness of Ferdinand himself" (K. H. Ansari, *John Webster: Image Patterns and Canon,* Kerala, India: Sterling, 1969, p. 50), to a delib-erate "gaucherie, . . . the disordered music of men reduced to the animal level" (McD. Emslie, "Motives in Malfi," *Essays in Criticism,* 9, 1959, 399), to a *charivari* mocking the Duchess' marriage and culminating in the Duchess' being taken out—not for a dance—but to her death (Ekeblad, "The 'Impure Art,'" pp. 261-66).

CHAPTER VI

1. G. E. Bentley, *The Jacobean and Caroline Stage,* II (Oxford: Clarendon Press, 1956), 906; IV, 862.

2. While G. R. Hibbard complains that the emphasis on suffering rather than on doing is a sign of decadence in tragedy ("The Tragedies of Thomas Middle-ton and the Decadence of the Drama," *Renaissance and Modern Studies,* 1, 1957, 41), Robert Ornstein more aptly notes that Middleton's concern was not "man's tragic relation to the universe" but the "relation between human appe-tites and the social environment which conditions them" (*The Moral Vision of Jacobean Tragedy,* Madison: Univ. of Wisconsin Press, 1960, p. 171).

3. As Norman Brittin observes, the stories of these women represent "pro-nounced contrasts on the theme of marriage" (*Thomas Middleton,* New York: Twayne, 1972, p. 119).

4. Whether Middleton intended the Duke to be considered as "utterly contemptible" (Richard Hindrey Barker, *Thomas Middleton,* New York: Columbia Univ. Press, 1958, p. 134) or as a "very graceful compliment" to King James, who also was about fifty-five (Baldwin Maxwell, "The Date of Middleton's *Women Beware Women," PQ,* 22, 1943, 339, 341), certainly the terror of this scene arises from the Duke's blind and fixed determination to impose his will upon another without regard for the consequences (Edward Engelberg, "Tragic Blindness in *The Changeling* and *Women Beware Women," MLQ,* 23, 1962, 21).

5. Line references to *Women Beware Women* are to the edition of Charles Barber (Berkeley: Univ. of California Press, 1969).

6. Christopher Ricks has described how the numerous commercial and monetary images connect and interpenetrate the world of money with the world of love "so that love becomes mercenary lust" ("Word-Play in *Women Beware Women," RES,* NS 12, 1961, 238). Both Muriel C. Bradbrook (*Themes and Conventions of Elizabethan Tragedy,* Cambridge: Cambridge Univ. Press, 1957, p. 244) and R. B. Parker ("Middleton's Experiments with Comedy and Judgement," in *Jacobean Theatre,* ed. J. R. Brown and Bernard Harris, London: Arnold, 1960, p. 192) are primarily concerned with the imagery of gluttony and its application to the theme of lust, greed, and sensuality.

7. "The Psychological Drama of *Women Beware Women," SEL,* 12 (1972), 376. If branding her "a shallow, witless fool" (Gamaliel Bradford, "The Women of Middleton and Webster," *Sewanee Review,* 29, 1921, 17) is an overstatement, she clearly "is not the stuff of which heroines are made" (A. H. Bullen, ed., *The Works of Thomas Middleton,* London, 1885, I, lxxv.)

8. Irving Ribner, *Jacobean Tragedy: The Quest for Moral Order* (London: Baylis, 1962), p. 143. Similarly, T. B. Tomlinson describes him as a smugly self-satisfied and insensitive man who has "for once done something far beyond the bounds of his normal, very limited activities" (*A Study of Elizabethan and Jacobean Tragedy,* Cambridge: Cambridge Univ. Press, 1964, p. 168). Una Ellis-Fermor, on the other hand, speaks of his initially virtuous character with the "promise of a fine flowering" (*The Jacobean Drama,* London: Methuen, 1936, p. 142).

9. Leantio is hoist with his own petard—"by an intrinsically mercenary nature which can cherish love only as a commodity and is therefore inevitably outbid for it" (Arthur Kirsch, *Jacobean Perspectives,* Charlottesville: Univ. Press of Virginia, 1972, p. 77), by "the acquisitiveness, the 'property consciousness' of the petty bourgeois" (Dorothea Krook, "Tragedy and Satire: Middleton's *Women Beware Women," SEL,* Scripta Hierasolymitana, 16, 1966, 102).

10. Critics have universally recognized the power of this scene. It is "the best example of wit in action and language" (Inga-Stina Ewbank, "Realism and Morality in *Women Beware Women," Essays and Studies,* 22, 1969, 68), a "tour de force, a triumph of sustained ingenuity" (Samuel Schoenbaum,

Middleton's Tragedies: A Critical Study, New York: Columbia Univ. Press, 1955, p. 118).

11. "The Pattern of *Women Beware Women,*" *Yearbook of English Studies,* 2 (1972), 87; see also Madeleine Doran, *Endeavors of Art* (Madison: Univ. of Wisconsin Press, 1954), p. 332.

12. The stage direction "Throw's flameing gold upon Isabell who falls: dead" appears in an annotation to the Yale copy of the 1657 edition. See J. R. Mulryne's edition (London: Methuen, 1975), p. 161.

13. To argue that Middleton "has no point of view" (T. S. Eliot, *Essays on Elizabethan Drama,* New York: Harcourt, 1932, p. 85), that he "failed to interpret" life (Helene B. Bullock, "Thomas Middleton and the Fashion in Play Making," *PMLA,* 76, 1961, 299), is to miss the point badly. The moral, as Charles A. Hallett aptly observes, "is stated epigrammatically in play after play. Craft, the antithesis to wisdom in Middleton's thought, is without exception ultimately condemned" ("Middleton's Overreachers and the Ironic Ending," *Tennessee Studies in Literature,* 16, 1971, 2).

14. Both George Williams (ed., *The Changeling,* Lincoln: Univ. of Nebraska Press, 1966, p. xiv) and Bradbrook (p. 214) describe the broad concept of transformation which characterizes the action as a whole. Specific claims for the "changeling" have been made for Antonio (F. S. Boas, *Introduction to Stuart Drama,* Oxford: Oxford Univ. Press, 1946, p. 241), for Beatrice (Katherine A. Hebert, "A Note on the Significance of the Title of Middleton's *The Changeling,*" *CLAJ,* 12, 1968–69, 66), for De Flores (William Empson, *Some Versions of Pastoral,* Norfolk, Conn.: New Directions, 1950, p. 50), and for Alsemero, Diaphanta, and Franciscus (Karl L. Holzknecht, "The Dramatic Structure of *The Changeling,*" *Renaissance Papers,* 1954, rpt. in Max Bluestone and Norman Rabkin, eds., *Shakespeare's Contemporaries,* Englewood Cliffs, N.J.: Prentice-Hall, 1961, p. 267).

15. Beatrice, as N. W. Bawcutt indicates, is not innocent at the beginning of the play (ed., *The Changeling,* London: Methuen, 1958, pp. liv–lv). She may be "surrounded by obsequious attendants" "like a princess in a fairy tale" (Dorothy M. Farr, "*The Changeling,*" *MLR,* 62, 1967, 588), but she is certainly not "naive to the point of ludicrousness" (William Archer, *The Old Drama and the New,* Boston: Small, Maynard, 1923, p. 98).

16. The central significance of the metaphor of sight is examined by Engelberg, p. 21. Both Thomas L. Berger ("The Petrarchan Fortress of *The Changeling,*" *Renaissance Papers,* 1969, 38) and Tomlinson (pp. 192–208) explore the function of the castle imagery. Perhaps the most perceptive analysis of the language of the play is by Ricks, who describes Middleton's extensive punning on five key words—"blood, act, deed, employed, and service"—each of which has a sexual meaning to establish the "moral and poetic themes" of the tragedy ("The Moral and Poetic Structure of *The Changeling,*" *Essays in Criticism,* 10, 1960, 292, 301); Michael C. Andrews sees a similar pun on sweet as a sexual metaphor as well as a term of approbation and endearment

("'Sweetness' in *The Changeling,*" *YES,* 1, 1971, 63). The symbolism of the ring is examined by Dorothea Kehler ("Rings and Jewels in *The Changeling,*" *ELN,* 5, 1967, 15–17) and J. Chesley Taylor ("Metaphors of the Moral World: Structure in *The Changeling,*" *Tulane Studies in English,* 20, 1972, 44–45).

17. Line references to *The Changeling* are to the edition of N. W. Bawcutt. Since the problem of authorship is not at issue in this discussion, I for the sake of brevity have referred to Middleton as the author of the tragedy.

18. Robert Jordan has suggested that their confrontation "reverberates with the echoes" of the myth of beauty and the beast ("Myths and Psychology in *The Changeling,*" *Renaissance Drama,* NS 3, 1970, 159).

19. David M. Holmes has argued at length that Alsemero is a superficial and hypocritical individual whose lust is masked "by a fair-seeming exterior. . . . In the last scene [he] becomes a grotesque moralizer" (*The Art of Thomas Middleton,* Oxford: Clarendon, 1970, pp. 174, 180, 184).

20. "Middleton and Rowley's *The Changeling,* V, iii, 175–77," *Explicator,* 26 (1968), Item 41. Barbara J. Baines reads Beatrice's first cry as one of sexual "death" (*The Lust Motif in the Plays of Thomas Middleton,* Salzburg, Austria: Universitat Salzburg, 1973, p. 114).

21. Pp. 37–38. The subplot "supplies a perspective, a background of contrasting moral coloration, that helps to clarify our judgment of the main plot." Empson, who along with Bradbrook was instrumental in the reappraisal, observes that the effect of the asylum scene is to "surround the characters with a herd of lunatics, howling outside in the night, one step into whose company is irretrievable" (p. 52). Its function is innuendo (Ricks, "Moral and Poetic," p. 301), anti-mask (Bradbrook, p. 221), burlesque (Matthew W. Black, ed., *The Changeling,* Philadelphia: Univ. of Pennsylvania Press, 1966, p. 5).

22. To assert that Middleton is "an observer without a philosophy, unable, or unwilling to evolve a theory" (Farr, p. 597) is to miss the point badly. On the other hand, Felix E. Schelling's comment on the "wholesomer general tone" of *The Changeling,* compared to *Women Beware Women,* is an equally partial view (*Elizabethan Playwrights,* New York: Harper, 1925, p. 173).

23. The reference to hell in the game of barley-brake points both backward to the last scream of the madmen to "catch the last couple in hell" (III, iii, 165) and forward to Vermandero's lament that hell circumscribes them in the final moments (V, iii, 164). See Richard Leven, *The Multiple Plot in English Renaissance Drama* (Chicago: Univ. of Chicago Press, 1971), p. 110.

CHAPTER VII

1. "Ford's Tragic Perspective," *TSLL,* 1 (1960), rpt. in *Elizabethan Drama: Modern Essays in Criticism,* ed. R. J. Kaufmann (New York: Oxford Univ. Press, 1961), p. 366. Una Ellis-Fermor's assertion that Ford's focus is "microscopic, . . . exclud[ing] everything beyond the area of a few minds" (*The Jacobean Drama,* London: Methuen, 1936, p. 228), seems quite wrongheaded; to the contrary, the spectators are constantly forced to consider the value

structure of the entire society, "full of intrigue and of an evil which is as pervasive as it is real" (Irving Ribner, *Jacobean Tragedy*, New York: Barnes and Noble, 1962, p. 163). H. J. Oliver has aptly noted that this Italy is a land where the principle of justice does not generally prevail (*The Problem of John Ford*, London: Cambridge Univ. Press, 1955, p. 88).

2. John Lawlor, *The Tragic Sense in Shakespeare* (New York: Harcourt, 1966), p. 14.

3. "Biblical Faith and the Idea of Tragedy," in *The Tragic Vision and the Christian Faith*, ed. Nathan A. Scott, Jr. (New York: Association Press, 1957), p. 30.

4. With "conventional ethics in conflict with immutable physical forces" (G. F. Sensabaugh, *The Tragic Muse of John Ford*, Stanford: Stanford Univ. Press, 1944, p. 93), the tragedy "postulates nature opposed to law, love opposed to morality" (George C. Herndl, *The High Design*, Lexington: Univ. Press of Kentucky, 1970, p. 263).

5. All line references in this essay to *'Tis Pity She's a Whore* are to the edition of N. W. Bawcutt (Lincoln: Univ. of Nebraska Press, 1966).

6. Arthur Kirsch complains, justly, I believe, that Annabella's impudence at this point is inconsistent "with what we have seen of her earlier in the play" and with "our acceptance of what happens to her at the end of the play" (*Jacobean Dramatic Perspectives*, Charlottesville: Univ. Press of Virginia, 1972, p. 125).

7. If one is not fully convinced by the assertion that Ford is portraying Giovanni's affliction as "religious melancholy in defect" (S. Blaine Ewing, *Burtonian Melancholy in the Plays of John Ford*, Princeton: Princeton Univ. Press, 1940, p. 72), there is no argument that Giovanni at this point is a confirmed atheist who does not believe his love is sinful (Alan Brissenden, "Impediments to Love: A Theme in John Ford," *Renaissance Drama*, 7, 1964, 100).

8. This moment is—according to Bawcutt (p. xxii)—"a symbol of the play as a whole"; for a full analysis see D. K. Anderson, Jr., "The Heart and the Banquet: Imagery in Ford's *'Tis Pity* and *The Broken Heart*," *SEL*, 1 (1962), 209-17.

9. Fredson Bowers, *Elizabethan Revenge Tragedy* (Princeton: Princeton Univ. Press, 1940), p. 210.

10. Mark Stavig, *John Ford and the Traditional Moral Order* (Madison: Univ. of Wisconsin Press, 1968), p. 96.

11. Herndl, p. 264; M. C. Bradbrook, *Themes and Conventions of Elizabethan Tragedy* (London: Methuen, 1936), p. 227.

12. "Love, Lust, and Sham: Structural Pattern in the Plays of John Ford," *Renaissance Drama*, NS 2 (1969), 164.

13. Kenneth A. Requa has recently maintained that Bonaventura's flight, his "culminating blunder," is the more serious "because it is rooted in despair" ("Music in the Ear: Giovanni as Tragic Hero in *'Tis Pity She's a Whore*," *PLL*, 7, 1971, 24).

14. There is enough critical smoke on this point to suspect a dramatic fire. On the one hand are those scholars like Stavig (p. 110) and J. A. Bastiaenen (*The Moral Tone of Jacobean and Caroline Drama,* Amsterdam: H. J. Paris, 1930, p. 103), who accept the Friar's morality without qualification. On the other, Robert Ornstein's perception of a "muddled moralist" (*The Moral Vision of Jacobean Tragedy,* Madison: Univ. of Wisconsin Press, 1960, p. 208) is mild compared to M. Joan Sargeaunt's assertion that he is "either a complete knave or a complete fool" (*John Ford,* Oxford: Basil Blackwell, 1935, pp. 124–25).

15. This aesthetic objectivity toward incestuous passion has occasioned charges that Ford was decadent (Gerard Langbaine, *An Account of the English Dramatic Poets,* London, 1691, p. 222; Vernon Lee, *Euphorion,* London, 1884, I, 102), that he was an ardent believer in free love (S. P. Sherman, "Ford's Contribution to the Decadence of the Drama," in *John Fordes Dramatische Werke,* ed. W. Bang, Louvain: A. Uystprusyt, 1908, pp. xii–xiii), that he reveled in his moral heresy (Wallace A. Bacon, "The Literary Reputation of John Ford," *HLQ,* 11, 1948, 197).

16. *John Ford and the Drama of His Time* (London: Chatto and Windus, 1957), p. 46.

17. For similar views, see G. F. Sensabaugh, "John Ford Revisited," *SEL,* 4 (1964), 212; Mary E. Cochnower, "John Ford," *Seventeenth-Century Studies by Members of the Graduate School, University of Cincinnati* (Princeton: Princeton Univ. Press, 1933), pp. 211–12.

18. *World Theater* (New York: Horizon Press, 1973), p. 188.

19. "The evil remains elusive" (Roger T. Burbridge, "The Moral Vision of Ford's *The Broken Heart,*" *SEL,* 10, 1970, 397), and every principal character wins our sympathy for his "readiness to suffer [his] fate with a measure of dignity" (Leech, p. 86).

20. Ralph J. Kaufmann has examined this point extensively in two articles— "Ford's Tragic Perspective," and "Ford's 'Wasteland': *The Broken Heart,*" *Renaissance Drama,* NS 3, 1970, 167–87; in the latter he writes that the irreducible tragic situation results psychologically from each character's being boxed in and entrapped by the other characters (p. 175).

21. Peter Ure, "Marriage and the Domestic Drama in Heywood and Ford," *English Studies,* 32 (1951), 213–14; see also Glenn H. Blayney, "Convention, Plot, and Structure in *The Broken Heart,*" *MP,* 56 (1958), 1–9.

22. All line references in this essay to *The Broken Heart* are to the edition of Donald K. Anderson, Jr. (Lincoln: Univ. of Nebraska Press, 1968).

23. It is hardly true that Orgilus does not resolve to seek revenge until the middle of the fourth act (Bowers, p. 212). Anderson aptly notes, however, that Orgilus, by delaying his revenge, makes it "doubly sweet"—both claiming Ithocles' life and depriving him of marital bliss (*John Ford,* New York: Twayne, 1972, p. 67).

24. George Saintsbury considers him so despicable that his very presence indicates that Ford "is not of the first order of poets" (*A History of English*

Literature, London: Macmillan, 1894, p. 407); to the contrary, Kaufmann
("Ford's 'Wasteland,'" p. 182) considers him an important "kind of alter ego
or reductive analogy to Orgilus." Ewing suggests (p. 57) that his personality
might have been suggested by certain portions of Robert Burton's *The
Anatomy of Melancholy.*

25. Ellis-Fermor, p. 232. Even more pointedly Herndl denounces the play
as a "structural monstrosity" (p. 277); for a counter view describing the
effectiveness of the triple plot, see McMaster, pp. 157–66.

26. Not infrequently this refusal to resolve conflicting values is attributed
to a decadence in Ford; his "frank enjoyment of sin" (T. B. Tomlinson, *A
Study of Elizabethan and Jacobean Tragedy,* Cambridge: Melbourne Univ.
Press, 1964, p. 265), for example, leads him to develop characters "defined
by sentimental rather than moral qualities" (Kirsch, p. 117). Catering to the
"putrid cravings" of a diminishing audience (Bastiaenen, p. 195), he attempts
"to deal with subjects outside his limited range" (Bradbrook, p. 260).

27. Brissenden, p. 95.

28. "The Jacobean Shakespeare: Some Observations on the Construction
of Tragedies," *Jacobean Theatre,* p. 40.

29. Penthea's dedication to honor leads the occasional critic to regard her
as "overhard and severe" (A. C. Swinburne, *The Complete Works of Algernon
Charles Swinburne,* ed. Edmund Gosse and T. J. Wise, London: Russell and
Russell, 1925, II, 381). Most, however, view her as an innocent figure "torn
between two rights" (Oliver, p. 65) whose tragedy "is to be betrayed by the
three men who love her" (Ornstein, p. 213).

30. Michael J. Kelly has argued that Calantha's flurry of actions provide
"the means for a man to transcend" the "stultifying stasis" of stoicism ("The
Values of Action and Chronicle in *The Broken Heart," PLL,* 7, 1971, 151,
154).

31. *Specimens of the English Dramatic Poets* (New York: Putnam, 1848),
Part 2, p. 29.

32. See further Ure (p. 211), Ornstein (p. 216), and Bowers (p. 211). Charles
O. McDonald explains the logic of Calantha's behavior in light of Tecnicus'
definition of honor ("The Design of John Ford's *The Broken Heart:* A Study
in the Development of Caroline Sensibility," *SP,* 59, 1962, 151), and Stavig
relates the final scene to the increasingly popular emblematic and symbolic
techniques of the mask (p. 144).

33. See also Sensabaugh ("John Ford Revisisted," p. 202).

Index

P₃